SUSTAINABLE PEACE

SUSTAINABLE PEACE
The Role of the UN and Regional Organizations in Preventing Conflict

Connie Peck

CARNEGIE COMMISSION ON PREVENTING DEADLY CONFLICT

CARNEGIE CORPORATION OF NEW YORK

ROWMAN & LITTLEFIELD PUBLISHERS, INC.
Lanham • Boulder • New York • Oxford

ROWMAN & LITTLEFIELD PUBLISHERS, INC.

Published in the United States of America
by Rowman & Littlefield Publishers, Inc.
4720 Boston Way, Lanham, Maryland 20706

12 Hid's Copse Road
Cumnor Hill, Oxford OX2 9JJ, England

Copyright © 1998 by Carnegie Corporation of New York

British Library Cataloguing in Publication Information Available

Library of Congress Cataloging-in-Publication Data
Peck, Connie.
    Sustainable peace : the role of the UN and regional organizations
in preventing conflict / Connie Peck.
       p.   cm.—(Carnegie Commission on Preventing Deadly Conflict
series)
    Includes bibliographical references and index.
    ISBN 0-8476-8560-8 (cloth : alk. paper).—ISBN 0-8476-8561-6
(pbk. : alk. paper)
    1. Peace.   2. United Nations.   3. Regionalism (International
organization)   I. Title.   II. Series.
KZ5538.P43   1998
341.7'3—dc21   97-26019
                                                               CIP

ISBN 0-8476-8560-8 (cloth : alk. paper)
ISBN 0-8476-8561-6 (pbk. : alk. paper)

Printed in the United States of America

⊗ ™ The paper used in this publication meets the minimum requirements of
American National Standard for Information Sciences—Permanence of Paper
for Printed Library Materials, ANSI Z39.48–1984.

ABOUT THE
Carnegie Commission on Preventing Deadly Conflict Series

Carnegie Corporation of New York established the Carnegie Commission on Preventing Deadly Conflict in May 1994 to address the threats to world peace of intergroup violence and to advance new ideas for the prevention and resolution of deadly conflict. The Commission is examining the principal causes of deadly ethnic, nationalist, and religious conflicts within and between states and the circumstances that foster or deter their outbreak. Taking a long-term, worldwide view of violent conflicts that are likely to emerge, it seeks to determine the functional requirements of an effective system for preventing mass violence and to identify the ways in which such a system could be implemented. The Commission is also looking at the strengths and weaknesses of various international entities in conflict prevention and considering ways in which international organizations might contribute toward developing an effective international system of nonviolent problem solving. The series grew out of the research that the Commission has sponsored to answer the three fundamental questions that have guided its work: What are the problems posed by deadly conflict and why is outside help often necessary to deal with these problems? What approaches, tasks, and strategies appear most promising for preventing deadly conflict? What are the responsibilities and capacities of states, international organizations, and private and nongovernmental organizations for undertaking preventive action?

The books are published as a service to scholars, students, practitioners, and the interested public. While they have undergone peer review and have been approved for publication, the views that they express are those of the author or authors, and Commission publication does not imply that those views are shared by the Commission as a whole or by individual Commissioners.

Published in the series:

BRIDGING THE GAP:
A FUTURE SECURITY ARCHITECTURE FOR THE MIDDLE EAST
  By Shai Feldman and Abdullah Toukan

THE PRICE OF PEACE:
INCENTIVES AND INTERNATIONAL CONFLICT PREVENTION
  Edited by David Cortright

SUSTAINABLE PEACE:
THE ROLE OF THE UN AND REGIONAL ORGANIZATIONS IN
PREVENTING CONFLICT
  By Connie Peck

Forthcoming:

The Ambivalence of the Sacred: Religion, Violence, and Reconciliation
  By Scott Appleby
Turkey's Kurdish Question
  By Henri J. Barkey and Graham E. Fuller

Opportunities Missed, Opportunities Seized: Preventive Diplomacy in the Post-Cold War World
  Edited by Bruce Jentleson
The Costs of Conflict: Prevention and Cure in the Global Arena
  Edited by Michael E. Brown and Richard N. Rosecrance

Reports available from the Commission:

David Hamburg, *Preventing Contemporary Intergroup Violence*. Founding Essay of the Commission, April 1994.

David Hamburg, *Education for Conflict Resolution*, April 1995.

Comprehensive Disclosure of Fissionable Materials: A Suggested Initiative, June 1995.

Larry Diamond, *Promoting Democracy in the 1990s: Actors and Instruments, Issues and Imperatives*, December 1995.

Andrew J. Goodpaster, *When Diplomacy Is Not Enough: Managing Multinational Military Interventions*, July 1996.

Jane E. Holl, *Carnegie Commission on Preventing Deadly Conflict: Second Progress Report*, July 1996.

John Stremlau, *Sharpening International Sanctions: Toward a Stronger Role for the United Nations*, November 1996.

Alexander L. George and Jane E. Holl, *The Warning-Response Problem and Missed Opportunities in Preventive Diplomacy*, May 1997.

A House No Longer Divided: Progress and Prospects for Democratic Peace in South Africa, Report of a Conference, July 1997.

Nik Gowing, *Media Coverage: Help or Hindrance in Conflict Prevention*, September 1997.

Cyrus R. Vance and David A. Hamburg, *Pathfinders for Peace: A Report to the UN Secretary-General on the Role of Special Representatives and Personal Envoys*, September 1997.

Preventing Deadly Conflict, Executive Summary of the Final Report, December 1997.

Gail W. Lapidus with Svetlana Tsalik, eds., *Preventing Deadly Conflict: Strategies and Institutions*. Proceedings of a Conference in Moscow, Russia, January 1998.

To order *Power Sharing and International Mediation in Ethnic Conflicts* by Timothy Sisk, copublished by the Commission and the United States Institute of Peace, please contact USIP Press, P.O. Box 605, Herndon, VA 22070, USA; (phone) 1-800-868-8064 or 1-703-661-1590.

Full text or summaries of these reports are available on the Commission's web site: http://www.ccpdc.org

To order a report or to be added to the Commission's mailing list, contact:
  Carnegie Commission on Preventing Deadly Conflict
  1779 Massachusetts Avenue NW, Suite 715
  Washington, DC 20036-2103
  Phone: (202) 332-7900   Fax: (202) 332-1919
  E-mail: pdc@carnegie.org

Contents

Figures

Tables

Foreword

This book seeks an integrative agenda for preventing deadly conflict by fostering a dynamic interplay between theory and practice. It delineates effective preventive diplomacy to keep disputes from turning into violent conflict and backs this up with a long-term approach to tackle the structural causes of conflict and the development of institutions to promote just solutions to underlying problems. It illuminates the fact that the most secure states are those which provide the greatest human security to their populations.

Following the lead of the Brundtland Commission, which linked environmental responsibility with economic development in an integrative concept of sustainable development, Peck links good governance with conflict prevention on a path to sustainable peace. Taken together, sustainable development and sustainable peace provide a comprehensive agenda for the international community in the decades ahead.

Prevention is best thought of not only as avoiding undesirable circumstances, but also as creating preferred alternatives. In the long run, we will be most successful in preventing ethnic, religious, and interstate wars by focusing on ways to avert direct confrontation between hostile groups and by promoting democracy, economic development, and the creation of civil institutions that protect human rights. This book clarifies the issues and international institutions pertinent to this great mission.

Among other assets, this work gives useful insights into the United Nations' potential for preventing deadly conflict. The UN is not a world government. It is an intergovernmental organization of sovereign states that works by seeking common ground among them to cooperate in their long-term self-interests. The UN Charter was written by experienced, thoughtful statesmen—largely from established democracies—who had been deeply influenced by two terrible world wars with a grotesquely distorted peace between them. Mindful of painfully missed opportunities, they carefully prepared a document that provided a bold vision of a better future and practical means of implementation.

The Charter set out ambitious objectives. Prominent among these were: achieving international security through the peaceful resolution of disputes, the rule of law, sanctions, and military action if necessary to suppress aggression; freeing colonial peoples, based on equal rights and self-determination; economic and social development; promotion of human rights and fundamental freedoms, regardless of race, sex, language, or religion; and fostering cooperation among diverse nations to attain common approaches to global problems. Now, with the cold war over and the world being drawn together by technological and economic forces, we need creative thinking to explore ways in which the UN might become more effective in these great tasks. This book is an excellent case in point.

Peck thoughtfully examines preventive diplomacy—the application of peacemaking methods prior to the outbreak of armed hostilities between disputing parties. Article 33 of the UN Charter states: "The parties to any dispute, the continuance of which is likely to endanger the maintenance of international peace and security, shall first of all, seek a solution by negotiation, enquiry, mediation, conciliation, arbitration, judicial settlement, resort to regional agencies or arrangements, or other peaceful means of their choice."

The UN must find effective ways to strengthen and institutionalize preventive diplomacy rather than reacting to crises that have spun out of control. The UN can best focus on early reconciliation of disputing parties' interests, primarily through diplomatic ingenuity. Can the UN create paths to conflict resolution that are visible, attractive, and useful before conflicts become large and lethal? Can the UN find effective ways to bring the world's experience to bear on a particular conflict at an early stage in its development?

The growing demand for UN intervention, not only in conflict between nations but also in serious internal conflicts, naturally challenges the capacity of the organization to respond. These new challenges also raise questions about the relationship between the UN as a global organization and the various regional organizations that relate to it. A variety of regional arrangements and agencies exist, some more effective than others. There are constructive possibilities for coordinating the efforts of regional bodies and the UN in conflict resolution. Regional organizations in Africa, Latin America, and Europe, such as the Organization of African Unity, the Organization of American States, the Council of Europe, and the Organization for Security and Cooperation in Europe, all need to be explored from this perspective. For the most part, they have not had major responsibilities in conflict resolution, but they could become much more effective in due course.

Peck seeks paths that might be desirable and feasible for strengthening regional capability to deal with conflicts. On the one hand, regional entities have the advantage in principle of intimate knowledge of the players and sensitivity to historical and cultural factors that bear on the conflict. On the other hand, they have the disadvantage that they tend to be emotionally engaged, tend to choose sides, and therefore have difficulty in establishing credible conflict-resolving functions. All this needs careful examination in terms of basic principles of conflict resolution and on a case-by-case basis in relation to the idiosyncrasies of particular organizations that have arisen over the years. In any event, strengthening the global–regional cooperative functions would have potential for a variety of purposes, and these are explored in this book.

Peck has worked creatively on the development of Regional Centers for Sustainable Peace—established under the auspices of either regional organizations or the UN. This would be one way to bring together the UN, regional organizations, nongovernmental organizations, and regional analytical centers. The proposed structure would integrate the most successful conflict prevention instruments, drawing widely on international experience and expertise, but ensuring that they are tailored to local needs and circumstances. The horizontal transfer of knowledge and experience within regions is a distinctive feature of this proposal, in which regional actors who have found solutions to their problems or developed successful models of good governance could assist their neighbors within the context of a regional effort aided, as necessary, by global support.

Regional centers would have two major foci. The first would be assistance in developing the structural processes for sustainable peace (good governance at all levels of society). The second would be maintaining peace through assistance in dispute resolution and the development of institutional structures that would allow groups to become more effective at resolving their own problems. Each center could provide an ongoing analysis of existing disputes to both the regional organization and the UN. Difficult as it is to create new institutions, the stimulus of looming disaster is powerful; the voice of reason, though small, is surely persistent.

Altogether, this book reflects an open-minded spirit of inquiry and innovation pertinent to great issues of the next century. It can have a stimulating effect on all those seriously concerned with preventing deadly conflict.

David A. Hamburg
Cochair
Carnegie Commission on Preventing Deadly Conflict

Preface

The tragic invasion of Kuwait by Iraq provided the initial impetus for this work. As chairperson of the Institute for Peace Research at La Trobe University in Australia, I began to think more seriously about how the international community might strengthen its capacity for preventive action at an earlier stage—before disputes escalated into crises. I became increasingly eager to see the developing knowledge about conflict resolution go beyond the academic realm to have a greater effect on practice. Accordingly, I approached the foreign minister of Australia, Senator Gareth Evans, to determine whether the Australian Department of Foreign Affairs might be interested in jointly pursuing a project in this area. Following exploratory discussions at the UN in 1991 (with support from the La Trobe Institute and the Australian Permanent Mission to the United Nations), I was seconded as a special consultant to the foreign minister and attached to the Australian Mission to the UN in New York to study how to strengthen the UN's capacity for preventive diplomacy and peacemaking.

The project involved extensive consultation with staff in the United Nations Secretariat and with diplomats from the permanent missions to the UN to determine how preventive diplomacy and peacemaking were carried out, the obstacles to a more systematic approach, and how such obstacles might be overcome. It soon became clear that some of the major impediments were related to the legacies of the East-West and North-South conflicts—coupled with a resource base that was insufficient to carry out the institution's enormous mandate. The result was that most disputes were given attention only when they reached crisis proportions—at the very time when, due to the powerful forces of conflict escalation, it was most difficult for a third party to be effective. No appropriate mechanism for early preventive action existed.

This initial work in 1992 led to a number of suggestions for strengthening preventive diplomacy and peacemaking within the UN; chief among them, a proposal for regional centers that could offer a more systematic approach to early prevention. It was proposed that the Department of Political Affairs be extended to the field, where it could be more effective, through the development of small, highly skilled teams that could travel around each region on a regular and routine basis to gain a better understanding of potential threats to peace and security, to establish rapport with relevant parties, and to quietly offer innovative ideas and assistance in resolving disputes before they escalated into crises.

Discussion papers outlining these ideas were circulated within the UN Secretariat and to the permanent missions, presented in seminars and conferences, and discussed extensively with those in decision-making roles within the system. As well, some of these suggestions were included in Gareth Evans's subsequent book, *Cooperating for Peace: An Agenda for the 1990s,* which was disseminated widely and launched in his 1993 address to the General Assembly.

At the same time, it was decided that a longer-term approach was also needed to raise awareness among UN staff and diplomats and to create the necessary support for a greater focus on prevention. Accordingly, a proposal for the establishment of a Fellowship Program in Peacemaking and Preventive Diplomacy was developed. Both the United Nations Institute for Training and Research and the International Peace Academy were approached as potential sponsors of such a program. Both were enthusiastic, but neither had the requisite funds or staff to develop the project. Thus, at the end of the consultancy in New York, with seed money from the Australian government, I transferred to UNITAR in Geneva, to raise the remainder of the funding and to organize the fellowship program. The first program was held in September of 1993 with further support from the Austrian and Swedish Ministries of Foreign Affairs, the Arthur Ross Foundation, and Rockefeller Family and Associates. Now in its fifth year, the UNITAR-IPA Fellowship Program in Peacemaking and Preventive Diplomacy is held annually in Austria, and has subsequently been supported by the governments of Australia, Austria, Germany, the Netherlands, Norway, Sweden, Switzerland, and the United Kingdom, as well as by a number of foundations and organizations, such as Carnegie Corporation of New York, the William and Flora Hewlett Foundation, the McKnight Foundation, and the United States Institute of Peace.

Astonishingly, this fellowship program represents the first time that the United Nations has ever provided advanced training to UN staff and diplomats to help refine their skills in conflict analysis, negotiation, and mediation. The UNITAR-IPA program thus represents an ongoing, major attempt to bring the latest knowledge about conflict and its resolution to those who are in a position to affect practice. Over the past five years, the many presentations and intensive discussions by senior UN staff and diplomats at these meetings has also greatly enriched my own thinking about these issues.

Since coming to UNITAR, I have been able to further expand my work on how the UN's peace and security role might be enhanced. A grant from the Ford Foundation supported a study, subsequently published as a book, entitled *The United Nations as a Dispute Settlement System: Improving Mechanisms for the Prevention and Resolution of Conflict* (Kluwer Law International, 1996). This project examined how the UN's interest-, rights-, and power-based approaches might be enhanced to complement one another more effectively.

The opportunity to organize and raise the funding for a colloquium to celebrate the fiftieth anniversary of the International Court of Justice provided a means for further consideration of ways to strengthen the UN's rights-based procedures. The meeting, which was held at the Peace Palace in The Hague, was addressed by eminent international lawyers and scholars, who offered a wealth of suggestions on how preventive diplomacy and dispute settlement through the Court might be refined. This led to a book, which I co-edited with Roy Lee, entitled *Increasing the Effectiveness of the International Court of Justice* (Kluwer Law International, 1997).

The current project began when David Hamburg and Jane Holl suggested that the kind of analysis I had been doing regarding the UN should be extended to regional organizations and relevant NGOs, such as the Carter Center, in order to provide a broader overview of the approaches that are evolving in the area of peacemaking and preventive diplomacy. The study was intended to provide a basis for drawing upon the best of these approaches to further develop the concept of regional centers. This work expanded the scope of the regional centers idea beyond preventive diplomacy and assistance in dispute settlement to encompass assistance in tackling the structural causes of conflict through the promotion of good governance. As will be argued here, Regional Centers for Sustainable Peace offer one way to integrate the peace and security agenda with the development, human rights and democratization agenda and hence to a process by which peace can be more effectively sustained.

This study, which investigates the work of seven actors—the UN, five regional organizations and the Carter Center—was carried out during 1995 and presented to the Carnegie Commission on Preventing Deadly Conflict in January 1996. It was revised in March 1997, following review and comments by five readers.

The opinions expressed in this volume are mine and do not necessarily reflect the view of the United Nations Secretariat, UNITAR, or any other United Nations organ or agency.

I would like to express my deepest gratitude to those who have provided help and encouragement over the last seven years. In particular, I would like to thank Gareth Evans, who courageously supported this work from the beginning, the late Peter Wilenski, Richard Butler, others at the Permanent Mission of Australia to the United Nations, and my colleagues at the La Trobe University Institute for Peace Research, especially Margot Prior and Eleanor Wertheim. I also owe special gratitude to the many UN staff and diplomats who have informed this work. Finally, without the support and assistance of project officers at Carnegie Corporation of New York, the Ford Foundation, the William and Flora Hewlett Foundation, the McKnight Foundation, and the United States Institute of Peace, as well as that of senior diplomats in supporting governments, this work could not have progressed as it has.

I would also like to thank Kluwer Law International for granting permission to adapt and include parts of my book, *The United Nations as a Dispute Settlement System: Improving Mechanisms for the Prevention and Resolution of Conflict.* The book was published in 1996 as volume 29 in Kluwer's series, Legal Aspects of International Organizations.

For their role in shaping the current project, I owe a particular debt of thanks to David Hamburg, president of Carnegie Corporation of New York, Jane Holl, executive director of the Carnegie Commission on Preventing Deadly Conflict, and John Stremlau, advisor to the executive director. David Hamburg's ability to provide encouragement and support at just the right moment is well known to all of those who have had the privilege of working with him. For their assistance in bringing this volume to publication, appreciation should also be expressed to Esther Brimmer, senior associate, and Robert Lande, the Commission's managing editor. The five anonymous readers who commented on the work, as well as the commissioners themselves, are also to be thanked for their helpful comments. I would also like to thank UNITAR's executive director, Marcel Boisard, for his constant encouragement and support and Elaine Conkievitch, who ably served as a research assistant for this project.

Originating with David Hamburg and Cyrus Vance, the Carnegie Commission on Preventing Deadly Conflict is a most timely initiative. It is composed of a distinguished group of commissioners and supported by an effective secretariat who have been working long and hard on examining the whole area of prevention. The Commission's final report and dissemination efforts are eagerly awaited and should provide real momentum for advancing more effective mechanisms for preventive action and moving the international community forward in the quest for sustainable peace.

Part One

Contemporary Conflict and Sustainable Peace

1

The Second Half of the Twentieth Century

AFTER TWO BRUTAL and ruinous world wars in the first half of this century, the leaders of the international community undertook a major initiative in preventive diplomacy—the creation of the United Nations. Their prescription for preventing violent conflict was a solid one. The sovereign states that joined the organization to "save succeeding generations from the scourge of war" agreed, as an obligation of their membership, to resolve their disputes peacefully. Article 33 of the UN Charter offered a menu of choices for resolving disputes before they turned into violence. It stated that "the parties to any dispute, the continuance of which is likely to endanger the maintenance of international peace and security, shall, first of all, seek a solution by negotiation, enquiry, mediation, conciliation, arbitration, judicial settlement, resort to regional agencies or arrangements, or other peaceful means of their own choice."

The Charter's prescription, however, went beyond the peaceful settlement of disputes to the wider issues that create the conditions for and sustain peace—and included social and economic justice, human rights, and respect for the rule of law. The preamble to the UN Charter stated:

> We the peoples of the United Nations determined . . . to reaffirm our faith in fundamental human rights, in the dignity and worth of the human person, in the equal rights of men and women and of nations large and small, and to establish conditions under which justice and respect for the obligations arising from treaties and other sources of international law can be maintained, and to promote social progress and better standards of life in larger freedom.

But even before this hopeful blueprint for an international dispute settlement system could get off the design board, a new danger to global peace and security sabotaged its promise. As noted by the Commission on Global Governance (1995):

> As the Charter was being negotiated and signed at San Francisco, the atomic bomb was being developed in Los Alamos, New Mexico, a thousand miles away. Few in San Francisco, including most of those who would play the role of founders, knew of this development. . . . The first atomic bomb was exploded over Hiroshima on 6 August 1945, just forty-one days after the Charter was signed. By the time the United Nations was established on 24 October 1945, the world that it was to serve had changed in fundamental ways.

For the next forty-five years, the nuclear threat and the cold war, which soon accompanied it, hung like a pall over the organization, gravely distorting the hopes that had been invested in it by the world's peoples.

The Effects of the Cold War

The founding fathers, in order to reach agreement at Dumbarton Oaks, had compromised between a fully democratic institution and one in which the Great Powers (who had prevailed in World War II) would have a disproportionate say in decision making—by being made permanent members of the UN Security Council, with veto power. But when the unanimity between the Great Powers, who were supposed to guide the organization, quickly dissolved into a bitter ideological struggle, the conflict regulation mechanisms set out in the Charter were never fully realized.

Since neither bloc wanted the United Nations to have a say in its geopolitical sphere, both refrained from bringing problems from its side of the divide to the Council, and when the rival bloc tried to have them considered, resolutions were vetoed before any action could be taken. Problems not involving the superpowers reached the Council's agenda only after they had attained crisis proportions, at which point it was usually too late to intervene effectively. Even when the Council did respond, its actions were limited to a narrow portion of its repertoire. As a result, the Council relied mostly on issuing resolutions (when they weren't vetoed), making appeals and recommendations, or urging and censuring recalcitrant parties. But because the Council waited until escalatory pressures were strong, these injunctions and admonitions were seldom effective.

When the United Nations was able to act, the focus was largely on containing and managing selected conflicts—as permitted by the superpowers. Too little attention was devoted to resolving the real issues and grievances that were behind such conflicts. Peacekeeping became the major area of innovation and the primary instrumentality for containing conflicts.

The cold war also constrained the Secretary-General and Secretariat. It eroded the ideal of the international civil service, and the Secretariat became bogged down in suspicion, secrecy and intrigue. Like the Council, the Secretary-General was restricted in what he could accomplish by powerful political considerations and restraints. Peacemaking was largely confined to setting the stage for peacekeeping and rarely went beyond this to search for real political solutions. Preventive diplomacy was virtually nonexistent.

The International Court of Justice, which had been designed to be the UN's principal judicial organ for dispute settlement, was also vastly underutilized. Until the end of the cold war, the Court decided only one contentious case on average per year, and only a handful of advisory opinions.

Thus, in spite of the obligation that the UN Charter imposed on member states to settle their disputes peacefully, they often did not do so. The ideological power struggle and the race to accumulate the largest arsenals of nuclear and conventional weapons had a profound effect on all regions of the world. Armed conflict continued to wreak havoc, both for the many who suffered directly from its devastation, and for those who suffered indirectly from the diversion of resources away from more pressing human needs.

The focus on the cold war and the absence of a truly viable multilateral forum, meant that future threats to peace and security were often neglected. The basic human needs of large segments of the world's population were given too little attention. Exponential population growth resulted in even more stress on the system, leading to growing poverty and social disintegration. Discrepancies between rich and poor widened, exacerbating social injustice and, in some cases, ethnic tension. With the penetration of mass media to all parts of the globe, these discrepancies became more apparent and led to increasing discontent—as disadvantaged and disenfranchised peoples aspired to be equal, and as individuals yearned for a better life for themselves and their families. Demands for access to political decision making and participation in the political process were seen as one way to achieve this goal, but entrenched power structures often stood in the way. Power struggles to gain political, economic, and cultural rights often ensued and ranged from nonviolent protest to intractable civil wars.

The macrolevel power struggle between East and West spilled over into many local and regional conflicts and caused them to grow in size and importance, with the superpowers often supporting (covertly or overtly) opposite sides. Both besieged governments and mobilized groups spent large amounts of money on arms, and often engaged in reciprocal acts of terror and terrorism, further exacerbating each other's fears. Government repression led to simmering discontent and reinforced aspirations for greater autonomy or political control. Communal militancy stimulated elites' fears of annihilation and made them increasingly repressive. Once entrenched, the cycle was difficult to break.

Excessive attention to the East-West conflict and the corresponding neglect of essential Charter goals, such as the promotion of "social progress and better standards of life in larger freedom," aggravated existing grievances. This created a macrolevel dispute between the "haves" and "have-nots" of the developed and developing world. The South faced diminishing resources, falling gross national product, and increasing disparities with the North, as much of Africa and parts of Asia and Latin America declined even further under a combination of destructive economic policies and ecological disasters. Moreover, the North-South debate created endless hours of adversarial discussion and recrimination and diverted time and attention away from problem solving.

The cold war was not the only villain. Legacies of historical dislocations and unaddressed past grievances smoldered beneath the surface in many parts of the world, and when stimulated by new grievances, erupted into conflicts. The anomalies of colonial expansion and dissolution left states with irrational borders, containing ethnic groups with no special affinity for one another, but often with strong ties to groups in other states. Pressures from rapid modernization and development added to the stress. Incompetent, corrupt, and repressive leaders failed to meet the needs of their peoples, even when they had the resources to do so, often preferring to squander their national budgets on armaments or divert them into their own bank accounts, the pockets of their relatives, or the country's elite.

Positive Developments Despite the Cold War

The news, however, was not entirely bad. A number of positive developments did occur, making many hopeful that, once the cold war was over, a "new world order" could take shape. During this period, large numbers of countries obtained independence from their colonial masters—a remarkable fact, although one destined to involve enormous transitional difficulties, first in the struggle for independence and then as newly formed and ill-equipped governments grappled with problems, many not of their own making. After independence, conflict often continued, as groups vied for control in the new power vacuum. Nonetheless, the long-term implications of this major exercise in self-determination led to the virtual end of colonialism and its gross injustices.

Cooperative relations between states and the network of international law that governs these relationships also deepened during this period. The development of treaties and conventions expanded to all aspects of interstate relations. The ease of international communication and travel led to an ever-increasing interaction and a network of acceptable rules became necessary for a smoothly functioning international system. Multiple forums evolved—internationally, regionally, and bilaterally—in which governments could exchange perspectives, explore ideas, and come to a consensus about problems. Despite what were sometimes serious disagreements, increased contact and understanding socialized representatives from widely divergent cultures into members of a common international community. These forums also contributed to conflict prevention, not only by elaborating rules by which all should abide, but also by allowing negotiations to occur over conflicting interests. Indeed, it could be argued that the existence of the United Nations and the outlet it provided for airing superpower tensions may have been, in part, responsible for the fact that the cold war never erupted into the nuclear nightmare so many feared.

Another remarkable development was the spread of democratic aspirations and ideals. Through a demonstration effect (accelerated by the modern media), people became aware that it might be possible to have a "voice" in how they were governed. A number of governments that were formerly autocratic acquiesced to the new trend for participatory democracy, as pressure from "civil society" became irrepressible. For those with no tradition or culture of democracy, however, transition was not without its problems, and sometimes raised hopes that were not met. Moreover, violent manifestations of these same aspirations also provoked conflict and in some cases created new grievances. On the whole, however, democratization was an important development and was accompanied by a corresponding growth of "civil society" as an emerging force.

The United Nations also made substantial inroads in establishing a set of rules for the interaction between governments and those they govern. The Universal Bill of Human Rights and the many declarations and conventions that followed it provided a recipe for conflict prevention and good governance. Although these standards were not universally applied, and many instances of gross human rights violations remained, significant progress was made in a number of countries.

Other developments were more remarkable for their absence. The kind of blatant cross-border aggression that had been so common in the first half of the century and that the UN had been designed to control, became so unlikely that even when Iraqi troops massed on the border of Kuwait, few expected them to carry out the threat. Moreover, when they did, the action drew universal condemnation as a breach of the paramount norm of the inviolability of borders.

The End of the Cold War

Rather unexpectedly the cold war ended, but its legacy of abuse and neglect was not so easily swept away. One superpower had bankrupted itself in its headlong race toward military superiority, and the other had spent vast resources on developing and producing expensive weapons, many of which would now have to be destroyed. As well, a myriad of new problems began to emerge.

The fragmentation of the Soviet empire, which followed the collapse of the bipolar system, led to a new set of threats. Newly independent states struggled with the simultaneous problems of a dual transition to democracy and a market economy, and with the reemergence of old aspirations and fears, released by the lifting of repression and exacerbated by the uncertainties of a new era.

Moreover, the world was still awash with weapons. The Great Powers, who were the largest manufacturers and exporters, were reluctant to engage in a rapid conversion of their arms industries for fear that it would lead to economic decline, and so continued major exports to the hot spots of the world. Many governments, whose social and economic problems were pressing, nonetheless committed large sums of money to purchase these arms. With the smuggling of nuclear material, horizontal nuclear proliferation emerged as another threat. A number of countries continued to develop and stockpile chemical and biological weapons. But most of the death toll in the developing world derived from the robust trade in small arms. And as confirmed in Rwanda, even the machete turned out to be a weapon of mass destruction.

Large segments of the world's population still lived in extreme poverty and were malnourished, unhealthy, and undereducated, with little prospect of improving their lot. The neglect of demographic and environmental problems led to a whole host of threats to security as grinding poverty, severe underdevelopment, economic stagnation, and rising expectations generated the necessary conditions for protest, rebellion, violence, and war. Also, there were new threats to security, as ozone depletion, global warming, deforestation, desertification, soil salinization, and species extinction endangered the health of the planet itself.

In the power vacuum left by the end of the cold war, the UN was no longer sidelined, but was instead suddenly required to take center stage. In a short space of time, the expectations, demands, and responsibilities placed on the international organization increased dramatically, while its resources remained frozen or were further cut. An organization whose peacekeeping budget was no greater than the combined budgets of the New York City police and fire departments (Commission on Global Governance, 1995) was being asked to become the world's police and fire department. Meanwhile, some of those who clamored for the organization to take on this enhanced role continued to be late in the payment of their dues or to withhold them altogether.

As a result, the UN has staggered under the unprecedented expectation that it should be able to deal effectively with a multiplicity of extremely complex and serious problems and that it should be able to do so with resources that are clearly inadequate to the task. The optimism that followed the cold war has evaporated and been replaced by a pervasive sense of pessimism, paralysis, and malaise.

Developing a More Effective Approach for the Next Century

If emerging chaos is to be contained, the gains of the last century sustained, and new opportunities pursued, there is an urgent need to reform and revitalize the international system. A major factor underlying the current impasse has been the inability of member states to identify and agree upon an appropriate methodology to match the new strategic environment. The UN's mandate and methodology were based on a collective security system created for a strategic environment where interstate conflict was considered to be the major threat to peace and security. But since the end of the cold war, only five of 96 armed conflicts have occurred between states—the other 91 have been within states (Wallensteen and Sollenberg, 1996).

Although there has been considerable discussion about what to do to adapt the United Nations to the new environment, a major reorientation has not occurred. The organization has continued to focus its efforts downstream on conflict management rather than upstream on conflict prevention. Rather than creating a new cooperative security approach, which could address problems more holistically and at an earlier stage, the UN Security Council has largely focused on trying to remold its collective security apparatus to respond when a problem can no longer be ignored. The limitation of applying these old practices to intrastate conflicts, however, has become apparent in the many setbacks that the organization and its operations have faced in recent years. These difficulties have contributed further to a crisis of confidence.

Lying at the heart of the dilemma are differing worldviews and prescriptions for the organization. The power struggle that has ensued between member states of the North and South in pursuit of these differing objectives is (at least, in part) responsible for the current paralysis in "political will," which is so often blamed for the UN's financial crisis, as well as the inability of member states to agree on or implement an appropriate reform agenda. Indeed, a recent study by Kim and Russett (1996) on voting patterns in the General Assembly highlights the differing goals of the two blocs:

> The North-South split now characterizes voting positions as much as the East-West split once did. The importance of North-South issues is not new, but during the cold war years it tended to be conflated with and be overshadowed by East-West issues as a source of division. The resurgence of North-South voting renews and strengthens a long-standing alignment, one now likely to dominate the UN for a substantial period in its future. Voting alignments are likely to be shaped by state preferences along developmental lines, and views of self-determination and economic development will reflect the continuing great differences between rich and poor nations.

Differing Perceptions in the North and South

These differing goals derive from the very different structural realities that separate the North and South. The South Commission (1990) summarizes these as follows:

> Three and a half billion people, three quarters of all humanity, live in the developing countries. By the year 2000, the proportion will probably have risen to four fifths. . . . While most of the people of the North are affluent, most of the people in the South are poor, while the economies of the North are generally strong and resilient, those of the South are mostly weak and defenceless; while the countries in the North are, by and large, in control of their destinies, those in the South are very vulnerable to external factors and lacking in functional sovereignty . . . Were all humanity a single nation-state, the present North-South divide would make it an unviable, semi-feudal entity, split by internal conflicts. Its small part is advanced, prosperous, powerful; its much bigger part is under-developed, poor, powerless. A nation so divided within itself would be recognized as unstable. A world so divided within itself should likewise be recognized as inherently unstable. And the position is worsening, not improving.

In order to characterize the resulting debate, the perceptions of North and South are sketched out below. Of course, neither the North nor the South is monolithic and widely divergent opinions exist on both sides (i.e., this characterization does not represent the views of some of the middle-level governments in the North nor of some of the rapidly developing states of the South). Nevertheless, however simplified, it is presented here to highlight the contrasting concerns of each side.

Perceptions in the South

Due to the bitter legacy of colonialism, the struggle for self-determination, and the structure and practices of current political and financial arrangements in the international sector, perceptions in the South are that the North remains largely in control of financial and political power, and thus continues to impose its will through various forms of neocolonialism. Members of the South, desiring at last to be the masters of their own fate, have typically responded by rejecting any attempts at coercive influence by the North. Many of the North's attempts to assist are now viewed with suspicion, since past examples (such as loans and the subsequent debt burden or the restructuring of economies) have, arguably, benefited the North more than the South. Representatives of the South have typically seen development as *the* major peace and security issue and have sought tirelessly to give it a higher profile on the international agenda. When the North failed to respond adequately, the South initially increased its demands to be heard—but more recently has succumbed to a resigned pessimism that the North will *never* grasp the significance of its problems or provide the necessary partnership to help overcome them.

Perceptions in the North

For its part, the North's preoccupation with the threat to its own security caused by the prolonged East-West conflict meant the most powerful governments did not give sufficient thought or attention to North-South issues, except where they intersected with East-West concerns. Severe resource shortages and grinding poverty in Africa, Asia, and Latin America seemed less salient or threatening than Soviet submarine-launched ballistic missiles off the coast of the United States or medium-range nuclear weapons within a few minutes (from launch to impact) of European cities. Following the cold war, the breakdown of the Soviet empire and Yugoslavia maintained much of the North's focus on Europe and the former Soviet Union, as well as on peace and security as traditionally conceived. Many in the North continued to see security problems and solutions largely in power-based, military terms, and the invasion of Kuwait and the subsequent enforcement action against Iraq reinforced this notion. Carrots and sticks were still viewed as the major tools of diplomacy, with coercive influence strategies typically given priority. The causes of conflict were attributed largely to bad leadership or ideological extremism rather than to real concerns or grievances. The linkage between peace, security, and development was unacknowledged or rejected. The depth and extent of problems in the South were not fully understood and demands from the South were often responded to by the North's own version of reactance*—which was manifested by withholding dues, as well as

---

Reactance is a psychological term that describes the tendency to react against pressure to comply with another party's wishes, in order to assert one's own freedom of action. Thus, contrary to the other party's intention, pressure sometimes can backfire.

by isolationist tendencies and a return to narrow definitions of national interest.

On the other end of the North's political spectrum, those who did see a credible connection between security and development and were aware of the depth of the South's plight were sometimes overwhelmed by the sheer magnitude of the problems, which seemed insurmountable, especially in a political climate where minimalist positions were normative and concepts of collective responsibility were too often rejected.

In the pursuit of these differing goals by those from the two blocs, a hard-bargaining rather than a problem-solving approach has prevailed and the outcome has been an entrenchment of oppositional arguments and a "hurting" stalemate. The UN and the problems it urgently needs to tackle have been held hostage to mutual attempts by both sides to exert their will. The sad result has been a corresponding "lack of will."

The Need to Develop a More Integrative Agenda

To overcome this impasse, a new *process* for conducting multilateral negotiations is urgently needed. A problem-solving approach will have to replace positional bargaining. To bridge and reconcile these differing worldviews, a better understanding of the problems and a more effective methodology are also required.

This book will seek to articulate a new, more integrative agenda. In order to base its suggestions on a sound diagnosis, it will draw upon two sources of knowledge and experience. The first is the scholarly literature on the root causes of contemporary conflict. David Hamburg (1994) has noted that

> A substantial body of careful empirical research on conflict resolution and international peacemaking . . . is at last beginning to emerge, and the results are providing new insights and guidelines useful to practitioners. It is apparent that there is no single approach to conflict resolution that offers overriding promise. Just as the sources and manifestations of human conflict are immensely varied, so too are the approaches to understanding, preventing and resolving conflicts. The field can benefit from a more dynamic interplay between theory and practice. The great challenge is to move with a sense of urgency to organize a broader and deeper effort to understand these issues, and above all, to develop more effective ways in the real world of preventing and resolving conflicts.

Although far from complete, the findings that are emerging from this research do, indeed, provide one starting point.

The second source is made up of the various kinds of procedures and mechanisms that have evolved within the international community to prevent and resolve conflict. The methods of conflict prevention of seven major actors (the UN, five regional organizations, and one NGO) will be examined.

These two sources will provide the foundation from which proposals for an integrative understanding of contemporary conflict and a corresponding methodology for preventing it will be proposed. Thus, this work will attempt to bring to life Hamburg's "dynamic interplay between theory and practice" by drawing on the knowledge obtained by scholars in studying conflict and the experience obtained by practitioners in their efforts to develop appropriate means for preventing and resolving it.

2

The Goal of Sustainable Peace

A S SUGGESTED IN THE previous chapter, sustainable peace has been elu-
sive in the twentieth century, in spite of a number of positive steps in
this direction. But as we approach the twenty-first century, a deepening
understanding of the causes of conflict and the new strategic environment
offer a new opportunity to reexamine how to attain this goal. To promote
sustainable peace, a clear vision will be needed of how to proceed, as well
as a determined and focused effort. The following chapters will attempt
to outline both a vision and some further steps for advancing sustainable
peace.

Both short-term problem solving and long-term structural approaches
to conflict prevention are required. More effective preventive diplomacy is
needed to keep disputes from turning into violent conflict—for example,
by offering assistance in dispute resolution at an *early* stage. But if peace is
to be sustained, it will need to be backed up by a long-term approach that
will address the structural causes of conflict and foster institutions that will
promote the kinds of distributive and procedural justice that have been
shown to make violent conflict less likely. In developing an agenda for
prevention, an understanding of the root causes of conflict should be the
first point of departure. Although summarized briefly below, the subject
will be covered in more depth in chapters 3 and 4.

Beginning with the Root Causes of Conflict

It is now widely agreed that the systematic frustration of human needs is
a major cause of conflict. Grievances and feelings of injustice are likely to

grow when individual and group needs for physical safety and well-being, access to political and economic participation, and cultural or religious expression are threatened or frustrated over long periods of time, especially when a group feels that it is being unfairly disadvantaged compared to other groups. In these cases, communal groups often mobilize along cleavages, such as ethnic, religious, or class lines, to express their grievances and seek redress. Typically, they begin with nonviolent protest, which may escalate to violence if their concerns are ignored.

Although contemporary grievances derive from contemporary factors, many of these have violent historical roots, related to practices of the past, including the injustices perpetuated by colonialism, state and empire building (where autonomous groups were forcibly incorporated into other entities), the decimation of indigenous peoples in the New World, or the mass migration of peoples. In many of these instances, little has been done to remedy the resultant imbalances, which are still manifest in systematic patterns of discrimination and injustice today (Gurr and Harff, 1994). It is these contemporary practices that need to be ameliorated if conflict is to be prevented.

Since it is the state that provides physical and cultural safety and regulates political and economic access, the prime objective of group mobilization tends to be *political access*. In cases where governments recognize, listen to, and accommodate dissatisfied groups, grievances may be lessened or resolved. Problems arise, however, when governments ignore or repress these concerns (Gurr, 1993).

In response to this analysis, the concept of "human security" has been advanced as the best foundation upon which "state security" can be built and, indeed, the evidence suggests that the most secure states are those that provide the greatest human security to their populations. Weak states are those that either do not, or cannot, provide human security. Moreover, this very weakness may lead political elites into a vicious cycle that further weakens their security and that of their people. In an attempt to increase their own security, governing elites amass the trappings of power, by investing heavily in military hardware or using repressive tactics. But diversion of money away from their people's needs or massive repression (although sometimes effective in the short term) tends to lead in the long term to greater discontent among the populace and increased vulnerability for the elite. Hence, assisting states in their capacity to enhance human security would seem to offer a promising approach to conflict prevention.

An Agenda for Prevention:
The Promotion of Good Governance

Recently, the linkage between development, democracy, human rights, and peace has also been more widely recognized and articulated than ever before (Boutros-Ghali, 1994, 1996). This synthesis is a useful one since it introduces a new element into the equation and the old North-South development-versus-security debate. That new element is the need for *a fairer process*—a process capable of reducing major grievances before they grow into problems. This approach suggests that what is needed to create the opportunity for both development *and* peace is *good governance,* which will allow people to determine their own priorities; safeguard and promote their civil, political, economic, social, and cultural rights; and provide a pluralist environment, within which they can live with one another in peace, with the freedom to develop in all ways.

Of course, to be effective, good governance must be instituted at all levels of society—local, national, regional, and international. Moreover, all levels will need to develop the protection of individual human rights, as well as the procedures and mechanisms necessary to adequately protect and balance the many contending demands of various groups.

Thus, it will be argued that one goal of prevention should be to assist in building human security through the development of an international architecture made up of the building blocks of good governance structures. This would mean providing assistance to local and national governments in the development of good governance, with special assistance for weak states and those in transition. It would also mean strengthening the governance structures and mechanisms available through subregional, regional, and international organizations—to create a "voice" for all peoples and a fairer distribution of resources within and between regions. The task would be to create a set of mutually reinforcing, self-correcting dispute settlement systems, through the development of interlocking good governance systems, which would operate effectively to prevent and resolve disputes in a constructive manner.

Following the lead of the Brundtland Commission, which blended environmental responsibility and development into the new and more dynamic concept of "sustainable development," it will be argued that the pairing of good governance and conflict prevention offers the best path to what, in this book, has been termed *sustainable peace.* It will be argued that together, the twin concepts of sustainable development and sustainable peace could provide a full, and more focused and acceptable agenda for conflict prevention for the international community for the twenty-first century. Since sustainable development has received considerable attention elsewhere, this book will focus more narrowly on sustainable peace, while acknowledging the importance of sustainable development as an intimately related concept.

Building Confidence through the Development of a Cooperative Security Methodology

Knowledge about conflict can also provide guidance on *how* change can be brought about. Indeed, the literature on conflict escalation clearly demonstrates that power-based, coercive methods of exerting influence, although very much the normative procedure used in noncooperative relationships, are typically (even in these relationships) *not* the most effective. They tend to create countercoercion, or reactance (the latter being a situation whereby the other party resists the attempt to influence in an effort to reassert its freedom). In any case, attempts at coercive influence often create a hostile relationship, making persuasion less, rather than more, likely. A much more effective methodology for influence exists in cooperative relationships, where socialization, assistance, and mutual problem solving provide powerful incentives for change. These processes are even more effective when they promote standards and norms that have been agreed upon by the parties. Indeed, this approach is the basis for all successful cooperative relationships.

Promoting Agreed-Upon Standards and Norms for Good Governance

It is encouraging to note that the first steps toward promoting good governance have already been taken. The creation of the more than 70 human rights instruments that the United Nations has endorsed over the past 50 years is one of the organization's major accomplishments and provides a wide consensus and agreed-upon basis for providing human security through the satisfaction of human needs. In fact, the Universal Declaration of Human Rights, the International Covenant on Civil and Political Rights, and the International Covenant on Economic, Social and Cultural Rights, as well as the declarations that have followed in their wake, offer the best available *blueprint for good governance,* specifying in great detail exactly how "human security" should be provided by governments. The key demands of individuals and communal groups to be discussed in the next two chapters are all prescribed as the *duty* of states in these documents. Moreover, even those states that have not signed the protocols have usually voted for them in the General Assembly and are obligated by virtue of their membership in the international community, which has endorsed these norms, to abide by their contents (Franck, 1990, 1994; Schachter, 1991).

Further, the connection between human needs (cast as "rights" in these conventions and declarations) and conflict prevention were clearly recognized by those who drafted the standards and provide a reminder to governments about *why* it is in their interest to guarantee human rights. The preamble to the Universal Declaration states: *"Whereas it is essential, if man is not to be compelled to have recourse, as a last resort, to rebellion against tyranny and oppression, that human rights should be protected by the rule of law"* (emphasis added).

But if "human security" and good governance are to be developed, the establishment of widely agreed-upon norms is merely the first step. What will be crucial in translating these norms into reality is the provision of *assistance* and the development of *positive incentives* to help governance structures at all levels move in this direction. Since, as discussed earlier, the state remains the major determiner of "who gets what" within a society (and since the Westphalian State does not seem likely to be replaced anytime soon), one of the major focal points for prevention by international and regional organizations should be the strengthening of human security by strengthening the capacity of states, through a process of socialization, assistance, and problem solving.

In order to examine how the UN and regional organizations have approached this goal and what methodology they have developed in this regard, chapters 5 to 11 will examine the evolving mechanisms of seven major actors in the area of conflict prevention: the United Nations, the Council of Europe, the Organization for Security and Cooperation in Europe, the Organization of American States, the Organization of African Unity, the Association of Southeast Asian Nations, and the Carter Center. (It should be noted that these actors merely represent a sample of those working in the field.) Although the sources of insecurity differ from region to region and each organization has responded in a unique manner to the challenges it faces, even a brief examination of these diverse approaches will be useful.

Providing Assistance for Good Governance

In the last few years, a new preventive methodology has been gradually evolving, both within the United Nations and regional organizations, and while it has not attracted much attention as such, it has, nonetheless, been received with enthusiasm by the consumers. It provides the seeds for a potentially useful and more integrative approach.

As will be elaborated in the following chapters, one major feature of the new methodology is the offering of technical *assistance* to member states. The United Nations Center for Human Rights, for example, has sometimes been unpopular with certain member states because of its involvement in monitoring human rights abuses, but it has received considerable praise and support from these same states for the development of its Advisory Services, Technical Assistance, and Information Branch—which has offered governments assistance in drafting constitutions, legislation, or bills of rights or in bringing national laws into conformity with international standards.

The UN's Electoral Assistance Division offers another kind of assistance, in this case, help across the whole range of electoral issues. The response to this service has been equally enthusiastic, as can be seen in the more than 60 requests for electoral assistance in a short period of time. In the last few years, regional organizations have also followed this model. Electoral assistance is now offered by the Council of Europe (COE), the Organization for Security and Cooperation in Europe (OSCE), the Organization of American States (OAS), the Organization of African Unity (OAU), as well as by a number of nongovernmental organizations.

Several regional organizations (the COE, OSCE, and OAS) have even more recently moved a step further by offering assistance in building democratic institutions. These programs prepare and support key institutional actors in the reforms needed to create good governance, and provide expert advice in developing the legal bases for the safeguard of human rights.

Yet another variation can be seen in the work of the OSCE High Commissioner on National Minorities, who offers assistance to OSCE participating states in finding solutions to minority problems. By visiting those concerned and discussion with all parties, he seeks to understand the basis for minority grievances, and then to offer specific recommendations to governments for change to legislation, regulation, or practice.

The Long-term Preventive Diplomacy Missions of the OSCE offer another kind of conflict-prevention assistance. Missions are typically small and deployed at the invitation of participating states, and they provide an "on the ground" presence that assists the national government in devising means of reducing tensions within the country.

What all of these assistance programs share is the availability of advice and options that governments are free to choose or refuse—but that they have usually accepted. Indeed, this type of assistance has been embraced by states with a wide range of governance structures. Such assistance is attractive to governments precisely because *it is low key and subject to their consent, and it also builds "local capacity."* Most important, this approach provides an acceptable basis for international organizations to become involved in conflict prevention *within* states. It ensures that when a government is ready to take even halting steps toward reform, there is international support to help it move in that direction.

An assistance approach does not replace the more legalistic structures that have been established by the UN and regional organizations to monitor and enforce human rights or the political leverage and action that are sometimes needed to influence states to comply with international law. Legal and political "backup" approaches remain important for governments that do not live up to their obligations, but the necessity to resort to them can be greatly reduced by providing knowledge, exposure to alternatives, and positive incentives for change.

Providing Incentives for Good Governance

It will also be argued that one of the most important incentives for change is group socialization. Indeed, the whole evolution of international law and governance can be seen in these terms. The United Nations, regional organizations, subregional organizations, bilateral relationships, nongovernmental organizations, as well as individual citizens all have an important role to play in socializing states to comply with the group norms that they have collectively developed to make conflict less likely. The development of group rules and norms (outlined in the charters, conventions, resolutions and practices of intergovernmental organizations (IGOs), as well as in bilateral agreements and treaties) and the use of mechanisms that monitor and respond when parties do not comply with the rules they have mutually established, have become powerful tools for influencing individual governments to conform to the norms, institutions, and practices of the larger community.

The necessary political architecture for socialization has begun to appear recently with the strengthening of regional and subregional organizations, and the institutionalization of representative political forums within each. These groups meet frequently and regularly to discuss potential and existing problems, consider ways to prevent these from growing into bigger problems, recommend a course of action to the governments involved, and urge them to respond (e.g., the OAU Central Organ, the OSCE Permanent Council, the OAS Permanent Council, as well as their corresponding higher level forums, which meet less frequently). The process provides ongoing corrective feedback, which helps governments understand and conform to the group's norms. This is a welcome development, especially when such forums focus their attention on prevention as well as on crisis management, as they have begun to do. In Europe, the Americas, and Africa (and to a lesser extent in the Asia-Pacific region), states are becoming (albeit guardedly) more open to the idea that regional organizations have a role to play in helping to resolve internal problems, as well as in assisting with the development of processes that are designed for conflict prevention. Indeed, it is interesting to note that some of the regional forums have developed further in this area than the UN Security Council, with its perennial problem of Great Power domination and its range of more coercive, collective security powers.

A related socialization process occurs when a critical mass of states with a common agenda for promoting good governance coalesces. Once ascendant, this agenda exerts a pull on the other members of the community who want to be accepted into the "club." This pull is particularly strong when accompanied by an expectation of related advantages. For example,

Eastern European and CIS countries have been eager to join the Council of Europe, and to meet its requirements for democratization and conformity with the principles of human rights, in order to have the option of joining other parts of the European architecture, such as the European Union, with its consequent economic advantages, or NATO, with its security umbrella. The rapid democratization in Eastern and Central Europe, Latin America, and Africa over the last ten years, derives, in part, from this kind of regional socialization of governments and peoples. Observation by citizens and governments of models of governance that appear to be more successful than their own, makes them wish to reform their own structures, in the hope that reform will bring them the same advantages.

A more strategic approach could also be used to provide positive incentives for movement toward better governance. Indeed, if the international community were to agree that good governance is a vital key to prevention, the Bretton Woods institutions and the various bilateral aid organizations could provide assistance for this purpose, so that governments could take steps in this direction. Financial assistance could, for example, be provided to help a government fight corruption, to strengthen an independent judiciary, to restructure and retrain their police force or prison personnel, to develop an electoral commission, to set up a parliament, to create a commission for minorities, or to develop an ombudsman's office.

Institutionalizing a Problem-Solving Approach

Scholars Ury, Brett, and Goldberg (1988) have identified three distinct methods that are used by parties in disputes—a power-based approach (where parties attempt to prove who is the most powerful); a rights-based approach (where they attempt to prove who is "right"); and an interest-based approach, also called "problem solving" (wherein parties attempt to reconcile their major interests through innovative solutions). The first two approaches tend to create zero sum (win-lose) outcomes; the latter is aimed at achieving a positive sum (win-win) outcome.

Analysis of the cost-effectiveness of these approaches in terms of efficiency and resource consumption has shown that the power-based approach is the most costly, whereas the problem-solving approach tends to be the least costly. Also, problem solving is likely to lead to the most sustainable outcome, since when grievances are addressed, problems that created the conflict are less likely to recur.

The search for sustainable peace will therefore need to be based on the establishment of the rule of law (a rights-based approach) and the institutionalization of problem solving (an interest-based approach) to replace violent conflict (a power-based approach). Thus, the methodology of problem solving will need to be institutionalized as a normative practice to replace the power-based approach and to act as a support to the rule of law at all levels of society.

Developing Regional Assistance Programs

Chapters 12 and 13 will propose that the locus of UN preventive action should be moved to the regional level, where access to the problems and those involved can be ongoing, and where cooperation with regional actors can be maximized through the establishment of UN Regional Centers for Sustainable Peace. Such centers could provide two types of conflict prevention services: assistance in dispute settlement and assistance in the development of good governance, but they would need to maintain an exclusive focus on early prevention.

Promoting Good Regional and International Governance

The concluding chapter will address the need to develop more effective regional and international governance. It will be argued that there is an urgent need to create a fairer process through institutional reform, which can offer greater access by all states to political and economic decision making and participation in the international system. Good regional and international governance could mutually reinforce good national and local governance. Revitalized regional and international institutions are needed to promote procedural and distributive justice within and between regions and to more effectively provide both operative and structural approaches to conflict. It will be maintained that greater democratization and pluralism at the regional and international levels must go hand-in-hand with greater democratization and pluralism nationally and locally.

For sustainable peace and sustainable development to become reality, however, the international community not only will need to establish a clear vision and methodology for achieving these objectives, but also will need to address the quintessential issue of providing resources for carrying out its new agenda. Chapter 14 will also emphasize the importance of endowing the international system with the means to accomplish these essential goals, before the world's structural problems become truly unsolvable—something that could happen in the twenty-first century—if we do not respond to this urgent imperative.

3

Diagnosing Contemporary Conflict

THROUGHOUT THE COLD WAR, the superpower confrontation and the nuclear threat it imposed took preeminence in the study of conflict. Even when regional conflicts were considered, the fact that one or both superpowers were involved caused scholars to focus on that involvement, rather than on the deeper origins of the problems. The end of the cold war and the realization that ethnic conflicts were a major problem confronting the international community and that they were not going to disappear anytime soon, caused many scholars (and funding institutions) to shift their focus from the East-West confrontation to the study of ethnic conflict. Their work is providing some useful data and insights that can assist in preventing and ameliorating such conflicts.

Studies of Contemporary Conflict

In a study by Wallensteen and Sollenberg (1996), 91 of the 96 conflicts which occurred since the end of the cold war were within a state. The total number of armed conflicts during this period and their regional breakdown is shown in tables 3.1 and 3.2. As can be seen from table 3.2, most armed conflicts were in Africa and Asia. Wallensteen and Sollenberg conclude that although interstate armed conflict has not disappeared, the balance has definitely shifted toward intrastate conflict. Further, they cautiously suggest that this finding indicates that the international system has been largely successful in its efforts to prevent interstate conflict. Since the main thrust of this book will be to consider how the international

TABLE 3.1
Armed Conflicts and Conflict Locations, 1989–95

Level of Conflict	1989	1990	1991	1992	1993	1994	1995
Minor	14	16	18	23	15	16	12
Intermediate	14	14	13	12	17	19	17
War	19	19	20	20	14	7	6
All Conflicts	47	49	51	55	46	42	35
All Locations	37	39	38	41	33	32	30

Source: Wallensteen and Sollenberg, 1996.

Note: Minor = At least 25 battle-related deaths per year and less than 1,000 battle-related deaths during the course of the conflict. Intermediate = At least 25 battle-related deaths per year and an accumulated total of at least 1,000 deaths, but less than 1,000 per year. War = At least 1,000 battle-related deaths per year.

community can go beyond its traditional approach to conflict between states to find and develop a new, acceptable methodology for preventing and resolving conflict within states, the focus of this review will be largely on the causes of intrastate conflict.

Particularly useful to developing an understanding of this type of conflict is an ongoing study by Ted Robert Gurr (1993, 1994), which assesses the political activity of 268 minority groups who are "at risk." Gurr defined such groups as those minorities that have collectively suffered or benefited from systematic discrimination in relation to other groups in the same state. His study includes not only disadvantaged, but also advantaged minority groups, such as the Tutsi in Rwanda and the white population in South Africa, since such groups are also "at risk." Indeed, throughout this discussion of minorities, it is important to note that in certain cases, minorities have also assumed and abused power. When they have, they can be even more vulnerable than disadvantaged minorities—since when they lose power, they can face the revenge of a discontented majority.

Table 3.3 provides a regional breakdown of the number of countries with minorities at risk, the number of minorities, the population of minorities per region and their percentage. It is notable that the two regions with the largest population of minorities—Asia and sub-Saharan Africa—are also those with the largest number of conflicts.

Gurr's longitudinal study tracks the political activity of these groups across five-year periods, from the end of World War II. It breaks this activity into three categories, according to severity: nonviolent protest, violent protest, and rebellion. The results show that all types of conflict increased sharply. *Nonviolent protest more than doubled. Violent protest and rebellion*

TABLE 3.2
Armed Conflicts and Conflict Locations by Region, 1989–95

Region	1989	1990	1991	1992	1993	1994	1995
Europe							
Minor	0	2	4	5	4	2	2
Intermediate	1	1	1	2	2	2	2
War	1	0	1	2	4	1	1
No. of Conflicts	2	3	6	9	10	5	5
No. of Locations	2	2	5	7	6	3	4
Middle East							
Minor	0	1	1	2	1	1	1
Intermediate	3	4	3	4	5	2	2
War	1	1	3	1	1	2	1
No. of Conflicts	4	6	7	7	7	5	4
No. of Locations	4	6	5	5	5	5	4
Asia							
Minor	7	5	5	7	6	6	5
Intermediate	6	7	5	6	5	7	6
War	6	6	6	7	4	2	2
No. of Conflicts	19	18	16	20	15	15	13
No. of Locations	11	11	8	11	8	8	9
Africa							
Minor	4	7	7	8	4	6	3
Intermediate	2	1	1	0	4	5	4
War	8	9	9	7	3	2	2
No. of Conflicts	14	17	17	15	11	13	9
No. of Locations	12	15	15	14	11	12	9
Americas							
Minor	3	1	1	1	0	1	1
Intermediate	2	1	3	0	1	3	3
War	3	3	1	3	2	0	0
No. of Conflicts	8	5	5	4	3	4	4
No. of Locations	8	5	5	4	3	4	4

Source: Wallensteen and Sollenberg, 1996.

Notes: Europe includes the states in the Caucasus. The Middle East includes Egypt, Iraq, Iran, Israel, Lebanon, Syria, Turkey, and the states of the Arabian penninsula. Asia includes Oceania, Australia and New Zealand. Africa includes Comoros, but not Egypt. Americas include the states in the Caribbean.

TABLE 3.3
Minorities at Risk in 1995 by World Region

World Region	Number of countries with minorities at risk	Number of minorities at risk	Population of minorities at risk (1995 estimates)	
			Total	Percent of regional population
Western democracies and Japan (21)	15	30	90,789,000	10.8
Eastern Europe and the NIS (27)	24	59	53,704,000	12.3
East, Southeast and South Asia (21)	19	57	441,732,000	14.4
North Africa and the Middle East (19)	11	26	94,263,000	27.3
Africa south of the Sahara (38)	28	66	226,695,000	36.9
Latin America and the Caribbean (23)	17	30	112,320,000	23.3
Total (149)	114	268	1,019,503,000	17.7

Source: Ted Robert Gurr, Minorities at Risk Project, Center for International Development and Conflict Management, University of Maryland at College Park, personal communication.

Note: Politically significant national and minority peoples of 100,000 or more in countries with 1995 populations greater than one million, based on current research by the Minorities at Risk Project, Center for International Development and Conflict Management, University of Maryland. Changing political circumstances and new information lead to periodic updates in the inclusion and exclusion of groups under observation. Numbers of countries above the one million population threshold are shown in parentheses in the World Region column. Most population figures for national and minority peoples are estimates, some are conjectural. Population percentages are calculated from UN estimates for all countries in each region.

increased by a factor of four. Grievances about discrimination and threats to group identity activated hundreds of protest movements. When coupled with historically grounded demands for the restoration of autonomy, the same grievances triggered 114 cases of rebellion. In 35 of these, groups resorted to terrorism, and in the other 79, guerrilla or civil wars were fought (Gurr, 1993). Almost half of the conflicts spanned three or more successive five-year periods and nearly all were located in the developing world. Ten of the regimes threatened by autonomy movements resorted to mass killings in separatist regions (Gurr and Harff, 1994). The resulting toll has been staggering. Of the 20 million killed in wars during this period, more than 70 percent died in wars involving ethnic conflict.

Gurr's study also notes significant differences across regions in the form and magnitude of communal conflict. Nonviolent protest was the most common form of communal action in western democracies, Latin America, Eastern Europe, and the former Soviet Union. Violent protest was more common in Eastern Europe and the Middle East than elsewhere. Most rebellions occurred in Asia, the Middle East, and Africa. The latter regions were the source of all but five of the short-term guerrilla and civil wars and all but one of the protracted communal wars that occurred since World War II.

The Minorities at Risk Study shows clearly that most problems begin with nonviolent protest and escalate into violent conflict. In authoritarian regimes, the escalation often occurs quickly, because the state is likely to be repressive rather than reformist, denying rather than addressing human needs. In democracies, the progression is slower; an average of thirteen years elapsed between the establishment of a movement and violent action. When the 79 groups involved in civil wars and rebellions were examined, 43 conflicts escalated from protest in a previous period and 28 escalated from lower to higher levels of rebellion. Gurr points out that this lag *should have provided ample time for governments to respond to communal grievances before violence erupted.*

The study's findings also challenge the conventional belief that religious extremism has become the major source of communal violence over the past decade. Although militant sects have become more assertive, their activity has not increased any more rapidly than that of other groups. In the 1980s, the average magnitude of conflict by militant sects was about the same as that of conflict by indigenous people and communal contenders, and considerably less than that of ethnonationalists. In that same decade, groups defined either completely or in part on the basis of religious cleavages accounted for one quarter of the total magnitude of conflict by all groups. While religious differences exist between many minorities and dominant groups, Gurr argues that this is more often a contributory factor, rather than a root cause of conflict.

The Causes of Protracted Social Conflict

As noted earlier, those who study conflict have shown that conflicts most often occur when basic human needs, such as the need for physical security and well-being; communal or cultural recognition, participation, and control; and distributive justice are repeatedly denied, threatened, or frustrated, especially over long periods of time (Azar, 1990; Burton, 1979, 1984, 1987, 1990; Galtung, 1980, 1990; Maslow, 1962; Mitchell, 1990;

Pruitt and Rubin, 1986; Sandole, 1990; and many others). Grievances and feelings of injustice accumulate—especially when one's identity group is perceived to be unfairly disadvantaged in relation to other identity groups.

Lake and Rothchild (1996) argue that collective fears for the future often motivate ethnic conflict, especially when there is "acute social uncertainty, a history of conflict, and fear of what the future might bring." These fears are greatest when they relate to physical security and well-being.

The need for recognition of communal and cultural identity, however, can also be important. Communal identity means, among other things, that individuals within a group share some combination of a common language, customs, religion, myth of descent, history, collective name, and association with a specific territory (which the group may or may not possess at the time) (Brown, 1993; Burton, 1990; Ryan, 1990; Smith, 1993).

Competition for scarce resources may also be at the core of ethnic conflict. In a world where resources are finite, their supply is often distributed unevenly, with dominant groups enjoying adequate satisfaction of these needs and nondominant groups suffering privation. "Property rights, jobs, scholarships, educational admissions, language rights, government contracts and development allocations all confer benefits on individuals and groups. In societies where ethnicity is an important basis for identity, group competition over resources often forms along ethnic lines" (Lake and Rothchild, 1996).

When groups fear for their physical or cultural safety or they are discriminated against on the basis of their ethnicity, they naturally mobilize to express their collective concerns and to seek redress. Previous experiences of exploitation and victimization strengthen a group's identity and shape its sense of collective injustice (Brown, 1996; Gurr, 1993). Although mobilization is most frequently on the basis of ethnicity, groups sometimes also mobilize around other identities, such as religion or class. When more than one identity differentiates the dominant from the nondominant groups, for example, a difference in ethnicity, religion, *and* class, the cleavage between groups is even greater.

In modern society, the denial or satisfaction of needs for physical security, recognition of group identity, and access to scarce resources is largely regulated by the state (Esman, 1990b; Esman, 1994; Lake and Rothchild, 1996). Thus, one of the first demands of identity groups tends to be for access to the political process.

When political elites recognize and accommodate the basic human needs of communal groups, disputes over the distribution of political and economic power tend to be managed satisfactorily (Azar, 1990; Gurr, 1993). But many governments are too fragile, partisan, authoritarian, or incompetent to do so and many also utterly fail to meet their population's basic human needs. Often through a distortion of modes of governance, political authority has been concentrated in the hands of the dominant group or a coalition of dominant groups, who use the state as a means of maximizing their own interests at the expense of others. To maximize their own power, these groups limit access by nondominant groups to political and social institutions (Azar, 1990). Indeed, Sisk (1996) proposes that the *role* of the state is a crucial predictor of the severity of conflict. He asks: "Does it stand above conflicts and mediate them, or does a group 'own' the state and use its power to the detriment of other groups?"

State weakness can also exacerbate interethnic fears. When states are no longer able to arbitrate between groups or provide guarantees of protection, concerns about physical security accelerate, causing groups to prepare for violence. In consequence, the well-known "security dilemma" begins to operate, as each side's preparation for potential conflict stimulate the other's fears and create a vicious cycle of escalation (Lake and Rothchild, 1996).

Factors such as a poor resource base or rapid population growth can also contribute to ethnic conflict since they exacerbate communal competition and constrain a government's policy options for responding. In some cases, there is simply not enough to go around—a factor that is particularly relevant to many protracted conflicts in the developing world. Sahnoun (1995) suggests that the divisions in Somali society derived in large part from the long-term struggle to survive. He proposes that insecurity itself was the common underlying factor, prompted by the threat of starvation or the prospect of diminishing access to resources. He comments further:

> In the next 50 years the world population will reach the 9 billion mark, with most of the increase occurring in the South. World economic output will quintuple over the same period. The joint pressure of these two trends on world resources will be devastating. We are already losing 10 million hectares of forest each year and 6 million hectares of arable land are blown away by the wind. Some non-renewable resources will disappear forever and some renewable resources such as drinkable water will become dangerously limited as the World Bank has just warned us. Erosion and desertification will compel entire populations to move from the areas they inhabit today. . . . we are entitled to ask ourselves: will the Somali scenario be repeated in these areas? Insecurity is, I believe, a paradigm which should be taken seriously.

Further, a state's linkage with the international system may also impact on its ability to meet basic human needs. Economic dependency within the international economic system limits the autonomy of the state and distorts the domestic economic and political systems through the formation of subtle coalitions of international capital, domestic capital, and the state. Stedman (1996) discusses how the ascendancy of neoclassical theories of economic growth, which were imposed by international financial institutions, forced rapid changes in the economy of many African states and contributed to the wave of political instability in the late 1980s. Another relevant factor is a state's political and military client relationships. In the usual formulation, powerful states provide protection in exchange for loyalty, but this arrangement sometimes leads states to pursue domestic and foreign policy directions that are not in the interest of their own citizens (Azar, 1990).

Historical Grievances

In outlining the roots of minority group grievances, Gurr and Harff (1994) delineate four major historical processes—conquest, state-building, migration, and economic development. The expansion of empires (such as the Russian, Austro-Hungarian, Ottoman Turk, Chinese, and Ethiopian) led to many autonomous people being forcibly incorporated into new entities. The European colonizers of Africa, the Middle East, and Asia carved up and created states with little regard for preexisting boundaries, and favored some groups over others, creating internal imbalances. (Even in the postcolonial period, many minority groups have felt that independence has not always helped their situation, with the dominant group seen as the new colonizer.)

European expansionism into the Americas and Australasia resulted in the physical and cultural decimation of many indigenous peoples. The subsequent plantation economies of the Americas created a need for cheap labor, which resulted in the importation of African slaves, whose descendants now form minorities in these regions. European colonization of Southeast Asia, the Indian subcontinent, and Africa created mass migrations of European settlers, as well as Chinese and Lebanese traders, and African and Indian laborers. More recently, the industrial economies of Europe, North America, Japan, and the Middle East have attracted large numbers of economic immigrants to provide cheap labor. These historical processes thrust together identity groups of unequal size and advantage. Dominant groups often capitalized on this to the detriment of minorities, creating lasting legacies of intergroup grievance. The sudden impact of one ethnic group on another through invasion, annexation, or migration gave rise to conflicts of interest in which the various groups sometimes sought to fulfil their aspirations through a struggle for political control (Gurr and Harff, 1994).

In some instances, governments attempted to "clean up the map" through such drastic measures as forced mass-population transfers or expulsions—with genocide being the ultimate excess (Ra-anan, 1990). These efforts to make states more homogeneous, however, have had a poor record of "success." Of the more than 180 states that exist today, fewer than 20 are ethnically homogeneous (as defined by having minorities that account for less than 5 percent of the population) (Welsh, 1993). Rather than "cleaning up the map," these practices simply resulted in deep and enduring scars of interethnic hostility.

Forced assimilation policies, also referred to as "cultural genocide," "ethnocide," or "cultural colonialism," have been another approach to erasing ethnic differences. In some cases, the state has banned the use of a particular language, religion or custom. More often than not, however, coerced assimilation has backfired, stimulating ethnic revival or secessionist movements (Ryan, 1990).

Mutually agreed upon assimilation projects, on the other hand, have had a much greater chance of success. The crucial factor, in these cases, has been that groups *wanted* to be assimilated into the dominant culture. Success has also been more likely when groups are more similar culturally or are migrants rather than ethnic groups living in their own territory (Nordlinger, 1972). Assimilation is not, however, a short-term project. Deutsch (1984) estimates that full assimilation of different ethnic groups (through intermarriage and blurring of ethnic boundaries) requires between 300 and 700 years. In short, unless targeted at people who are willing to acquire a new civic identity, assimilation projects have typically created rather than prevented conflict.

Various other state-building policies have also exacerbated grievances. "Hegemonic control" has been common in imperial or authoritarian societies (although it can also occur in democratic states when the majority party has complete control). Its intention is to keep individuals or groups in their place through a policy of containment. Hegemonic control has typically made ethnic demands for greater political or economic rights either "unthinkable" or "unworkable," since the state's internal security apparatus threatens all those who dare to oppose it. Of course, when any hegemonic system breaks down, the history of suppression adds to the stock of grievances, leading to an even more robust backlash (McGarry and O'Leary, 1993).

Thus, many contemporary conflicts are the current manifestation of a cycle of historical grievance. Although led by modern political entrepreneurs, who are also articulating modern grievances, their intensity is related to deep-rooted beliefs in a separate identity that were never completely extinguished by state policies of repression, eradication, or homogenization. Severe political and economic discrimination often leaves a durable legacy of reverberating echoes of conflict.

Finally, previous violence between groups also contributes to animosity and fear, which can last for generations. When sudden changes in the political or economic environment lead to new levels of insecurity, assessing the intentions of the other side becomes difficult. In the absence of information, groups often fall back on past beliefs about the other group. When

memories or stories (whether true or not) of atrocities exist, these beliefs
can stimulate fear and influence behavior. This is one way in which past
conflict makes future conflict more likely (Lake and Rothchild, 1996).

Contemporary Grievances

In spite of the importance of historical grievances in predisposing parties
to conflict, contemporary circumstances are what is most likely to trigger
conflict. When people interact on a daily basis with others whose language
is different, whose cultural traditions are hard to comprehend, and whose
backgrounds teach them to behave differently, they develop an awareness
of the differences between themselves and the other group. When they
have to compete socially and economically with another group, differences
in interests naturally occur (Ra-anan, 1990). When one's ethnic identity
determines one's security, one's life chances, and one's opportunity, it is
not surprising that this identity unites groups more solidly than any other
in terms of perceived common interests and destiny (Esman, 1990a).
Thus, ethnicity splits groups into "us" versus "them," "insider" versus
"outsider," and "in-group" versus "out-group" (Brown, 1993). As previously mentioned, the more distinctions there are between groups, the
more obstacles there are to intergroup understanding. When groups are
treated differently or suffer discrimination, these cleavages are widened
and grievances begin to build.

The Minorities at Risk Study provides useful data about the kinds of
contemporary grievances that lead groups to advocate demands for autonomy, greater political access within states, and greater economic or cultural
rights. The findings will be reviewed below.

Demands for Political Autonomy

Groups which seek *political autonomy* typically want control over their
own governance. They may desire total secession and independence in a
new state, union with a kindred group elsewhere (in a neighboring state,
for example), or greater regional autonomy within the existing state. In
the Minorities at Risk Study, over half of the groups studied expressed
demands for greater autonomy during the 1980s and the more secessionist
of these demands led to some of the most protracted wars of the period.

Gurr found that the strongest historical factor predicting demands for
autonomy was that the group had once governed its own affairs. Sixty-
three of the groups based their claims on having been autonomous until
they were conquered by a modern state. Nineteen had broken free from
existing states or empires but were reincorporated. Thirty-three had been
transferred from one state to another against their will during the breakup

of an empire or during decolonization. The two contemporary factors most likely to intensify groups' demands for autonomy were (1) pressure by the dominant group on group lands and resources, and (2) pressure on cultural distinctiveness.

Demands for Greater Political Access

Demands for greater political rights can take many forms, ranging from the demand for greater participation in political decision making at a central level, to the demand for equal civil rights, or simply to the demand for replacement of unpopular local officials or policies. Access to greater political rights is instrumental in gaining access to economic, social, and cultural rights. By gaining access to political rights, groups become more able to develop and enforce laws that will determine their economic opportunities as well as their cultural and social status.

In studying what led groups to demand greater access to political rights, Gurr's study examined the difference between each minority and majority group, as well as the level of discrimination that the minority group experienced. To operationalize political differences between groups, the study rated each group's access to positions of national or regional political power; access to civil service positions; recruitment into the military and police service; voting rights; rights to organize political activity on behalf of the group's interest; and rights to equal legal protection.

It also examined whether these differences were due to an active policy of discrimination. Discrimination was rated on a five-point scale based on whether members of the group were systematically limited in their enjoyment of political rights or access to political positions in comparison with other groups in their society.

The study's results demonstrated that a significant number of minority groups *are* disadvantaged politically and many are disadvantaged due to *deliberate* policy. The most important finding is that demands for political rights result primarily from discrimination. That is, it is discriminatory policies that most often lead groups to demand access to political decision making.

Demands for Economic Rights

A group's demands for greater economic rights may include a call for a larger share of public funds; improved working conditions; access to higher status jobs; better salaries; better education; access to positions in the military, police, and government bureaucracies; or the protection or return of group lands or other resources. Groups may also want access to wealth, including land, capital credit, foreign exchange, and business licenses; eligibility to compete for government construction and supply contracts; and opportunities for employment in the private sector. Or groups may want a fairer distribution of public services, such as housing, health facilities, roads, water supply, and electricity.

In studying what leads groups to demand access to greater economic rights, Gurr assessed economic differences between the minority and the majority groups, as well as the level of economic discrimination. Economic differences were determined by coding inequalities in income, inequalities in land or other property, access to higher or technical education, presence in commercial activities, presence in professions, and presence in official positions. Gurr found that demands for economic rights arise from the same kinds of conditions that motivate demands for political rights. That is, economic discrimination was largely responsible for political activity to demand economic rights.

The data also suggest that discrimination had a greater impact on the extent of minorities' disadvantages than did cultural differences. Gurr (1993) concludes that *"Policies of neglect and deliberate exclusion are substantially responsible for the persistence of contemporary inequalities"* (emphasis added).

Not surprisingly, the study found that political and economic differences between groups are closely related, as are political and economic discrimination, demonstrating a consistent connection between the two conditions, which he terms a "syndrome of inequality." It also appears to be rare for a group to experience more severe economic discrimination than political discrimination, probably because minorities who have gained political access can use their power to remove discriminatory economic barriers. Gurr suggests, therefore, that it may be more rational for governments to initiate reform by providing political rights, than by providing economic rights.

Demands for Social and Cultural Rights

In the social and cultural arena, demands may be related to one's language (such as for it to be given official status or used in educational settings, government services, or judicial proceedings). Other demands may revolve around freedom of religious belief or practice, equal status in legal matters and in community treatment, or protection from threats or attacks by other communal groups.

In studying what led groups to demand greater social and cultural rights, the study examined the extent of the cultural differences between the minority and majority groups. It found that a greater cultural difference and previous conflict with other communal groups were the best indicators of increased demands for social and cultural rights.

Only a moderate relationship was found with regard to cultural differences and political and economic differences. Also, the data showed only a weak relationship between cultural differences and political and economic discrimination. Gurr concludes that although cultural differences are frequently used to explain and justify the unequal status of particular minorities, the evidence suggests that this is not usually the case.

Gurr (1993) summarizes his data by noting that "two different kinds of dynamics drive the political grievances of contemporary minorities. Political and economic disadvantages motivate communal groups to demand greater access to the political system and greater economic opportunities, whereas a history of political autonomy leads groups to attempt secession." These issues will have to be addressed by governments if conflict is to be prevented.

Factors That Cause Groups to Mobilize to Express Their Grievances

Disadvantaged peoples do not automatically think that the inequalities they experience are unjust, and even when they do, they do not automatically demand redress. Thus, some groups experience grievances over long periods of time without mobilizing. Scholars have suggested several factors as conditions necessary for mobilization, as outlined below.

Ethnic Geography

Concentration of an ethnic minority in a specific region reinforces ethnic identity and makes it more likely that they will be able to organize. In particular, ethnic geography helps to determine the kind of goals that will be pursued. Groups that are concentrated are more likely to pursue separatist or secessionist goals than groups that are geographically scattered. Since political institutions may already exist that can be used for such activities, supporters and resources are easier to organize, and there is little opposition (Levine, 1996). In contrast, pursuit of political or economic rights within the state are more likely where members of ethnic groups are scattered (Levine, 1996). Thus, ethnic geography may determine what a group demands.

Leadership and Political Organization

For a group to mobilize, there must be leadership and a political organization that can voice its grievances and convince group members that they should act. Leadership is also necessary in bringing the group's interest to the attention of governments or others. Sustained collective action requires the articulation of a specific set of demands and a plan of action.

Of course, the nature of leadership is also vitally important. Moderate leadership may help steer communal groups toward satisfactory agreements with governments in which their needs are addressed. But ethnic activists and political entrepreneurs may also emerge (not only within communal groups but also in governments). When they do, their actions can quickly polarize multiethnic societies and dramatically increase the likelihood of conflict. Ethnic activists typically discourage interethnic contact and urge intraethnic association, while political entrepreneurs may use the "ethnic card" to draw electoral support. (Even moderate politicians may embrace this agenda, when extremists otherwise might "outbid" them.) Memories and myths from past conflict situations are evoked to highlight the opposing group's villainy and justify the rightness of their own cause. In this way, political entrepreneurs often "reflect and stimulate ethnic fears for their own aggrandizement" (Lake and Rothchild, 1996).

When collective interests are segmented among subgroups, there may be many contenders for a group's allegiance, leading to competition and factional fighting within a movement. In such cases, a group may be mobilized, but multiple leadership can make it difficult for governments or international organizations to know how to respond.

Changing Circumstances That Provide New Threats to the Group

Often a triggering event or set of events creates the momentum necessary for mobilization and it becomes the turning point at which individual victimization of a group's members is collectively recognized (Azar, 1990). A common trigger is the emergence of a new threat to the vital interests or established expectations of the group (Esman, 1990a). This may occur when there is a sudden change in the political or economic environment—for example, during periods when empires or federal states collapse and new states are formed, or when there is a sudden change to the economic system, such as rapid industrialization, the introduction of market forces into regulated economies, or the integration of the economy into a world market with radically different relative prices (Esman, 1990a; Levine, 1996). When states fail to make accommodations for such changes, groups may mobilize to demand more effective governance, leading to a struggle for greater power or autonomy. When the organizational or communication systems between groups break down in an environment of mutual distrust, disputes may begin to escalate to overt conflicts.

Weak or ineffective states are the most likely candidates for such problems. If a state is strong, it can listen to and address the grievances of minorities, or alternatively, it can seek to suppress them (Azar, 1990). In either case, it will have the means required. If a state is weak, however, it may be able to do neither. This suggests that one point for prevention might be the strengthening of weak states through assistance in the development of more effective governance so that they are able to pursue accommodation of minority groups. This will be discussed in more detail in chapters 12 and 13.

The breakdown of old states can also trigger a sense of insecurity in ethnic groups, which fear that the new state may repress them in new ways. As Lake and Rothchild (1996) note: "When multi-ethnic polities fragment, as in Yugoslavia and the former Soviet Union, the relevant political space alters rapidly and the various ethnic groups that once counted their numbers on a national scale must now calculate their kin in terms of the new smaller territorial units, and may find themselves in a stronger or weaker position." Chechens in Russia, Abkhaz and Ossetians in Georgia, Albanians in the former Yugoslav Republic of Macedonia, Armenians in Azerbaijan, Croats in Bosnia-Herzegovina, and Serbs in Croatia and Bosnia-Herzegovina have all claimed self-determination as a defense against the feared consequences of a new status quo (Shehadi, 1993).

Changing Circumstances That Offer New Opportunities for the Group

Mobilization can also be stimulated when there appears to be a political opportunity for collective benefit if the group can organize itself. Changes in circumstances that are favorable to the group's interests, such as the end of colonial rule, the introduction of democracy in a previously authoritarian state, or the coming to power of a moderate government, sometimes causes communal groups to state their claims more loudly in the hope that, at last, they may be heard.

In such circumstances, however, the danger is that the group may raise its expectations more quickly than the state is able to respond. As a result, dissatisfaction rapidly increases, even when conditions are improving. Disappointment based on what was expected rather than actual gains may, in turn, create a new coalescing of grievances (Esman, 1990a). Thus, as Sisk (1996) notes: "Transitional moments, both in terms of changes in structure of international relations and in terms of relations among groups within states, are moments of promise and peril. Ethnic relations can improve or worsen."

Demonstration Effects

Another possible trigger is the "demonstration effect." In this case, one group's mobilization stimulates another's through observational learning and modeling. Protest movements in Western Europe and North America during the 1960s, the Islamic revival in the Middle East, and indigenous rights movements across the globe, are examples of how mobilization can spread from group to group through a demonstration effect.

Group Identity, Grievances, and Leadership As Necessary Conditions for Mobilization

The evidence suggests that three factors—group identity, deep-seated grievances related to the group's collective status, and the existence of leaders are *all* essential to the development of group mobilization. If grievances and group identity are both weak, there is little chance that a group can be mobilized by any political entrepreneur. On the other hand, the combination of shared grievances with a strong sense of group identity and common interests provides a tinderbox for spontaneous action, whenever external control weakens. The combination can trigger powerful political movements and sustained conflict, which can be organized and focused by group leaders capable of giving plausible expression to group grievances and aspirations. Of course, factors such as resources; size of group membership; ethnic geography; quality of leadership, organizational, economic, and communication skills; status in the larger society; and commitment to "the cause," all contribute to how successful a group is in asserting its claims convincingly and having its needs met (Esman, 1990a).

Factors That Affect Government Responses to Communal Grievances

Apart from the fact that conflict tends to increase group solidarity and a sense of common interest, there was no strong tendency shown in the Minorities at Risk Study for communal movements to become either more radicalized or more moderate over time. Instead, the data demonstrated that the direction in which a minority is likely to move *depends on the response of the government* to the group's expression of grievances. Thus, if the government is willing to seek solutions, the communal group is likely to respond in kind, and if the government adopts hard-line or repressive tactics, communal groups are more likely to do so as well.

Addressing Grievances

Gurr (1993) concludes from his work that when governments listen to grievances and act to address them, problems *are* ameliorated. Confirming this notion, Lake and Rothchild (1996) argue that prevention of ethnic conflict requires governments to *reassure minority groups of their physical and cultural safety, as well as to accord them respect.* They state:

> Stable ethnic relations can be understood as based upon a "contract" between groups. Such contracts specify among other things, the rights and responsibilities, political privileges, and access to resources of each group. These contracts may be formal constitutional arrangements or simply informal understandings between elites. Whatever their form, ethnic contracts channel

politics in peaceful directions. Most importantly, ethnic contracts contain "safeguards" designed to render the agreement self-enforcing. They contain provisions or mechanisms to ensure that each side lives up to its commitments and feels secure that the other will do so as well.

These arrangements and safeguards will be the subject of the next chapter.

Democratic states, in particular, are adept at this kind of accommodation, responding to the protests of many of their communal groups and thereby heading off serious conflicts. As Levine (1996) notes: "It is no accident that, while democracies have not always responded peacefully to separatist challenges, most peaceful secessions have involved democracies." She attributes this to "the presence of democratic institutions, flexible attitudes toward constitutional arrangements, and established traditions of civil discourse." Although she acknowledges that democratic forms of government are not a guarantee that political conflicts will be peacefully resolved, she notes that "it does improve the odds." "Minorities in general and regionally concentrated minorities in particular are more likely to be fairly represented in democratic systems" (Levine, 1996). Sisk (1996) agrees that although democracy is difficult, it offers the greatest hope for long-term peaceful conflict management. But he notes that even when it is not present, there are effective strategies that can manage ethnic tensions.

Ignoring or Repressing Grievances

How governments respond is conditioned by how they perceive their own interests. Governments in multiethnic states, such as the Russian Federation or India, may fear that giving in to the demands of one region could lead to "chain reactions" in other regions and even to the ultimate collapse of the state (Levine, 1996). Governments may be especially fearful of losing, through secessionist movements, regions with particular economic or military value (Levine, 1996).

Some studies have shown that governments also tend to have an exaggerated fear of disloyalty among minority groups. Minorities are often viewed as a kind of Trojan horse (Ryan, 1990). This sense of insecurity is especially strong when a majority group within a state represents a minority within a region, as with the Israelis in the Middle East, the Loyalists in Ireland, the Greek Cypriots of the Eastern Mediterranean, and the Sinhalese in the Indian subcontinent (Ryan, 1990). These fears strongly affect government responses to communal demands.

In order to control the mobilization of dissatisfied groups, governments sometimes adopt heavy-handed military or police actions against members of dissatisfied groups, often under the auspices of special legislation, such as martial law or a state of emergency. Even without special legislation, individuals may be tortured in detention centers, be murdered by death squads, disappear, or be deprived of the basic requirements of life.

Success is sometimes claimed for severe repression, but the record shows that gains from repression are usually short lived. Although it may temporarily quash the expression of demands, it typically adds to the intensity of outgroup grievance and hostility, and may lead to other forms of violence (such as terrorism) or resurgence of even more intense protest at some later time. The moderate parts of a communal movement are discredited, in favor of more radical voices (Ryan, 1990). Unfortunately, governments often draw the wrong conclusions, leading to the same errors being repeated over and over.

Governments also sometimes try to deal with group grievances by simply denying that a problem exists. They may claim that unrest is being caused by outside forces, or by a subgroup that does not represent the minority group as a whole. They may even go so far as to deny that an ethnic minority exists. Past Turkish governments, for example, called the Kurdish people "mountain Turks" and deleted all references to the Kurds in books and atlases. The former Bulgarian government claimed that members of their Turkish minority were ethnic Bulgarians who had simply adopted a foreign culture (Ryan, 1990). Ignoring grievances, however, does not make them go away and governments who choose this path do not resolve their problems.

The Spread of Intrastate Conflict

Intrastate conflict does not always remain within national boundaries. Many factors can cause it to spread, including the fact that ethnic groups are often dispersed over more than one state. In Gurr's (1993) database, 122 ethnopolitical groups had ethnic kindred in a neighboring state. Thus, conflict in one country can have repercussions in another, due to cross-border movement by rebels and refugees, the mobilization of ethnic kin in adjacent states, or the subsequent reciprocal repression of minorities in neighboring states.

"Ethnic overhang" problems manifest themselves in various ways. Nation-states may be artificially divided after a war, as occurred in Germany, Vietnam, and Korea. In other cases, the ethnic group may be divided among several states and not form a majority in any of them, as occurred with the Kurdish population after World War I. The most frequent problem arises when a dominant group in one state is separated from a minority of the same group in another state, which causes a desire to redraw existing boundaries. Ryan (1990) notes that Hitler's attitude toward neighboring states was, in part, inspired by *Volksgemeinschaft,* the idea of a single German state that would contain all those who were living as minorities in Poland, Czechoslovakia, and elsewhere. States also sometimes use such logic to legitimize their call for control over "lost territory."

A study by Tillema (1989) showed that 40 civil or regional conflicts from the end of World War II to 1988 attracted major military interventions by foreign or colonial powers. Protracted minority conflicts, especially the mass murder of indigenous people, created political pressure for military intervention by third parties, as occurred in East Bengal, Cambodia, and Uganda.

Brown (1993) details further means by which ethnic conflicts can spread. The first occurs when multiethnic states begin to fragment and one group is successful in seceding. In such cases, other groups may also seek independence or more autonomy (the Russian Federation, for example, fears that if it allows Chechens to secede, other groups in the federation may want to do likewise). A different kind of chain reaction can occur in the case where a state fragments and allows a region to secede and form a new state, but a minority group in that region then tries to secede from the newly independent state and rejoin the original state (for example, when Croatia seceded from Yugoslavia, Serbs in Croatia wanted to secede from Croatia and join Serbia). A variation of this occurs when a state fragments, allowing a region to secede and form its own state, but a minority group in that region wants to secede from the newly independent region and join its brethren in a third state (for example, when Azerbaijan seceded from the Soviet Union, some Armenians in Nagorno-Karabakh pursued their desire to secede from Azerbaijan and join Armenia). A fourth kind of problem occurs when an ethnic group comes to the defense of its ethnic brethren who are being discriminated against in a neighboring state (for example, if Serbia took steps to drive ethnic Albanians from Kosovo, Albania might try to defend them). Yet another problem can evolve when a state fears the establishment of a new ethnic state on its border, because of the danger that its own minority population might seek to join the new state or have more autonomy (the recent creation of an independent Kazakhstan, for example, could create Chinese fears that Kazakhs in China might wish to develop ties with their newly independent brethren or agitate for more autonomy). Complications can also be created when an ethnic group is spread over two or more states and discrimination against the group in one state causes those in the other to become more militant (for example, Iraqi treatment of its Kurdish population appears to have intensified Kurdish militancy in Turkey). Finally, states may become involved in ethnic conflicts for strategic reasons, as occurred in Africa and Asia during the cold war. Other factors may also play a role, such as the opportunity to harm or embarrass a rival, a prior commitment to protect a minority, or a desire for access to an important raw material.

Ryan (1990) notes that there is considerable evidence that external intervention (except by an international organization) is likely to cause a conflict to escalate: "If a state intervenes for mainly instrumental reasons the conflict will be seen as something to be exploited rather than resolved. As a result there will often be a lack of sensitivity to the local issues, sides may be taken and new issues will be introduced into the conflict. If, on the other hand, affective reasons for intervention are important then such intervention will be biased and will merely escalate one side of the argument." Levine (1996) supports this argument, noting that external support gives the weaker party the ability to challenge the stronger and has deleterious effects for political settlements by making political rhetoric more radical and compromise more difficult.

Another reason for expecting intervention to result in escalation is counterintervention as occurred in Lebanon, Cyprus, and Angola. As Northedge and Donelan (1971) observe: "Intervention always tends to lead to counter-intervention of some sort, if there is time and opportunity for it. When this happens, the effect of intervening is often that the intervening state wins nothing; that both the intervener and the counter-intervener incur great costs; and that the dispute itself is simply protracted and raised to a higher level of violence."

Summary

Clearly, a complex set of factors is involved in prompting minority groups to make demands and initiate political activity in the hope of achieving some sort of autonomy, and/or access to political, economic, and cultural rights. Many of these factors relate to historical and contemporary neglect or discrimination on the part of majority groups and governments, whose actions (often over long periods) have frustrated and threatened the basic human needs of minority groups.

How minority groups and governments approach the problem is vital to the outcome. While there is a tendency for both to adopt a power-based strategy, the evidence suggests that an excessive reliance on this approach, especially in its more violent manifestations, typically leads to countercoercion, and ultimately, to further frustration of both groups' interests. Accommodation and problem solving appear to offer a more promising direction for those on both sides of the asymmetrical power balance.

4

Finding Structural Solutions to Conflict

I T IS ARGUED HERE that the building blocks of sustainable peace and se-curity are well-functioning local, state, regional, and international systems of governance, which are responsive to basic human needs. Sustainable peace thus involves the institutionalization of participatory processes in order to provide civil and political rights to all peoples. It requires adequate legal, enforcement, and judicial protection to ensure that all citizens are treated equally and fairly and that their human rights are safeguarded. It involves equitable economic development and opportunities so that economic and social rights can be provided. Finally, it entails the development of pluralistic norms and practices that respect the unique cultures and identities of all. Sustainable peace also requires education of dominant groups to convince them that their own long-term security interests lie in the development of a just society. Van der Stoel (1994), the OSCE High Commissioner on National Minorities, comments on the benefits of such an approach:

> The first observation is that the protection of persons belonging to minorities has to be seen as essentially in the interest of the state and of the majority. Stability and security are as a rule best served by ensuring that persons belonging to national minorities can effectively enjoy their rights. If the state shows loyalty to persons belonging to minorities, it can expect loyalty in return from those persons who will have a stake in the stability and well-being of that state. My second observation is that solutions should be sought as much as possible within the framework of the state itself.

Outlined below are four major types of structural reform that governments can use to address the concerns of their minority groups, each corresponding to the demands discussed in the preceding chapter. They include
(1) territorial reform to satisfy demands for greater autonomy and control,
(2) electoral reform to meet demands for greater access to political decision making, (3) balanced distributive policies to provide opportunities
for disadvantaged groups to satisfy demands for greater economic rights,
and (4) policies of cultural pluralism that allow groups to develop their
own identity and that address demands for cultural rights.

Of course, policy development must be carefully tailored to the unique
problems facing each society. This means that those contemplating such
reforms will need a good understanding of the root causes of problems
within that society and also a good knowledge of the benefits and risks of
particular methods to be chosen.

Territorial Methods for Providing Political Autonomy

Given that control of one's own destiny is a powerful and, some argue,
fundamental human need, it is not surprising that ethnic groups who are
victims of internal oppression and who have a highly developed sense of
their own distinctiveness want to govern themselves (Ryan, 1990). Horowitz (1990a), however, points out that those who think secession or partition is a good alternative have not looked closely at the record. Normally,
demands for secession are highly threatening to the dominant group because they challenge the majority's core (nationalist) ideology. Even when
independence or autonomy is achieved, "grinding and devastating wars"
are usually the price paid by all concerned (Gurr, 1993). Indeed, between
1948 and 1991, of the 30 groups that fought protracted wars for political
independence (if decolonization is excluded) only one new state, Bangladesh, was formed from an existing state. Until the disintegration of the
Soviet Union, Singapore was the only country that was peacefully parti-
tioned throughout the entire post–cold war period and, in this case, it was
Malaysia that initiated the division. Nevertheless, as noted by Ryan
(1990), since the breakup of the Soviet, Yugoslav, and Ethiopian empires,
"secession has become a growth industry."

Although self-determination was introduced by Wilson at the Versailles
Conference as a means of managing ethnic conflicts, the principles of territorial sovereignty and self-determination are contradictory principles in
international law, and neither international law nor practice has allowed
for an unqualified right to secede from an existing state. In fact, Ryan
(1990) notes that if the governments of the world were to accept the principle of self-determination wholeheartedly, they would largely undercut

their own legitimacy. Hence, states and intergovernmental organizations have generally limited the principle of self-determination to the decolonization of colonial peoples.

As McGarry and O'Leary (1993) note, the principle of self-determination begs four important questions: (1) "Who are the people?" (2) "What is the relevant territorial unit in which they should exercise self-determination?" (3) "What constitutes a majority?" and (4) "Does secession produce a domino effect in which ethnic minorities within seceding territories seek self-determination for themselves?" Jennings (1956) comments further: "On the surface [the principle of self-determination] seems reasonable: let the people decide. It is in fact ridiculous because the people cannot decide until somebody decides who are the people."

Gurr (1993) examined the outcome of 30 cases of ethnonationalists who fought protracted wars for national independence or for unification with their ethnic kin in the post–World War II period up to 1990. He reports that 14 groups achieved some form of regional autonomy, but only after considerable losses. These conflicts lasted *14 years on average,* and in some cases, hostilities continued long after autonomy agreements were implemented. Three other groups were, at the time of his study, involved in long-term negotiations that may lead to power sharing or autonomy. Seven ethnic groups suffered massive defeats and in six other situations, serious conflicts were continuing or escalating. In the latter 13 cases, the conflicts lasted an *average of 25 years.* In brief, the search for political autonomy is not automatically successful and, even when achieved, it is often at enormous cost.

Moreover, as numerous authors point out, secession often creates as many problems as it solves. Even when partition is achieved, ethnic groups are often so geographically mixed that it is impossible to draw clean boundary lines. Typically, remnants of each group are left on the wrong side of the border. Large-scale exchanges of populations are sometimes carried out, but this is costly in economic and human terms. Populations on the move are also highly vulnerable to massacre, as was exemplified during and after the partition of the Indian subcontinent. Dividing land and natural resources fairly among the groups after partition is also complex and leads to new problems. Prospects are ripe for irredentas—claims to retrieve land and people on the other side of the border. Further, because partition puts international boundaries between the contenders, it can convert what was a domestic ethnic conflict into an even more dangerous international conflict (McGarry and O'Leary, 1993). Finally, new forms of ethnic conflict can emerge from secession. Separating out one group does not separate out all groups.

Thus, the only circumstances in which partition is likely to lead to a stable solution is when there are no large or disaffected subgroups within the seceding area, and the great majority of the population within a seceding area favors secession. Such situations, however, seldom occur (McGarry and O'Leary, 1993).

Partition, therefore, seems suitable only as a policy of *last resort,* when all forms of power-sharing arrangements have been tried and failed (Horowitz, 1990b; Lijphart, 1990). Even in such cases, both sides need to carefully weigh the costs. Governments must consider whether allowing a discontented minority to go its own way might make their state easier to govern and be preferable to what could become a 25-year war. Secessionist movements must weigh the uncertain prospects of success against the probable grievous cost to their peoples (Ryan, 1990).

Sisk (1996) notes that both governments and the international community "face a fundamental choice: allow partition and political divorce, or create new more viable structures for living together in a common polity." Where the enmity is especially bitter, however, peaceful coexistence may be virtually impossible. If the possibility of political divorce is, indeed, to be considered, Sisk argues that the international community should establish clear guidelines about when and under what circumstances secessionist efforts will be supported or opposed.

Given the overall record, however, more moderate forms of control and self-determination within an existing state are easier to attain and offer a better alternative. The next section will outline what forms this alternative might take.

Granting Different Degrees of Autonomy within the Existing State

While partition generally limits the choices of separating parties, autonomy usually creates greater latitude for negotiation. Cataloguing some of the many issues that autonomy can cover, Gurr (1993) lists:

> The group's right to teach and use its own language, to practice its religion, and to protect traditional values and lifeways from assimilationist pressures; guarantees of group control of its land, water, timber and mineral resources; powers to ensure that resource and commercial development take place in accordance with group preference; greater funding from the central government for development, education, and medical and welfare assistance; communal control of internal security and the administration of justice; the right to participate in state decisions affecting the group, and if necessary to veto or modify the implementation of those decisions; protection of the rights of members of the communal group who do not live within regional boundaries.

Of course, state officials may have many reasons for resisting accommodation on these issues, such as previous commitments to assimilation, fear of losing the dominant group's economic and political control or opportunities, concern that accommodation will lead other groups to demand more autonomy, or fear that it will lead to the minority group's eventual secession (Gurr, 1993). But de Nevers (1993) contends that, while governments often fear that regional autonomy is the forerunner to secession, "the historical evidence suggests that this is rarely the case." Following the granting of regional autonomy, the local population more often becomes occupied with internal politics rather than with secession.

The major kinds of autonomy arrangements relevant to conflict prevention include *regional autonomy,* where the state devolves powers to subordinate units; *federalism,* where a balance of power coexists between two jurisdictions on different issues; and *confederalism,* where the central state exists because of powers devolved to it by its members (Coakley, 1993). Notably, in these arrangements, relations between the center and its regions need not be symmetrical. Asymmetrical arrangements are sometimes a useful means of granting special privileges to regions that want additional autonomy.

Regional Autonomy

As Coakley (1993) notes, "The regionalist strategy is based, at least in part, on the premise that ethnic protest can be undercut by the concession of at least a symbolic degree of regional autonomy." It involves the devolution of authority from the center to regional power. The major problem with regional autonomy arrangements, which makes them somewhat less attractive to minority groups, is that the center retains the power to limit or withdraw the autonomy, should it choose to do so. Thus, some sort of guarantees normally need to be built into such agreements.

Regional autonomy arrangements can vary widely in the amount of power devolved, as well as in their in intent. In some cases, autonomy may be granted to provide the ethnic group with its own decision-making mechanism. In other cases, the state may use regionalism as a way to dilute regional ethnic distinctiveness by combining two groups in the same region (Coakley, 1993).

Gurr's data suggest that, on balance, regional autonomy agreements can be a useful way to manage intrastate conflicts. The Minorities at Risk Study records 11 instances where autonomy was given to communal rebels following an active conflict. Seven of these led to conflict de-escalation and four did not. However, in two of the failed cases (Baluchistan and Southern Sudan), civil war began or resumed when the central government abrogated previously agreed-upon autonomy arrangements. A third case was negotiated without the participation of the nationalist group (the 1987 accord in Sri Lanka, which was negotiated between the Indian and Sinhalese governments without the participation of the Tamil nationalists). The fourth case was that of the Sikh state of Punjab, where intermittent conflict has continued in spite of an autonomy arrangement (Gurr, 1993).

The success of autonomy agreements is based on a careful balancing of the division of powers and responsibilities between communal and state interests, which is usually arrived at after long negotiations. Detailing this further, Gurr (1993) states: "Balancing means, first, that the majority party among the ethnonationalists gains enough advantages to develop a vested interest in the new regional government, and second, that state officials make a good-faith effort to keep their commitments. Transformation of secessionist conflicts is decisively achieved only when political trust in autonomy arrangements has been established on both sides, and tested in the peaceful resolution of subsequent disputes."

The power of regional autonomy to satisfy needs enough to terminate conflict suggests that it might have an even more effective role if it were used as a *preventive* strategy. Indeed, Gurr's study shows that most people who have gained regional autonomy in the past fifty years have attained it through processes that are less destructive than civil wars. For example, many of the autonomy agreements in western democracies, although sometimes punctuated by violent protest, were achieved by essentially peaceful political contention.

Federalism

Federalism describes an arrangement whereby the division of powers between two levels of government (the periphery and the center) is written into the constitution and therefore is formally guaranteed. Any changes must be mutually agreed upon, since constitutional amendments usually require the consent of both levels.

Although federalism did not originate as a response to ethnic diversity and many examples exist in states that are not multiethnic, federalism has, nonetheless, been adopted as a method for dealing with ethnic diversity. In addition to providing an arrangement for regions to govern themselves, it also allows multiparty fluidity and interethnic cooperation by remaking legislative majorities and minorities through the adjustment of territories. In multiethnic states, federalism may take several forms. It can be used to give federal autonomy to concentrations of ethnic groups, as in the former Soviet Union with its 15 republics, each with its distinctive (although by no means pure) ethnic character, or in the former Czechoslovakia, with its separate Czech and Slovak republics. In the Canadian model, with its twelve provinces and territories, of which one is predominately French speaking and the others predominately English speaking, the ethnic minority is given federal autonomy (Horowitz, 1990b). On the other hand, where ethnic groups are widely dispersed, federal boundaries can contain heterogeneous populations. In Malaysia, for example, there are 12 federal states, all of which are multiethnic, although in varying degrees.

Problems can occur at the federal level, however, if minorities are not sufficiently represented. Thus, federalism may be more effective when maintained by some kind of power-sharing arrangement at the federal level (McGarry and O'Leary, 1993). Power sharing will be discussed in detail later in this chapter.

Governments, however, often fear the costs of federalism and do not see its potential benefits. The major concern is that federalism will pave the way for separatist independence. Horowitz (1990b) proposes that one practical way for governments to prevent a region from wanting to become separate is to keep a substantial proportion of the population of that region occupied in rewarding roles at the center. As Lake and Rothchild (1996) note: "In conceding to ethnic minority leaders and activists a proportionate share of cabinet, civil service, military, and high party positions, the state voluntarily reaches out to include minority representatives in public affairs, thereby offering the group as a whole an important incentive for cooperation."

As well, the creation of new political institutions and competition at the local level will not only provide better access to political and economic opportunities, more effectively address local grievances, and provide a mechanism for negotiating with the central authorities, but it also creates political competition within ethnic groups, a situation that is likely to dilute the conflict between minority and dominant groups (Levine, 1996).

Confederalism

Confederalism is often an intermediate stage. It may be a step between federalism and independent statehood, as a formerly federalist system disintegrates; or in the opposite direction, it can be a step along the way from independent statehood to federation. In the cases of the former Soviet Union, the former Yugoslavia, and the former Czechoslovakia, confederalism was used as an attempt to halt a slide from federation to disintegration by devising a looser form of association. Two examples of a movement in the opposite direction are the Swiss Confederation, which has, in effect, become a federation, and the European Union, which may eventually become a federation by first going through a confederal stage (Coakley, 1993).

Improving Political Access to Decision Making

At first glance, it would seem that democracy should in theory be the ideal form of governance for providing the kind of procedural justice that is needed to ensure that all groups have some control in decision making that affects their lives. Democracy should ensure that grievances can be expressed and addressed through participation in the system. A number of factors, however, complicate the situation. These include the problems faced by states in transition to democracy, and the problems of democracies in multiethnic societies.

The Problems of Transition to Democracy

Austin (1992) describes the spectrum of governments in today's world as mature democracies, dictatorships, new democracies, reforming autocracies, and partial democracies. With the growing trend toward democratization, many states can now be placed in the last three categories, being neither wholly repressive nor wholly democratic. He notes that "many of these halfway houses are under governments that frequently engage in undemocratic behavior even within the framework of parliamentary control. They hold elections and tolerate some opposition, but they also rely on government patronage, control of the media, corruption, the appeal to communal loyalties, a heavy-handed treatment of opponents, and an array of electoral malpractice."

The evidence from these cases suggests that a true culture of democracy grows slowly and does not emerge overnight, especially when states have a long history of authoritarian rule (Austin, 1992; Snyder, 1993, among others). Weak democracies, therefore, must nurture the process by creating the necessary attitudes, structures, and procedures that stabilize and strengthen a democratic system. Indeed, it is generally accepted that only by supporting weak democracies and encouraging their efforts can the ground for strong democracies be prepared (Snyder, 1993). Once started, however, the transition process can be self-correcting. The presence of an active opposition, a free press, and an involved citizenry make an emerging democracy better able to learn from its mistakes than an authoritarian regime.

An important factor in how well emerging democracies work to prevent ethnic tension appears to be the nature of their transition process. Much of the literature on this topic supports the idea that transitions are more likely to succeed if democracy is approached *gradually,* if the authoritarian regime is liberalized rather than overthrown, and if pluralist groups and associations are allowed and encouraged to develop. Gradual transformations to democracy, such as occurred in South Africa, typically occur only when moderates are stronger than radicals in both the original regime and the opposition movements. This allows more moderate ethnic policies to be negotiated (Austin, 1992; Snyder, 1993).

On the other hand, when a regime is overthrown suddenly, power struggles between the opposition parties are likely to develop. Negotiated solutions are often thrashed out hurriedly and consequently risk being unstable. In such cases, political leaders may seek to exploit or exacerbate ethnic tensions for personal gain. As Snyder (1993) points out, "The problem . . . is not democracy *per se,* but the turbulent transition to democracy" in which there are no conflict regulating institutions to accompany the increase in nationalism that tends to occur as groups express long-term or newly emerging grievances. To avoid these dangers, Austin recommends against pushing democracies too fast. Rather, they should be allowed "to proceed at their own pace, encouraged, but not goaded."

Ultimately, as de Nevers (1993) argues, *ethnic tension can best be prevented by creating an environment that encourages political moderation and that allows a workable distribution of power.* Political leaders must be helped to realize that it is in their interest to avoid adopting extremist strategies and instead to search for negotiated solutions to problems. De Nevers (1993) outlines a number of other conditions that enhance the prospects that ethnic conflict will be constructively managed during the process of democratization. The outlook is better when the ethnic groups are relatively equal in size and power, when the previous authoritarian regime was not dominated by an ethnic minority, when the main ethnic groups were united in opposition to the previous regime, when the leaders of large ethnic groups are moderates rather than extremists, when external ethnic allies are not present, and when the army is loyal to the state rather than to a particular ethnic group. These factors are givens. The most important condition, however, is a matter of strategic choice: a willingness to address ethnic issues *early* in the transition process through the writing of a new constitution.

In summary, democracies have a better long-term chance of reducing ethnic conflict than authoritarian regimes, but democracy is *not* a panacea (Rothstein, 1992). *How* ethnic problems are managed is of critical importance. While the legacy of previous ethnic problems and the nature of the transition to democracy are both important factors, careful attention to ethnic concerns and grievances early in the constitutional process and *inclusion of ethnic groups in a satisfactory power-sharing arrangement are vital to preventing serious conflict in the new state.*

The Problem of Ethnic Parties and a "Permanent Majority"

In societies based on "civic nationalism," which are not divided sharply along ethnic or communal lines, voters often shift their party or allegiance based on policy issues or personal preference for a given candidate. But in multiethnic societies, where "ethnic nationalism" is the accepted norm and where ethnic parties exist, communities tend to vote uniformly along ethnic lines. Thus, if there is a 60–40 breakdown between two ethnic groups, the majority group always wins (Horowitz, 1990a). This "permanent majority" problem results in a democracy that does not really work. As Horowitz (1990b) so aptly comments, under these conditions, an election is no more than a census.

Frequently, the permanent majority acts in its own self-interest and pays little attention to the minority. Since the minority is permanently excluded from participation, it may seek some form of adjustment through violent protest, secessionist movements (if the group is territorially concentrated), a coup (if the group has sufficient representation in the armed forces), or a power struggle for central control (Horowitz 1990b). Conflict along these lines has occurred in such places as Lebanon, Nigeria, Northern Ireland, and Sri Lanka.

Such systems may profit from a power-sharing arrangement to make them work as true democracies. Indeed, Lijphart (1990), one of the most ardent advocates of power sharing, argues that power sharing is really the *only* solution to this problem.

The Power-Sharing Approach

Lijphart (1990) notes that there is no detailed blueprint for a power-sharing constitution. Power sharing is a general set of principles and not a set of specific rules or institutions. As such, it can be compatible with a wide variety of institutional alternatives, if the designers of the power-sharing system are creative.

Lijphart has catalogued some of the essential requirements: (1) participation in government (central and local) of the representatives of all significant groups, (2) a high degree of autonomy for these groups, (3) proportionality, and (4) the availability of the minority veto over issues of particular importance to minority groups. He notes that all four are essential and need to be part of the package: "Although proportional representation is empirically associated with and encourages a broadly inclusive coalition government, it does not guarantee it. Hence, it is necessary to make a separate provision for it. Furthermore, there is no logical or empirical link between proportional representation and the minority veto, and these two elements of power-sharing should therefore also be explicitly introduced as part of the total power-sharing system" (Lijphart, 1990).

Since power-sharing arrangements require joint rule by the representatives of different ethnic groups and a collegial decision-making body, they are most easily managed in a parliamentary system with proportional representation. Power sharing in a parliamentary system allows for grand coalition cabinets to be formed with representatives of different parties. Such systems tend to operate more effectively than presidential systems, since the latter results in power being concentrated in the hands of one person who, in a multiethnic society, is typically a member of the dominant ethnic group. The only way that power sharing can work in a presidential system is to share or rotate the presidency and other high offices among the various groups, but this has not proved a very satisfactory method (Lijphart, 1990). Therefore, Lijphart (1990) asserts, "If a new power-sharing system is to be created, the presumption should be clearly in favor of parliamentary rather than presidential government."

In any power-sharing arrangement, joint decision making is taken on issues of joint concern, but decision making is carried out by each separate group on group-specific issues. If there is clear territorial concentration, it may be possible to institutionalize group autonomy through regional autonomy or federalism. If the groups are dispersed, however, it may be necessary to set up a nonterritorial form of autonomy or a combination of territorial and nonterritorial forms, as will be discussed below.

Lijphart argues that a proportional system of voting is much better than plurality, majority, or "mixed" systems, which combine elements of proportional representation and plurality. In particular, "winner-takes-all" systems should be avoided, since in multiethnic societies they leave the losers with little stake in the system (as in the 1992 Angolan election).

Rather than predetermining what proportions various groups should have, Lijphart contends that the ballot box should determine the balance of representation. Proportional systems based on the ballot box provide a self-adjusting mechanism that avoids the kinds of problems that contributed to the downfall of the Lebanese government, where certain numbers of seats had been allocated to different ethnic parties, but were not adjusted as changes took place in the population. Indeed, proportionality can be used as a basic standard for decision making, not only for political representation, but also for such things as deciding public service appointments and allotment of public funds. Such a system minimizes conflict since it defines how power is to be shared. It also permits groups not defined along ethnic lines to be represented. Finally, it allows for internal splits within parties to be appropriately translated into a "voice" in government.

A limited minority veto may also be necessary to keep minority participants from being constantly outvoted or overruled by the majority. Of course, the minority veto is usually not strongly favored by majorities, and if overused, it contains a danger that a whole power-sharing arrangement could collapse. Hence, such veto power would appear to be most effective when used sparingly and restricted to issues where a minority's vital interests are at stake.

Lijphart (1990) identifies nine factors that make it more likely that power sharing will be successful: (1) the absence of a majority ethnic group; (2) the absence of large socioeconomic differences among the ethnic groups; (3) ethnic groups of roughly the same size, so there is a balance of power among them; (4) not too many groups, so that the negotiations will not be too complicated; (5) a relatively small population, so that decision making is less complex; (6) the presence of external dangers that promote internal unity; (7) geographically concentrated ethnic groups, so that, among other things, federalism can be used to promote group autonomy; (8) prior traditions of compromise and accommodation; and (9) cross-cutting group loyalties that reduce the strength of ethnic loyalties. These are not, however, decisive factors. Even when all of these conditions are present, power sharing is not ensured. Conversely, even when they are not present, success is still possible.

Creative policymakers can also make adjustments to power sharing to accommodate different situations. In cases where ethnic groups are geographically dispersed, a combination of semiautonomous regions and optional cultural councils may be useful, as has been demonstrated in Belgium. The Belgian constitution prescribes a combination of territorial and nonterritorial autonomy through three autonomous regions (similar to states in a federation) and two autonomous cultural communities that are governed by cultural councils—each responsible for its respective linguistic group.

There are also a number of creative ways to manage the problem of minorities that are too small to be part of a power-sharing cabinet. These include an autonomous region (if the group is geographically concentrated); a cultural council; representation as advisory members of the cabinet with the right to participate in cabinet decisions that are of special importance to them; or representation on a special council to advise the cabinet on minority issues, with each small minority having a permanent representative on the council.

One major obstacle to establishing power sharing is that it is more difficult for majorities to accept. Short-term thinking and a lack of understanding of the causes of conflict sometimes lead majority parties to the age-old error of overlooking minority interests. In Switzerland, the lesson was only learned after centuries of internecine war. To avoid such problems in the future, Lijphart (1990) concludes, governments must "engage in a form of political engineering; if they wish to establish or strengthen democratic institutions in their countries, they must become power-sharing engineers."

Building Multiethnic Coalitions

A somewhat different approach seeks to adopt electoral reforms that will break the nexus between ethnic or communal identities and political

parties, through either the inclusion of incentives for intergroup cooperation or by finding ways to break down intragroup solidarity so that individual group members do not congeal along group identity lines in their
voting. Horowitz (1990b) is the main proponent of this approach. In an
article comparing the problems in Sri Lanka and Malaysia, he notes that at
the early stages of state-formation, the situation in Malaysia looked more
ominous in terms of interethnic conflict. However, the conflict-manage-
ment strategy that was adopted in Malaysia was much more effective than
that in Sri Lanka.

Horowitz details how several electoral factors not only allowed the Sinhalese to win a permanent majority but caused the two Sinhalese parties
to compete with one another in becoming increasingly pro-Sinhalese and
opposing any proposals to address the growing grievances of the minority
Tamil population. The conditions that made this system so inhospitable to
interethnic accommodation were the largely homogeneous constituencies
in the Sinhalese south and the first-past-the-post system in single-member
constituencies, which translated small swings in Sinhalese popular votes
into large swings in seats (increasing the intensity of the competition
among Sinhalese parties). Although, in 1978, new electoral rules were
adopted that somewhat ameliorated the problem, the reforms came too
late. As Horowitz notes: "Sinhalese and Tamil opinion had so polarized
that, in the short term at least, no electoral system could foster moderation.
In addition to accommodative arrangements, therefore, timing must be
taken into account."

By contrast, in Malaysia, three factors affected the balance of incentives
toward interethnic cooperation. The first was that the Malaysians began
working on interethnic accommodation *early* in relation to independence.
A second difference was that Malaysia's ethnic populations were more dispersed, with more heterogeneous parliamentary constituencies. This created a situation in which ethnic Chinese voters could punish Malay
extremists and reward moderates. As well, Chinese and Malay parties
could exchange votes at the constituency level and win. Where there were
more Malays than Chinese, a Chinese party could urge its voters to vote
for a friendly Malay candidate and vice versa. Thus, although parties
evolved along ethnic lines, there were countervailing incentives that fostered interethnic coalitions. A third reason for the comparatively better
outcome in Malaysia was the early formation of a permanent multiethnic
coalition that occupied the center of the ethnic spectrum. The result was
that more extreme Malay and non-Malay parties lined up on the flanks and
locked the Alliance party into the middle. Horowitz concludes that, "taken
together, Malaysia and Sri Lanka show that small differences can produce
big differences; that once a multiethnic coalition gets going, multiethnicity
can become a habit; that interethnic accommodation does not preclude
major structural changes in ethnic relations; and that in the absence of

accommodative arrangements, governmental actions that could otherwise have been either endured or modified can be so provocative as to produce violent responses."

He comments that under conditions of democratic elections, the most reliable way to bring about interethnic accommodation is to make politicians reciprocally dependent on the votes of members of groups other than their own. Thus, heterogeneous constituencies, together with incentives for vote pooling across ethnic lines, are a key to moderate behavior and can be part of the deliberate design of electoral reform by creating new heterogeneous districts or rules.

Tailoring Power Sharing to the Problem

Sisk (1996), however, argues that rather than engaging in an either-or debate regarding whether the Lijphart or Horowitz approach is the right one, it makes more sense to consider the various components of each as a series of possible power-sharing options that can be tailored to individual situations "like a grand puzzle which when pieced together, carefully meets a divided society's particular needs." He deconstructs each of these two broad approaches described above into ten components, and he provides a brief analysis of what is known about the situational variables for choosing one over the other, as well as the possible risks. Sisk argues that international mediation involving such arrangements has not always been guided by a coherent analysis of the match between solutions and the nature of the problem, and he proposes that there is no substitute for "intimate scholarly and policymaker knowledge" about whether a given power-sharing practice is likely to have an ameliorative or potentially adverse effect on a given conflict.

Addressing Economic Discrimination

As discussed previously, lack of access to political rights is not the only issue that can generate ethnic grievances. Many groups who have suffered economic discrimination also want to have their physical needs better met and want access to greater economic opportunity. In the same way that democracy is sometimes considered the panacea for greater political access to decision making, development is often considered the key to minority groups' economic concerns. But just as a more nuanced answer is needed regarding how to structure democracy in multiethnic societies, so a more sophisticated answer is needed with regard to development policy.

Indeed, as Azar (1990) notes, development can sometimes exacerbate rather than ameliorate ethnic problems when rapid-growth strategies result in the "deepening of the dual economy in which the *modern* sector becomes prosperous with the assistance of foreign capital and through state protection and promotion, while the *traditional* sector stagnates or even deteriorates as wealth is intentionally transferred to the modern sector. The urban and rural poor are further marginalized during the process of uneven economic development, thus sowing the seed for, or accelerating, the process of protracted social conflict in many parts of the Third World."

Such problems are likely to occur along rural-urban as well as regional lines. When these boundaries also describe ethnic divisions, protracted social conflicts may develop. Azar concludes: "There is ample empirical evidence that demonstrates a causal link between distorted patterns of development plus communal discrimination on the one hand, and protracted social conflict on the other. To effectively address protracted conflict, one must attend to the links between development strategies and ethnic/communal cleavages."

Azar suggests several ways that governments can minimize such problems. The first is through sectoral balance. He notes that disadvantaged communities are often clustered in distinct economic sectors. Governments need to be careful to ensure that scarce resources are managed in such a way that sectoral balance is achieved. Neglecting the agricultural sector, for example, in favor of the modern, industrial sector is likely to inflame preexisting tensions. Regional balance should be another aim of a state's development strategy. Since economic discrimination toward a given region can also deepen social conflict, this may involve giving priority to disadvantaged groups in order to favor more balanced overall development.

Azar points out that development strategies that promote regional, sectoral, and communal balance should also be accompanied by increased attention to population control and ecological management. He notes the relationship between uneven economic development and the breakdown of population equilibrium among communal groups. Communal groups with low income or education tend to have higher birth rates, whereas communal groups with higher income and education have lower rates. As a consequence, demographic balance among communal groups is changed, leading to increased demands for redistribution of political and economic power and, ultimately, to conflict. Population problems can, in turn, harm the ecosystem, as occurred in Ethiopia, Somalia, Sudan, and some sub-Saharan states, where such problems exacerbated protracted conflict and triggered humanitarian disasters.

Because development strategies are largely based on vested economic and political interests rather than rational national objectives, it is not always easy to alter them to ensure communal, regional, and sectoral balance, or to preserve ecological balance. Progressive reform of sociopolitical structures is required to allow a more balanced distribution of power, which can then lead to institutions that can foster broad-based economic development. Power-sharing arrangements and devolution of power through regional autonomy can both assist in this process and thus provide the right kind of conditions for a development policy that will better meet human needs and reduce ethnic tension.

Land reform is another kind of distributive policy. Arat (1991) notes that among the 22 countries whose landless peasants constitute more than one-quarter of their population, 15 have experienced revolution or protracted civil conflict in this century. She quotes Huntington as saying, "No social group is more conservative than a landowning peasantry, and none is more revolutionary than a peasantry which owns too little land or pays too high a rental."

Distributive policies can also operate at a more individualistic level. For example, members of a disadvantaged group can be given greater access to economic opportunities. Going beyond the dismantling of the legal basis for discriminatory practices, this policy creates special rights for members of minority groups through such things as quotas for government hiring, special loans, or special recruitment for entry to university. The affirmative action legislation introduced in the United States in the 1960s is an example. In such cases, the dominant group is asked to temporarily accept the policy in order to achieve a more stable and just society. It is easiest to implement these measures in times of economic growth, since they can be supported from that growth and therefore require less encroachment on the dominant group's entitlements (Horowitz, 1990b).

Horowitz (1990b) cites Malaysia's effort at this kind of distributive policy as a particularly sweeping and robust example. Following the riots of 1969, which were attributed to Malay economic grievances, an extensive program called the "New Economic Policy" was put into place. Its aim was to achieve ethnic proportionality in employment and a 30 percent Malay share in company ownership by 1990. Measures were brought in to increase the availability to the Malay population of loans, government contracts, licenses, and franchises. According to Horowitz, most Chinese political leaders shared the view that augmenting Malay economic resources was necessary. Moreover, the policy was supposed to bring about the changes only through future opportunities without expropriating existing businesses. Horowitz concludes that after more than two decades of this policy, dramatic changes in economic power were achieved without major disruptions to the economy or the government.

With all types of distributive policies, there is, of course, a danger of backlash from the dominant group, with governments being accused of "reverse discrimination." Therefore, such policies need to be accompanied by public education programs to help constituencies understand the efficacy of distributive policies in guaranteeing their own security. Levine (1996) suggests that "adroit trade-offs" may be needed, whereby, for example, rich regions are promised more investment or autonomy later in exchange for assisting poorer regions in the short term. Even so, as Horowitz (1985) cautions, it is possible that if the climate is not right, redistribution programs targeted at minority groups, rather than regionally or sectorally, may have a reverse effect and actually cause more ethnic conflict than they ameliorate. Indeed, Levine (1996) cautions that wealthy regions may even develop secessionist movements when they believe that they are being asked unfairly to support poorer regions through redistribution policies.

Of course, some countries are so uniformly poor that there is little wealth to be distributed. Thus, economic grievances may stem not only from *relative* deprivation, but also from *absolute* deprivation or from relative deprivation in an international sense. Austin (1992) notes that *poverty is a basic structural restraint on any movement toward political reform.* He quotes General Wojciech Jaruzelski of Poland as saying, "Bread without democracy is bitter, but democracy without bread is fragile." Debt burdens, falling commodity prices, trade restrictions, natural disasters, excessive expenditure on armaments, war, and other structural problems such as poor roads, inadequate telecommunications, lack of skills, and the fragility of the private sector all contribute to whole states being poverty stricken. In this case, better distributive policies need to be viewed in the international context. This issue will be taken up again in the final chapter.

Another type of distributive policy that should be considered at the national level concerns the redistribution of expenditure within government budgets. In the mistaken belief that their ethnic problems can be controlled through a strong military, many states commit inordinately large proportions of their budgets to military expenditure. Reallocating even part of these funds toward social policy initiatives that address the root causes of these same conflicts would be much more effective (see the 1994 UNDP Report for suggestions about how this could be done).

When compared with their nondemocratic neighbors, democracies, on the whole, seem to perform better in achieving some distributive gains and balancing the conflicting demands of rapid growth and improved equity, especially when governments are able to limit corruption and are not victimized by deteriorating international or internal conditions (Rothstein, 1992). Thus, Gurr's finding that access to political decision making usually precedes a minority group's achievement of greater access to economic opportunity suggests that a stepwise approach to economic reform should be pursued. That is, redress for economic grievances can be achieved faster when minority groups have gained some form of decision-making "voice" in government.

Addressing Cultural Grievances

As discussed in the previous chapter, threats to a group's cultural identity through containment or assimilation are also a potent source of conflict. Containment policies, in which groups are kept separate but unequal, may be based on the dominant group's religious beliefs, economic interests, or security concerns. Whatever their source, Gurr (1993) notes that "much of the recent increase in communal protest and rebellion is rooted in reactions to discredited policies of containment . . . globally they are a source of bitter grievances and escalating conflict."

Similarly, assimilationist policies that encourage group members to subordinate or abandon old communal identities and to adopt the language, values, and behaviors of the dominant group, even through incentives, are also coming increasingly under attack. Although accepted by some, they are rejected by others, who are not willing to sacrifice their cultural and social autonomy in exchange for the dominant culture. Gurr (1993) concludes, "Historically, assimilation has ended some conflicts by eroding the communal basis for intergroup hostility. But the failures of assimilation have also provided the motivation for new and potentially destructive rounds of intergroup conflict."

Many communal groups are shifting toward a preference for pluralism. Pluralism means equal individual and collective rights, including the right to separate or coexisting identities. Communal advocates of this policy want recognition and promotion of each group's history, culture, language, and religion. Of course, pluralism also has economic and political ramifications. Economically, it means a shift away from programs to help individuals and toward programs to assist ethnic groups. Politically, it implies the emergence of ethnic politics with guarantees that communal interests will be represented in decision making. As Gurr (1993) states,

> Pluralist policies may be more complex and expensive to implement than policies of assimilation, but pluralism is not fundamentally inimical to state interests in democratic societies. Democratic politics are premised on competition among, and accommodation of, contending interests of parties, classes, and associations; organized communal interests can be dealt with by the same principles and procedures. Pluralism is an approach with great potential for redirecting intergroup conflict into institutionalized and constructive channels.

The problem is that pluralism challenges assimilationists' commitment to a homogeneous society and can create a backlash that may push politicians dependent on majority views into a retreat from pluralism.

Ryan (1990) suggests that, in general, successful multiethnic societies are those that respect the right of open cultural expression, including cultural autonomy for schools and religious institutions, the recognition of minority languages as official languages, and the use of these in the media, in official transactions, and in the courts. The 1967 Welsh Language Act, for example, gave the Welsh language equal status with English. The Welsh have their own television channel and bilingual road signs. In 1971, Canada adopted a policy of bilingualism and biculturalism, overseen by a minister of state for multiculturalism. Australia also has a policy of multiculturalism with a multicultural television network with mixed programming for its various minorities.

Such policies do not, as some governments fear, undermine national unity. As Walzer (1983) concludes, "Ethnic citizens can be remarkably loyal to a state that protects and fosters private communal life if that is seen to be equitably done."

Developing Institutional Mechanisms That Support Reform

Reforms are more likely to be sustainable if attention is given to the development of institutional mechanisms that support them. The military, police, and judiciary, as well as other government bodies, may need to be restructured and their staff retrained in order to ensure fair treatment of all groups. Adequate representation by minority groups in such institutions also helps to strengthen reform. The task, however, is not an easy one, since these sectors of the community often constitute entrenched power bases in their own right, and restructuring requires courage, resolve, and sufficient support from other segments of the community and/or from the international community.

Inexpensive conflict resolution mechanisms such as ombudsmen, conciliators, or neighborhood mediation centers can also serve a useful role in allowing grievances to be aired, assisting parties in finding acceptable solutions that can defuse local problems, and making recommendations to governments regarding necessary structural changes.

Timing

Timing is crucial to structural reform. A number of authors stress the importance of making reforms *as early as possible,* before ethnic tensions become a major problem. Timing is also important in terms of how policies of accommodation are pursued. From the government's side, they must be implemented "cautiously but persistently over the long term, slowly enough not to stimulate a crippling reaction from other groups, persistently enough so that minorities do not defect or rebel" (Gurr, 1993). From the side of the communal group, Gurr notes that the nonviolent pursuit of group interests is a strategic virtue, as is a willingness to compromise about the specifics of accommodation. He points out that when groups pursue a strategy of sustained violence, they alienate other groups that would be more helpful as allies, and harden positions so that accommodation and settlement become increasingly difficult to achieve. Thus, communal groups who want to minimize the time required for their needs to be met would be well advised to be persistent in the pursuit of their interests through constructive, nonviolent methods.

It is essential for all groups to bear in mind that prevention and accommodation are much more cost-effective than conflict. Data on civil wars show that they are particularly difficult to terminate (Lickleider, 1995; Mason and Fett, 1996). Unlike war between states, when violence occurs within a state, the members of the two sides must live next to each other and work together to form a common government after the killing stops. Lickleider asks, "How can you work together, politically and economically, with the people who killed your parents, siblings, children, friends or lovers?" (Lickleider, 1995).

Summary

The evidence suggests that ethnopolitical conflicts do not have to be intractable. All but one of the 24 communal minorities that were politically active in the Western democracies and Japan in the post–World War II period made gains over the past two decades, due to strategies of accommodation and the kinds of solutions suggested here (Gurr, 1993). These include specific reforms to guarantee full civil and political rights, programs to reduce poverty, programs to give recognition and resources to minority cultures and languages, and the granting of greater autonomy and state subsidies for indigenous peoples and ethnonationalists. These policies of addressing ethnic grievances have, in turn, contributed to a substantial decline in most forms of ethnic conflict in the states involved, improving both stability and security. As Evans (1994) argues, "Policies that enhance economic development and distributive justice, encourage the rule of law, protect fundamental human rights, and foster the growth of democratic institutions are also security policies. They should be recognized as such and receive a share of current security budgets and future 'peace dividends'."

Part Two

The Role of the UN, Regional Organizations, and NGOs in Promoting Sustainable Peace

5

The United Nations

IN ORDER TO SAMPLE the current state of practice in promoting sustainable peace, the next seven chapters will examine the evolving roles of the UN, five regional organizations, and one NGO—the Carter Center. Particular attention will be given to the peaceful settlement of disputes, as well as to the mechanisms that each has developed to promote human rights and democracy. Of course, these organizations work in other areas, even in related fields, such as disarmament and development, but these will not be reviewed here.

Moreover, this set of organizations is by no means comprehensive; there are many others working on various aspects of sustainable peace whose important work is not covered here. Nonetheless, the seven that are sampled offer testimony to the wide variety of emerging approaches. Certain older mechanisms, such as the International Court of Justice, were created to settle disputes between states. Others, such as the OSCE High Commissioner on National Minorities, are more recent innovations, developed to address disputes within states. This overview is necessarily sketchy and cannot do justice to the breadth and complexity of these organizations or the situations that they have helped to resolve.

It is also important to bear in mind the slow, complicated, and cumbersome multilateral decision-making process by which such mechanisms come into being—where member states, with differing interests, are required to agree. This tortuous process is also responsible for what has *not* been done. It is hoped that this overview will highlight, at least implicitly, some of the difficulties involved in designing appropriate mechanisms for sustainable peace in a multilateral world still dominated by Westphalian states and their governments, whose interests are not always perfectly aligned with those of their populations.

On the more positive side, this review demonstrates that certain groups of states are increasingly able to agree on group norms and practices that can socialize governments within their collectivity into more normative and constructive behavior. The results provide hope that it may be possible to develop collective norms and procedures that can begin to promote sustainable peace. Further, exposure to approaches that are being developed elsewhere should provide a source of ideas for generating locally relevant instrumentalities.

Obstacles to the Development of Preventive Diplomacy

Following the end of the cold war, the UN did attempt to evolve an agenda for the new strategic environment. The 1992 Security Council Summit and the Secretary-General's *An Agenda for Peace* outlined a set of approaches to peace and security that, among other things, included "preventive diplomacy." Paradoxically, however, in the ensuing debate, the more "preventive diplomacy" was discussed, the more resistance to the concept grew. Preventive diplomacy—which was not clearly defined or operationalized—faced opposition from several quarters for quite different reasons. Because it was not yet fully articulated, different sectors of the community were able to project different meanings onto the term. Hence, before considering how a more effective and widely acceptable approach to prevention could be created, it will be useful to examine how the concept was construed by different sectors within the system and what their concerns have been.

The conceptual confusion in *An Agenda for Peace* between "preventive deployment" and "preventive diplomacy" did not help matters. Preventive deployment was inappropriately listed as a subcategory of preventive diplomacy, whereas it would have been more appropriate to categorize these as two distinctively different types of *preventive action*. This blurring of methodologies suggested that preventive diplomacy might sometimes be a power-based approach.

The greater problem, however, was created by the context of the debate and the sudden emergence of the Security Council's ability to exert its power, once the logjam of the cold war was broken. The new capacity of the Council to reach consensus and take powerful actions, as exemplified by the Gulf War, created considerable hope in some parts of the organization that *finally* the United Nations would be able to develop its long-dormant collective security system, with peacekeeping and peace enforcement as its principal modus operandi. Many of those who were enthusiastic about the expansion of the Security Council's power were not, however, especially favorable toward preventive diplomacy. Believing that what the system needed was more "teeth," they viewed preventive diplomacy as a "soft" option and were skeptical about its efficacy. Proposals for a rapid deployment force or strengthened peacekeeping capacity received more attention than those for prevention.

Enthusiasm for the Council's newly realized ability to wield power was not, however, universal. For those who had experienced colonial domination, the renewed eagerness that they detected for strengthening the peace and security agenda of the Council, stimulated old fears about interventionism and Great Power hegemony. Now that the Security Council could actually wield power, the Great Power privileges of permanent membership and the power of the veto, along with the Council's lack of adequate representation and consultation, were increasingly called into question. The perception grew that the Council was applying different standards to different cases, and that, in certain instances, its actions were taken to pursue the geopolitical aims of its permanent members, rather than the organization as a whole.

These concerns quickly affected perceptions of "preventive diplomacy," which became a lightning rod for fear of interventionist intent. Concern grew that preventive diplomacy could become the thin edge of a neocolonialist wedge. This was fueled by those who inappropriately equated the term with "early warning"—which, regrettably, also took on an unfortunate connotation when it became associated in the minds of some with espionage—rather than with trying to understand the root causes of conflict. The fear was that "early warning" information gathered by the Secretariat might be turned over to the Security Council, which would impose some sort of unwanted coercive intervention. Such apprehensions were also exacerbated by the focus on "late prevention" rather than "early prevention," and by proposals for a UN satellite, UN embassies, and the fact that the Office for Research and the Collection of Information (which was established to carry out "early warning" among other things) had been modeled after a similar unit in the U.S. State Department. Arguments about nonintervention, sovereignty, and the dangers of "internationalizing" a problem, were mounted in response. Since preventive diplomacy was not yet developed, it became a line in the sand that could be drawn.

Member states of the South were also disappointed by the seeming lack of interest by many in the North in the South's social development needs and concerns, and they worried that the UN's new preoccupation with peace and security (and the huge cost of peacekeeping) would drain resources and energy from efforts to resolve what they saw as the root causes of conflict. As the financial crisis within the system deepened, their concerns intensified. Thus, in the debate between the peace and security agenda and the social development agenda, preventive diplomacy became linked to the peace and security side of the debate, and its linkage to the social and development side remained largely unexplored.

A third level of resistance came from those who simply lacked a clear operational vision of what preventive diplomacy might mean. Bureaucratic inertia and commitment to old practices, both administratively and politically, meant that the old ways of doing things became reified and were difficult to change. The crisis orientation of the Council and the Secretariat and the difficulties of managing crises of immense complexity meant that all of the available resources were devoted to these demands and there was little time for conceptualizing how prevention might be incorporated or practiced.

Some support for prevention was, however, forthcoming from middle-level, developed countries, which wanted to see both the peace and security agenda *and* a social development agenda advanced in a way that would truly address the root causes of conflict, and also would create institutions and norms that could lay down the foundation for lasting social justice. Gareth Evans, in his book *Cooperating for Peace: The Global Agenda for the 1990s and Beyond,* outlined such a vision of "cooperative security." Unfortunately, this conceptualization of prevention had difficulty competing with the fears, paralysis, and general skepticism that accompanied the developing malaise within the system.

As a consequence, there remains a great need to further articulate a new agenda for prevention that would address the root causes of conflict, be more acceptable to member states, and create the conditions for durable peace. This will be the subject of chapters 12, 13, and 14.

Which UN Organ Should Have Primary Responsibility for Preventive Diplomacy?

In order to overcome the fears that have been expressed, it is important to clarify how preventive action should be structured and which UN organ should assume primary responsibility for its implementation. Although the UN Charter gives primary responsibility for the maintenance of international peace and security to the Security Council, in reality, the Council is *not* the best structure for carrying out preventive diplomacy.

Although both the UN Charter and the 1988 Declaration on the Prevention and Removal of Disputes and Situations and on the Role of the United Nations in this Field urge the United Nations to become involved "early in a dispute or situation" or "at any stage of a dispute or situation," the fact is that most disputes do not reach the Security Council's agenda until they have escalated into armed conflict. In other words, many disputes are not considered by the Council until it is *too late* for their peaceful resolution.

The major inhibiting factor is the Council's potential range of coercive or punitive action. It is not surprising that member states are often reluctant to relinquish control over the process and outcome of their disputes to a Security Council with such powerful instruments and whose members are sometimes perceived to be pursuing their own geopolitical interests. Thus, discussions about the rights of "sovereignty" and concerns about "internationalizing" a dispute often mean that most states prefer to maintain control over how their disputes will be resolved, at least until such time as the situation becomes desperate.

As well, the kinds of actions that the Security Council can offer are not well suited to dispute settlement at an early stage. The notion of the Council as a kind of arbiter causes parties to engage in adversarial debate rather than problem solving. Mutual recrimination and positional arguing by each side to convince the Council of the "rightness" of its case may further harden positions and inflame a situation. Moreover, when Council members are forced to declare their sympathies, support for one or both sides may widen the dispute or encourage hostilities.

Moreover, the Council is so overwhelmed in its attempt to manage the many full-blown crises with which it is already seized that, even if disputes were brought to it at an early stage, it would be unlikely to add them to its agenda—even though they might well be next year's crises.

What is needed instead is a *less political and more professional approach* to UN dispute resolution, which can assist member states in the implementation of Chapter VI ("Pacific Settlement of Disputes")—by offering the right kind of acceptable assistance for resolving disputes at an early stage. As well, a parallel mechanism is needed that can focus on preventing and ameliorating the structural causes of conflict. It will be argued in chapter 13 that such programs should be developed within the UN Secretariat under the aegis of the Department of Political Affairs.

The Development of Preventive Diplomacy within the Secretariat

In the early years of the UN, when the organization was smaller, it was generally considered that the Secretary-General would be able to personally provide whatever was needed in terms of good offices and mediation. However, as the demands on the Secretary-General grew, as the number of member states expanded, and as disputes and conflicts proliferated, it became increasingly unrealistic to expect the Secretary-General to be able to respond to all emergent and emerging situations, while at the same time carrying out the many other functions and duties required of him.

Over time and out of necessity, secretaries-general began assigning senior staff or diplomats to be personal representatives or envoys to assist in providing good offices and mediation. These assignments were typically ad hoc in response to crises and the choice of personnel was usually limited to a small number of trusted individuals. Frequently, however, these individuals did not have sufficient resources (in terms of personnel or infrastructure) to back them up. Fact finding also evolved as a mechanism for gathering information and, in some cases, as a forum for diplomatic initiatives. But once again, fact finding was largely an ad hoc procedure. On short notice, staff members who had not worked together before were hastily assembled from various parts of the Secretariat and sent to the field to fulfill a particular mission. In many cases, they were unfamiliar with the situation and with its political, historical, or cultural context. Once they had reported back, they often returned to their previous posts with little continuity or follow-up.

These ad hoc arrangements for providing good offices and other peaceful means of dispute settlement, together with the Council's focus on crisis situations, meant that the Secretary-General and his senior staff were swamped with situations that had deteriorated to the point where they could no longer be ignored—or, in many cases, controlled. As the system was structured and practiced, handling the conflicts that were already on the agenda was more than they could manage. There was no time and no structure for early preventive diplomacy and even late preventive diplomacy was often neglected.

Thus, UN Secretariat efforts were focused on peacemaking rather than preventive diplomacy and until the end of the cold war they were concentrated largely on negotiating cease-fires, troop withdrawals, deployment of peacekeeping forces, and the repatriation of refugees, rather than on tackling the issues at the heart of the conflict. Since the end of the cold war, the record has been considerably better. The UN has been able to assist in brokering a number of comprehensive political settlements (e.g., Cambodia, El Salvador, Guatemala) and has helped to implement them through comprehensive peacekeeping operations (e.g., Namibia, Cambodia, El Salvador, Mozambique).

Preventive diplomacy, however, has not enjoyed a similar development. The first attempt to consider a formal mechanism for preventive diplomacy occurred after the war in the Falklands/Malvinas, which took the UN by such surprise that it is said that no map of the islands was available in the Secretariat when the invasion began. In response, the Office for Research and the Collection of Information (ORCI) was eventually set up to (among other things) establish a system of early warning. Six staff members were assigned to collect and analyze information to provide early warning and recommendations to the Secretary-General. Several others were assigned to develop a more quantitative system, based on "early warning indicators" and the development of a computer model for prediction of crises. Although it seemed to be a good beginning, a number of problems plagued these attempts.

One of the major difficulties was the separation of early warning from early action. Essentially, there was no effective system of early action to respond to the early warning signals. Political officers in ORCI sent early warning signals (sometimes repeatedly) about a number of deteriorating situations to the Executive Office of the Secretary-General, but because his office was so overburdened and had no capacity for early preventive action, little was done. Another problem was created when the already small number of early warning staff was reduced, by "borrowing" them for peacemaking tasks.

The development of a more sophisticated quantitative system also did not materialize (although subsequent efforts in the humanitarian field have now shown promise). There was insufficient knowledge and little agreement about what kinds of indicators might be most useful for prediction, and computer programming expertise was lacking.

Moreover, ORCI was established with the belief that preventive diplomacy could be carried out from UN Headquarters in New York. The assumption was that if only the right information about "early warning indicators" could be collected and programmed to provide prediction, then staff members sitting at their desks in midtown Manhattan would be able to predict where problems might erupt around the world. The concept, however, was unidimensional. Even if it had worked to predict *where* crises would erupt, it would not have provided the more qualitative analysis needed to understand *why* a given dispute was occurring or *what might be done* to ameliorate the situation. Such information cannot be derived from computer models, since it requires "on-the-ground" knowledge of the circumstances and the actors.

Even before *An Agenda for Peace* was released, however, Secretary-General Boutros Boutros-Ghali acted to reform parts of the Secretariat's structure. ORCI was abolished and its information collection and analysis functions were reassigned, along with responsibility for peacemaking to the new Department of Political Affairs (DPA). The Department of Peacekeeping Operations was given responsibility for setting up and managing peacekeeping operations, and the Department of Humanitarian Affairs was created to provide a more effective response to humanitarian problems, through better coordination of humanitarian agencies. It was hoped that the three departments would be able to work closely together to provide a more integrated approach to peace and security.

With regard to its peacemaking and preventive diplomacy functions, DPA established six regional divisions: two for Asia (one for West Asia, the other for East Asia and the Pacific); two for Africa (called the Africa I and II Divisions); one for the Americas; and one for Europe. A director was appointed to head each division, which was comprised of several staff members. But due to a hiring freeze, recruitment was limited to those staff members who needed reassignment following the abolition of other posts and the department was not permitted to recruit new staff from the best applicants both inside and outside the system. Thus, staff were assigned to these important and sensitive positions, not on the basis of their ability and knowledge, but rather on the basis of their availability. Of course, an attempt was made to choose those with suitable experience, but they were not always available. As a consequence, staff members have varying levels of experience and expertise; some are competent at political analysis and knowledgeable about their region; others are less so. In all, more than fifty staff members now work in these six divisions.

Although what now exists is a quantum leap forward, some of the problems inherent in ORCI remain and a number of bureaucratic, structural, and resource problems (largely outside the department's control) have continued to inhibit its optimal functioning. Thus, although information collection and analysis is located in DPA, the decision to take early action still resides largely in the Executive Office of the Secretary-General, thus creating a schism between those who gather and analyze information and those who decide whether action should be taken and, if so, what type of action. Further, although the number of staff for collecting and analyzing information grew, there were still no permanent staff for carrying out preventive action. Cost-cutting within the Secretariat (carried out to meet the demands of member states) meant that many senior positions were abolished, depriving the organization of much of its experienced staff. Although senior Secretariat staff had begun to take a more active role in providing good offices under the direction of Secretary-General Pérez de Cuéllar, this downsizing meant that the old practice of using ad hoc special or personal representatives or envoys was necessary once again. Although not ideal for peacemaking, it is even less appropriate for "early" preventive diplomacy. As will be discussed more fully later, early prevention requires permanent staff dedicated to prevention (whether they be DPA staff or permanent, special or personal representatives or envoys) to continuously follow developments, to spot emerging problems before they achieve crisis proportions, and to offer quiet assistance and advice in helping to resolve problems before they escalate. Permanent staff would be able to identify problems before they have reached the crisis threshold of salience normally required to appoint an ad hoc special representative. Moreover, permanent staff could offer assistance quietly, whereas the appointment of an ad hoc special representative necessarily calls attention to the problem and "internationalizes" the issue in a manner that many governments find unacceptable.

Moreover, the difficulties of obtaining an understanding of the complex problems of the region from UN Headquarters in New York remained and were exacerbated by the department's woefully inadequate travel budget. In 1995, a mere $260,000 was allotted for travel for all six divisions (with only $40,000 and $45,000 allotted for the Africa I and Africa II Divisions, respectively). Although political officers are assigned to track specific countries on a daily basis, funds have been so short that, in a number of cases, political officers have never been to the region that they are supposed to be covering. Even senior staff members have often been inhibited in their ability to travel to the field to obtain an adequate assessment of developing situations. In the absence of sufficient resources to even visit the field on a regular basis, the debate about whether preventive diplomacy staff should be based in the region or at UN Headquarters has remained theoretical.

An equally serious problem has been that while the department's staff in the six divisions were, in theory, engaged full time in preventive diplomacy and peacemaking, in practice, much of their time had to be devoted to other tasks, such as providing background papers and briefing notes for the Secretary-General to help him conduct relations with member states. With their remaining time, the staff necessarily continued to apply most of their effort to crisis situations. Hence, directors and their staff have been hard-pressed to keep up with the rush of events and, even in the area of peacemaking, there has been insufficient time to adequately prepare information or to consider decisions carefully. This crush of work has also resulted in little time for the development of a proactive or creative approach or for adequate consultation among staff.

Exacerbating these problems further, the infrastructure that supports DPA has been less than ideal. There has been an inadequate number of research assistants and virtually no access to outside consultants or experts. Moreover, the system has had little means of improving itself. There have been few means of accessing the body of knowledge and expertise that has been developing over the past years outside the UN in the growing field of conflict resolution. There has also been little systematic analysis or overview of UN efforts at good offices, which could preserve the lessons of peacemaking so that the UN's methodology of dispute resolution could be improved and refined.

Thus, although the UN's role has expanded in the area of peacemaking, the organization has simply not been given adequate resources to allow it to develop and adapt its procedures to conflict prevention. The collection and analysis of information continues to be carried out from New York, with no real capacity for early action; and, in spite of the tireless efforts by its staff, DPA is still unable to fully carry out preventive diplomacy. Thus, regrettably, until member states can agree on what should be done and provide sufficient resources, this situation is likely to persist.

The Role of the International Court of Justice in Peacemaking and Preventive Diplomacy

As the principal judicial organ of the United Nations, the International Court of Justice is designed to hear contentious cases *between* sovereign states and to provide advisory opinions to the authorized organs of the UN. Like the UN's other peaceful methods for the settlement of disputes, recourse to the Court is largely voluntary. States can accept its jurisdiction in one of three ways. The first is through the "optional clause" (Article 36[2] of the Court's statute). This allows member states to declare that they recognize the compulsory jurisdiction of the Court, although they can also exempt certain areas from jurisdiction. The second is through the consent of a state to take a dispute to the Court as part of a special agreement or *compromis* (Article 36[1]). A final avenue is through compromissory clauses in treaty agreements, which stipulate that any dispute arising therefrom must be referred to the Court (Article 36[1]). Since there are now hundreds of such treaties, most states, in one way or another, have accepted limited jurisdiction of the Court (Rosenne, 1995). Since contentious cases brought before the Court are typically those related to the peaceful settlement of disputes between states, they will be the main focus of this discussion. Rosenne (1995) provides a description of the Court's methodology in contentious proceedings, which is summarized below.

The Court's Methodology in Contentious Cases

When parties agree to bring a case to the Court, an agreement is filed with the Court in which the dispute is defined and the questions that the Court is asked to decide are detailed. Alternatively, proceedings can be instituted unilaterally. In such cases, there is usually no agreement between the disputants that the case should be brought to the Court or as to what the claim is. Such an application, therefore, lists the parties, the subject of the dispute, the basis for believing that the Court has jurisdiction, the nature of the claim, and a statement of the grounds upon which the claim is based.

When the Court's registrar receives an application, he or she ensures that it complies with the Court's procedural requirements, then opens a folio in the Court's general list. The registrar subsequently sends the application to the judges and the respondent government and contacts all members of the UN through the Secretary-General, so that they can notify the Court if they wish to intervene in the case. Finally, he or she also issues a press communiqué. If the parties have not given the case a name, it is given a "nonprejudicial" name.

Once agents (those formally entrusted to represent each party) have been appointed, the president of the Court attempts to determine the parties' views (through meetings and other communications) on matters such as the amount of time required to file the first round of written pleadings. If the parties cannot agree, the Court or the president decides.

A formal procedure is available that allows any party to file a preliminary objection with regard to admissibility and the Court's jurisdiction (this must be filed within the time limit that has been set for the first written pleading). When this occurs, the proceedings on the merits are suspended and the Court decides on the objection after the adverse party has been given an opportunity to present its written observations. Normally, a hearing is then held, wherein the party who raised the objection acts as the applicant. The case is terminated if the court accepts any objection; if none are accepted, the proceedings on the merits then resume.

Requests for provisional measures can also be made by either party at any time, and if made, they take precedence over everything else. Provisional measures are decided after the adverse party is given an opportunity to submit its written observations, but may also involve oral proceedings.

Written proceedings on the merits of the case can be filed consecutively or simultaneously, but in unilateral proceedings, consecutive filing is usual, with the applicant being the first to file. The first written pleading or memorial normally contains a statement of all relevant facts, a statement of law, and other relevant submissions. The counter-memorial from the opposing party typically includes an admission or denial of facts in the memorial plus additional relevant facts, the party's observations concerning the statement of law in the memorial, and a statement of law in answer, as well as other relevant submissions. The memorial and the reply are filed by the applicant; the counter-memorial and rejoinder by the respondent in consecutive filings (if the filings are simultaneous, they are typically limited to memorials, counter-memorials, and replies). The Court's rules state that the reply and rejoinder should not simply restate the arguments, but instead should highlight the issues that still divide the parties. When the counter-memorial, reply, and rejoinders are made, the nature of the dispute becomes clearer, since both perspectives have now been presented.

Written pleadings are filed in the registry, and after being translated into the two official languages of the Court, copies are then delivered to the members of the Court, the other party, and other interested parties that have been authorized to receive them. The written pleadings are not made public until the oral proceedings begin (if both parties agree) or otherwise at the termination of the case. Any government can ask the Court to make written pleadings available to it.

Following written pleadings, the case becomes ready for hearing and is entered into the Court's list for oral proceedings. In situations where more than one case is on the list, the Court typically hears cases on the basis of what it deems to be the relative urgency of each—since the Court hears only one case at a time.

The oral proceedings are usually public. The customary order for addressing the Court is for the applicant to present its oral argument first, followed by the respondent (in cases of simultaneous written pleadings, the order may be decided by the Court). Oral arguments are not intended to cover the same ground as the written pleadings, but instead are to be directed at the essential issues that still divide the parties. After a short interval, a second round of oral argument takes place. Witnesses and expert witnesses may be called, but seldom are. The Court as a whole (through the president) can ask questions, or individual judges may also ask for explanations. Each agent presents a "final submission" at the end of the argument and the president declares the hearing closed. No further evidence can be presented after this.

Members of the Court are given a short time to study the arguments, and then brought together for in camera deliberation in which the president outlines the main issues that require decision and preliminary views are expressed. The judges then have a few days in which to prepare a written note, giving their tentative views on the answers to the questions that have been put forward in the first discussion. The notes (which are later destroyed) are circulated and provide an idea of where the majority opinion seems to lie. The judges then deliberate orally, in reverse order of seniority. Once this process is completed, a drafting committee of three judges, whose opinion appears to be similar to the majority, is asked to prepare a preliminary draft judgment. This is then circulated to the members of the Court, who make written suggestions for amendments. The drafting committee decides whether or not to accept proposed amendments and a fresh draft is produced. At further meetings, each paragraph (in both English and French versions) is read aloud and left unchanged or amended. An amended draft judgment is then distributed and given a second reading, where amendments can still be made. A final oral vote is taken in inverse order of seniority. Decisions are based on a majority of judges present, with the president having a deciding vote, in the event of a tie.

The parties are then called back to the Court for a public meeting, at which the authoritative text of the judgment is read. Signed and sealed copies are given to the agents and a copy sent to every member state of the UN, to the Secretary-General, and to every state entitled to appear before the Court, as well as to the press. Judges may append "individual" opinions of either a concurring or dissenting nature. The vote of each judge in a given case is (since 1978) a matter of public record.

Use of the Court

The Court has in the past suffered from much the same problem faced by the Security Council. On the whole, member states have been reluctant to relinquish decision-making control to a third party. Only 59 of the 185 member states of the United Nations (less than one-third) have agreed to the Court's compulsory jurisdiction under the optional clause, and many of these have limited its jurisdiction by making exceptions. Of even greater concern, only one of the five permanent members of the Security Council (the United Kingdom) has currently endorsed the optional clause for compulsory jurisdiction.

Use of the Court has, nonetheless, grown significantly in the last few years. In 1995, the Court had a record number of thirteen cases before it. Indeed, this increase in popularity has posed a problem for both the Court and those states with cases on its docket. In 1994–95, for example, the Court decided only two cases (Boutros-Ghali, 1995), although the record was much better for 1996. If member states are required to wait long periods before their case is considered, the much-welcomed increase in the use of the Court could reverse itself.

Increased use of the provision for smaller ad hoc chambers should make the Court both more attractive to member states and more efficient. This provision, which states that the judges to constitute such a chamber shall be determined by the Court, with the approval of the parties, was used for the first time in 1981 by the United States and Canada. Initially, the procedure was subject to some concern, because it essentially allows states to choose which judges will hear a case. The fear was that unrepresentative chambers could produce judgments that would not be supported by the full Court. This concern, however, has subsided, as the quality of the chambers' decisions appears to have been maintained. The importance of the chambers provision lies in the fact that it offers another dispute settlement option to member states; this may be more acceptable to those concerned about exercising greater control, since it provides additional control over the process.

Another variation is the use of a *compromis,* or special agreement, whereby states can ask the Court to lay down and define the relevant legal principles that are applicable to the resolution of the dispute in question. After the Court has done this, the parties can use the judgment as the basis for a negotiated settlement. Indeed, many of the recent maritime delimitation cases were resolved in this way. As Rosenne (1995) states:

This method of dividing a dispute into segments, with the Court determining with binding force the legal issues and leaving to the parties the closing settlement on the basis of that decision, combines some of the best features of both judicial and diplomatic means of dispute settlement. It is quite probable that this method of submitting portions of disputes by mutual agreement to the Court (or variations on this theme) will prove to be of continuing and increasing importance because of the advantages it offers by combining authoritative and binding legal guidance with the freedom of parties to negotiate the conclusive settlement between themselves.

Another interesting way the Court has been used to support dispute settlement is through a diplomatic innovation in which two states formally agree to refer a dispute to the Court, if they are unable to settle it on their own by other means. This allows the parties to try other methods, such as negotiation or mediation, but with a powerful backup procedure to ensure that the dispute will ultimately be resolved. Knowing that they will have less control, if the issue is turned over to the Court, disputing parties have a greater incentive to negotiate with one another in good faith. If direct efforts fail, taking the case to the Court seems less of an inimical act, since it is a matter of prior agreement.

Hence, the International Court of Justice provides a range of judicial possibilities for resolving disputes between states, and the streamlining of its procedures, as will be discussed at the end of this chapter, should make it an ever more viable dispute settlement mechanism.

The UN's Human Rights Machinery

In the area of human rights, the first task that the UN undertook was to set international standards for the observance of human rights and, indeed, its achievements in this area are exceptional. As Childers and Urquhart (1994) note, "If nothing more had been done in forty-five years at the United Nations than the negotiation and adoption by from 51 to 180 states of the nearly 70 instruments of the International Bill of Human Rights, this alone would fully justify the existence of the organization."

Regrettably, however, member states have not been as laudable with regard to their implementation. From the mid-1970s onward, the UN began to be more involved in monitoring states' compliance with human rights and responding to violations. But the effort has too often been hindered by states' reluctance to establish effective mechanisms for ensuring compliance, due to fears that their own human rights shortcomings might be exposed to international scrutiny or be used for political point-scoring by others.

For this and other reasons, the human rights machinery has evolved in a complex and ad hoc manner, with no overall strategic plan. In cases where political intransigence led to little being done, a new body was simply set up to do the job. Thus, the current UN human rights system is made up of a wide range of disparate bodies that often do not interact as meaningfully as they should and have overlapping mandates with different and sometimes inconsistent approaches. The most relevant of these for the advancement of sustainable peace will be briefly reviewed below.

Human Rights Monitoring: The UN Commission on Human Rights

The Commission on Human Rights, which began with 18 members, has now grown to 53. In contrast to the commissions of regional organizations, it is composed of governmental representatives rather than independent experts. Although many of the delegations are headed by senior diplomats, some of whom have considerable expertise in human rights, the commission acts as a political body in which decisions are made along political lines. The commission's major product consists of resolutions and decisions that often involve lobbying and horse trading.

From 1946 to 1966, the UN commission maintained that it had "no power to take any action in regard to any complaints concerning human rights" and although it received complaints, it did nothing about them. One Secretariat official at the time termed it "the world's most elaborate waste basket," and others have concluded that this practice contributed to a significant loss of credibility by the UN in human rights matters (Alston, 1992b).

From 1967 to 1978, the situation gradually changed as a number of developments led to the adoption of two separate procedures: ECOSOC Resolution 1235 stated that violations could be examined and responded to in a public debate at the commission's annual meeting, and ECOSOC Resolution 1503 called for situations that revealed a consistent pattern of gross violations of human rights to be pursued with governments in private. But while these procedures engendered high hopes, they accomplished relatively little during their first decade in operation. The Carter administration's commitment to human rights, however, finally mobilized public opinion, and pressure was exerted on the commission to use its new procedures more effectively.

Today, the commission meets once a year for a six-week session. Several hundred delegates debate and produce around 90 resolutions and decisions, which are painstakingly negotiated in the presence of representatives from scores of NGOs. Strohal (1993) notes that diplomats are often less concerned about achieving effective protection and promotion of human rights than "in reaching *consensus* or conducting bilateral feuds in multilateral surroundings." The commission's procedures are outlined below.

The Private Procedure

Although based on individual complaints, this procedure is not intended to provide redress to individual victims. Instead, its objective is to use complaints as a means of assisting the commission in determining situations that involve "a consistent pattern of gross and reliably attested violations." Every year, each of the five members of the Communications Working Group of the Sub-Commission on the Prevention of Discrimination and the Protection of Minorities sorts through the complaints that have been received. Each is responsible for a particular kind of violation and that individual goes through all of the relevant communications on that topic. If the forwarding of a given communication is recommended, the other members of the working group have the opportunity to examine it and to agree or disagree as to its admissibility (the decision being made by majority vote). If, however, the member decides not to make a recommendation, the others have no say in the matter. The sub-commission then examines the communications referred to it by the working group in closed meetings.

From the tens of thousands of complaints received in an average year (the number has been as high as 300,000), the sub-commission usually refers eight to ten countries to the commission. (Sometimes it also identifies a few cases that will be considered the following year, in order to put the governments concerned "on notice.") Once a case has been referred, the government is invited to submit written observations and/or to defend itself before the commission. Complainants, however, are not informed or given an opportunity to participate, resulting in a clearly one-sided procedure.

The next stage is for the commission itself to establish the Communications Working Group, which drafts recommendations for action. The range of action that the commission can invoke includes: keeping the country "under review," sending an envoy to seek further information and report back to the commission, appointing an ad hoc committee that will conduct a confidential investigation aimed at finding a "friendly solution," or transferring the case to the public 1235 procedure. At the end of its deliberations, the chairman announces which countries have been considered and which have been dismissed. No information is provided on the nature of the allegations or the action taken by the commission.

Although secrecy makes this procedure difficult to assess, Guest (1990) concludes that "confidentiality has not persuaded governments to cooperate with the UN." Since the commission and sub-commission meet only once a year, the procedure typically takes between two and three years from the time when complaints are received until the commission responds.

The Public Procedure

This procedure allows the commission to hold an annual *public* debate on issues involving gross violations of human rights. Various actions can be taken to investigate claims, including the appointment of a special rapporteur, special representative, expert, independent expert, working group, or commission delegation. In other cases, the Secretary-General is asked to make direct contacts and report to the commission through a representative.

The selection of rapporteurs, however, is often a political process, and in some cases, the target country has even been involved. Moreover, the mandates given to special rapporteurs are often uncertain or intentionally ambivalent, and rapporteurs are frequently left to choose their own methods. Normally, they adopt either a documentation approach, where the goal is to record the facts and to provide a reliable historical record; a prosecutorial/publicity approach, in which they attempt to gather as much evidence as possible to support a condemnation; or conciliation, where they try to find solutions that will improve the situation (Alston, 1992b). Once the commission has received the report, it usually debates the matter and passes a resolution. In some cases the mere threat of a resolution has resulted in a constructive response from the government involved.

One criticism of this procedure has been the uneven focus of its attention, which has led to accusations of a "double standard." Most investigations have occurred in Latin America and Asia, and until 1995, the Great Powers escaped scrutiny. Regional solidarity has also helped African and Arab states avoid examination. Finally, the commission has only acted in cases involving serious repression. Alston (1992b) notes that, as a general rule, for the commission to act, "it seems that blood needed to be spilled, and in large quantities." Evaluating the effectiveness of this procedure in terms of saving lives, he comments that "the response time is too great, the potential sanction too distant (or un-immediate), and the range of other relevant pressures in most situations too vast. . . . As a measure for dealing with issues on an emergency basis the 1235 procedure is deeply flawed, especially because of the fact that the commission meets but once a year." He notes further that it is difficult to accept that, "After almost half a century of concerted efforts, the principal UN procedures for responding to violations are quite as embryonic, marginally effective and unevenly applied as they are."

Thematic Procedures

Another development is the investigation of human rights abuses of a particular type. A number of special working groups or special rapporteurs has been appointed to consider particular types of abuses and include the Working Group on Enforced or Involuntary Disappearances, the Special Rapporteur on Summary or Arbitrary Executions, the Special Rapporteur on Torture, the Special Rapporteur on Religious Intolerance, and the Working Group on Arbitrary Detention. Although they use a range of methods, routine requests for information are the most common. In this case, the essence of plausible allegations is sent to the government concerned, with a request for information. A second method is an "urgent action" procedure. The technique was introduced in 1980 when the person slated to be the next chairperson of the Working Group on Enforced and Involuntary Disappearances (an Iraqi) himself disappeared. The procedure allows the chairperson of a group to contact a government to request information as a matter of urgency, and to appeal for the human rights of a particular person or group to be respected. Each year, hundreds of urgent cables are transmitted to governments and thousands of letters are sent. In some cases, this technique has been effective in protecting individual victims from further harm (Strohal, 1993). On-site country visits are a third method, which allows a rapporteur to be in touch with victims' family members, witnesses, and NGOs, as well as with governments. A fourth method is the "prompt intervention" procedure, whereby a cable is sent to the relevant official. In the case of the Working Group on Enforced or Involuntary Disappearances, a cable may be sent to the minister for foreign affairs, requesting that immediate protection be given to relatives of missing persons or witnesses to disappearances and their families. For the Working Group on Enforced or Involuntary Disappearances, about one in ten of the routine requests has established the whereabouts or fate of the individual in question, and about one in five of the urgent inquiries has yielded results (Donnelly, 1993). Thus, the thematic procedures have been useful in keeping some pressure on those governments that are the most frequent violators of human rights.

The Sub-Commission on the Prevention of Discrimination and the Protection of Minorities

The Sub-Commission on the Prevention of Discrimination and the Protection of Minorities is a body of 26 "independent experts," who are nominated by governments and elected by the Commission on Human Rights. No criteria have been set for evaluating the qualifications of candidates, and although prohibited, a number of "independent experts" have, over the years, been found to be in the employment of their governments. The sub-commission was originally created to provide analysis and advice to the commission through studies, but its role has evolved over time.

Although the protection of minorities was one of the two dimensions of the sub-commission's original mandate, it has turned out to be "a near-impossible task" (Eide, 1992). The sub-commission's draft of a clause on minorities for the Universal Declaration of Human Rights was deleted by the commission, although it was later introduced as Article 27 of the International Covenant on Civil and Political Rights. Other proposals of the sub-commission with regard to minorities were either ignored or rejected by the commission. The drafting of the two-page Declaration on the Rights of Persons Belonging to National or Ethnic, Religious and Linguistic Minorities, which was finally approved by the General Assembly in 1993, had been on its agenda since 1979, its slow progress being due to a lack of enthusiasm by the government delegations on the commission. More recently, however, the new Working Group on Minorities has been set up with a broad mandate to promote the implementation of the declaration.

The sub-commission has had more success in other areas, including the Convention on the Elimination of All Forms of Racial Discrimination, which was adopted in 1965. In 1981, it succeeded in having its Declaration on the Elimination of All Forms of Intolerance and of Discrimination Based on Religion or Belief adopted by the General Assembly. Following a sub-commission study on states of emergency, the Commission on Human Rights called on the sub-commission to propose measures "to ensure respect for human rights under states of siege or emergency." Since 1987, a member of the sub-commission has been given the task of preparing "an annual report listing all states which have proclaimed, extended, or terminated a state of emergency, as well as the grounds given, the duration, and the measures adopted."

Another working group, relevant to intrastate conflict, is the Working Group on the Rights of Indigenous Populations, which was formed in 1982 and hears presentations each year by representatives of these populations. Since 1988, the working group has been developing a Draft Universal Declaration on Indigenous Rights, which is currently being studied by the commission.

Like the Commission on Human Rights, the sub-commission's major output is resolutions, which NGOs are often involved in drafting. Indeed, one of the sub-commission's major contributions has been its opening of a multidimensional dialogue with victims and NGOs, which is otherwise rarely found in the UN system.

In summary, although the development of a more expert group has had some positive influences on the human rights commission, its subservience to the commission and the influence of governments in the appointment process has eroded some of the potential that such a body might have had, if it had been more independent.

The Human Rights Committee

Following the ratification of the International Covenant on Civil and Political Rights, which came into force in 1976, the Human Rights Committee was established to consider reports on progress in achieving the observance of human rights by the states that had ratified or acceded to the covenant. As of July 1997, 138 states had done so (personal communication, Center for Human Rights, 1997). These states are legally bound to submit reports on the measures they have adopted in regard to legislative, judicial, and administrative matters, to give effect to the rights recognized in the covenant. The reports are examined by the 18 Human Rights Committee members, who serve in their personal capacity as human rights experts.

The committee is not a court, but it has the right to question states regarding their reports. In addition, under the First Optional Protocol of the covenant, states can recognize the competence of the committee to consider complaints from individuals against state parties regarding alleged violations of human rights. Typically, the committee meets in three sessions per year to consider these matters.

It is interesting to note that the draft covenant, which was prepared in 1954, envisioned a quasi-judicial Human Rights Committee, with considerably more power than that which was ultimately approved. By the time the Third Committee of the General Assembly debated and proposed its implementation twelve years later, the majority was opposed to making the procedure for interstate communications obligatory. The lowest common denominator was decided upon; that is, the committee's only compulsory role would be to study and comment generally upon the reports of state parties. The functions regarding complaints were made entirely optional and those concerned with individual complaints were even separated from the covenant and placed in an optional protocol (Opsahl, 1992).

The Reporting System for States

States that have acceded to or ratified the covenant are obligated to provide their first report within one year of the covenant's entry into force for that state and subsequently whenever the committee "so requests." The committee has, to date, adopted a five-year interval for subsequent reports. Parties are required to submit reports on the "measures they have adopted," "the progress made in the enjoyment of those rights," and the factors and difficulties affecting the covenant's implementation.

One problem, however, is that states are frequently late in putting in their reports. In order to persuade governments to comply, the committee has recently decided to publish in its report to the General Assembly the names of states that had more than one report overdue, along with the number of reminder notices (as many as 21 notices have been sent to some countries). When a country does send in its report, consideration of it takes place in a public meeting in the presence of representatives of the state concerned. The meeting attempts to establish a "constructive dialogue" between the committee and the state party by raising issues that need further consideration. The representatives of states that are submitting their initial reports are given time to prepare answers to these issues. In the case of periodic reports, the committee identifies in advance the matters that might most usefully be discussed. Although NGOs can send observers, they do not have the right to formally address the committee.

An important recent development has been the issuing of comments reflecting the views of the committee following the process. These are sent to the government and published in the committee's annual report. They provide an overall evaluation of each state's report and of the dialogue with the delegation, and they note factors and difficulties that affect implementation. They also note "positive aspects of the report," "principal aspects of concern," and "suggestions and recommendations." Often, these are quite specific and direct. States are asked to keep the committee informed of their progress in following its recommendations and are reminded of the availability of advisory services through the Center for Human Rights.

Since 1991, the committee has used an emergency procedure, asking state parties to submit reports urgently on a given situation. In 1993, the committee decided that when a report revealed a grave human rights situation, it could request the Secretary-General to inform the competent organs of the UN, including the Security Council. This development provides an important new link to the rest of the system.

Complaints under the Optional Protocol

As noted above, in states that have acceded to or ratified the Optional Protocol of the International Covenant on Civil and Political Rights, individuals who claim that their rights have been violated under the covenant can submit written communications to the committee. Of the 138 states that have ratified or acceded to the covenant, 92 have accepted the optional protocol (personal communication, Center for Human Rights, 1997).

When "communications" are received, a special rapporteur and working group examine them for admissibility. A communication is only admissible if it concerns one of the rights and freedoms recognized in the covenant, if submitted by or on behalf of the alleged victim, if it is not anonymous, if all domestic remedies have been exhausted, and if it is not being considered under another international procedure. State parties are often invited to reply regarding admissibility, and complainants may also be asked for further information. Thus, it can take between six months and a year before the working group declares a communication admissible.

At this stage, the state party is asked to submit "written explanations or a statement clarifying the matter and the remedy, if any, that may have been taken by the state." If the state fails to respond, its failure is taken as an admission of culpability. The committee does not have adequate resources to carry out independent inquiries, fact finding, oral hearings of the parties and witnesses, nor to take steps toward mediation or settlement of the matter. It may, however, ask the victim for further clarification. Such "written communications" are considered on their merits during closed meetings. The final decisions of the committee (called "views") are, however, made public. In expressing its "views," the committee also provides recommendations about individual reparation and preventive measures for the future.

Since the Optional Protocol came into force in 1977, 716 communications concerning 51 states have been registered for consideration. Of these, the committee found violations of the covenant in 142 cases (Report of the Human Rights Committee, 1996). In the past, the committee simply submitted its findings to states, asking them to report on their compliance. There were no formal follow-up procedures. Only about half of the governments involved responded, and of these, only a little over one-fourth submitted replies that were fully satisfactory and displayed a willingness to accept the committee's view and remedy the situation. To help overcome this problem, the committee, in 1990, established a special rapporteur to follow up on its findings. In 1993, the committee decided further that information on follow-up activities should be made public. In 1994, it decided that publicity should be given to responses in its annual report to the General Assembly through "a separate and highly visible" section and in its press communiqués.

A number of further problems have constrained the use of the Optional Protocol. Lack of public knowledge of the availability of the procedure and the lack of a fact-finding mechanism both weaken its effectiveness. There is no provision for pleadings or conciliation; the only means of enforcement is the committee's moral authority, and the pressure of public censure. Finally, the severe shortage in resources has meant that a backlog of communications has recently been accumulating.

The Committee on Economic, Social, and Cultural Rights

As of July 1997, 136 states had ratified or acceded to the International Covenant on Economic, Social, and Cultural Rights (Center for Human

Rights, 1997). Although the covenant came into force in 1976, the Committee on Economic, Social, and Cultural Rights was not established until 1987. The committee adopted a reporting and review procedure similar to that of the Human Rights Committee. States were asked to put in initial reports, and thereafter were required to submit reports every five years. The committee meets once a year to consider these. States are invited to respond to questions and, at the end of the hearing, the committee provides an overall view of a state's progress, including an evaluation of its report and response to questions, the factors and difficulties impeding its implementation of the covenant, the positive aspects of the state's progress with implementation, the principal subjects of concern, and a set of suggestions and recommendations.

Because the Covenant on Economic, Social, and Cultural Rights was not based on a significant body of domestic jurisprudence, the committee faces a number of difficulties in making recommendations, including the lack of conceptual clarity; the ambivalence of governments toward economic, social, and cultural rights; the absence of national institutions in this area; the complexity and scope of the information needed to supervise compliance; the largely programmatic nature of some of the rights; the more limited relevance of formal legal texts and judicial decisions; and the paucity of NGOs with interest in the area (Alston, 1992c).

The committee also experiences many of the same problems that face the Human Rights Committee in terms of lateness of reporting. Too many states seem to approach the task not as a part of a continuing process of improving their domestic realization of economic, social, and cultural rights, but rather as a "diplomatic chore." The committee has recently warned governments that, if it is not able to obtain the information it requires, it will request that the state concerned accept a small mission to collect the information necessary for the committee to carry out its functions in relation to the covenant.

The committee also found itself faced with a chronic problem of a few states putting off their presentations by saying that their representatives could not be present. In response, it decided that on the third occasion of this excuse, it would simply proceed with the consideration of the report whether or not a representative of the state party was able to attend. Every state that had been using this ploy sent a representative to the subsequent meeting.

More recently, the committee has asked the Center for Human Rights to begin a file for each country and has invited "all concerned bodies and individuals to submit relevant and appropriate documentation to it." At each meeting, the committee has also made a practice of holding a Day of General Discussion with experts in the area to try to further clarify the norms involved in the treaty. More resources, however, are needed if the committee is to function maximally.

The UN High Commissioner for Human Rights

Following the recommendation of the World Conference on Human Rights held in Vienna in 1993, the Office of the UN High Commissioner for Human Rights was established by General Assembly Resolution 48/141. This idea was first advanced in 1951 and formally proposed by the Commission on Human Rights in 1967, but due to a minimalist approach, it did not secure the approval of the General Assembly. Only recently has sufficient consensus and concern with gross violations prompted its adoption.

The High Commissioner was appointed in 1994 by the Secretary-General at the rank of Under-Secretary-General for a four-year term. This is meant to be the "United Nations official with principal responsibility for United Nations human rights activities." In essence, the UN High Commissioner for Human Rights has both the coordinating job as head of the Center for Human Rights, as well as the diplomatic function of a roaming special representative of the Secretary-General. This office provides a much-needed link between the human rights machinery, the Secretary-General, and the Security Council. It will, however, be important for the High Commissioner to take advantage of the mandate to present cases of gross violation to the Secretary-General and through this person to the Security Council. It remains to be seen whether the Security Council will then respond in a timely fashion. During 1995, the High Commissioner visited over thirty states on all continents to hold discussions with government officials, members of parliament, the judiciary, NGOs, academics, the press, and the public on issues such as the ratification of treaties, cooperation with the UN's human rights mechanisms, inclusion of human rights in national laws, the establishment of national institutions to protect human rights and to urge the following of recommendations regarding human rights violations (Boutros-Ghali, 1995a).

Human rights field presence either in the form of field operations or field offices is one of the recent innovations of the High Commissioner. This ranges from a staff of one in the Malawi office to more than 120 staff members in Rwanda. In 1992, there were no human rights field activities, now there are eight. More staff members are now deployed in the field than in New York or Geneva. Nonetheless, financial problems continue to haunt these activities. In Burundi, for example, where according to the Special Rapporteur of the Commission on Human Rights, hundreds of thousands of people have been killed, the original field project called for a human rights observer mission with 35 staff members, but funding could only be found for five. Four more have since been added, but as the High Commissioner points out, this is "far from sufficient" (Report of the United Nations High Commissioner for Human Rights, 1996).

The High Commissioner is also charged with coordinating human rights activities and initiatives, and at the time of this writing, he has undertaken a restructuring of the Center for Human Rights to create a more "functional framework for integrating and consolidating activities" in the field of human rights. As well, he has begun to work more closely with other UN agencies and programs, regional organizations, national institutions, academic institutions, and nongovernmental organizations. Moreover, the High Commissioner and the center have held meetings with the World Bank to discuss the "right to development" to consider how the two institutions might cooperate more closely and to present a more comprehensive approach (Report of the United Nations High Commissioner for Human Rights, 1996).

Although it is too early to fully evaluate the impact of this new post, the High Commissioner for Human Rights is an important addition to the existing human rights machinery and this coordinating role alone may assist in increasing the effectiveness of this complex machinery.

Assistance in Human Rights

Recently, a significant effort has been made to help governments implement human rights reform by providing them with technical assistance. Although the Center for Human Rights has been active in human rights education from its inception, the formation (in 1987) of the Voluntary Fund for Technical Cooperation provided a major impetus for it to provide assistance to governments. The 1993 World Conference on Human Rights made a strong plea for this program to be strengthened and for its funding base to be expanded. As a result, the Advisory Services, Technical Assistance, and Information Branch was created.

Because of government sensitivities about interference in their internal affairs, the branch typically waits for governments to approach it before taking action, although some countries are also referred by the Human Rights Commission, the Human Rights Committees, or special rapporteurs. Once a government has approached the branch, a field visit is carried out by one or more experts who assess the human rights needs of the country through in-depth discussion with a range of interlocutors. The team collects and studies copies of the country's constitutions and laws. In some cases, it recommends that assistance begin with a small, discreet initiative; in others, it recommends a comprehensive "country program." A legal agreement is then signed to ensure that the parties are willing to follow through on the proposed program.

For countries in transition, the branch can provide *constitutional assis-*

tance through the advisory service of experts, through conferences and seminars, or simply by making relevant documents available. Advice may be offered on drafting legislation, constitutions, or bills of rights. In order to bring national laws into conformity with international standards, experts and specialized staff are available to assist governments in the reform of legislation related to human rights and fundamental freedoms. Commentary on drafts is provided and recommendations are made, which include comparative reference to similar laws in other jurisdictions.

In addition, the branch has been involved in the training of judges, magistrates, lawyers, prosecutors, police officers, and prison personnel. It also plans to begin training armed forces regarding human rights. It provides training and an advisory service to parliamentarians on national human rights legislation, parliamentary human rights committees, and the role of parliament in promoting and protecting human rights. The branch also offers its services to governments considering or in the process of establishing national human rights institutions, including financial assistance, training and assistance in the drafting of reports to United Nations treaty bodies, and training on the effective investigation of human rights violations.

The service has recently introduced courses for media professionals on topics such as the situation of the press, public perceptions of human rights through television, access to information, the problems of censorship, the role of the press in the development of a pluralistic society, and obstacles to human rights reporting. A range of training initiatives has been established for primary, secondary, and tertiary students, aimed at assisting in the building of a human rights culture. Finally, the branch translates documentation into local languages, assists in the computerization of national and regional human rights offices, and provides support to national libraries as well as to national or regional human rights documentation centers.

Although this new approach is exceedingly promising, the sharp increase in demand has already caused a critical shortage of resources, both in terms of staff and finances. The branch has 27 project officers, and its director estimates that it needs twice that number to adequately meet recent requests.

Electoral Assistance

In 1992, with the growing trend toward democratization, the Electoral Assistance Unit (now a division) was established under the Department of Political Affairs. In its first 30 months of operation, it provided more than 50 member states with some form of electoral assistance. In spite of the sensitivity of this task, *no* complaints have been made by any member state regarding interference in its internal affairs and requests for these services have been on the increase.

To obtain assistance, a member state must send a request to the division. A needs assessment is then carried out by a small team, which travels to the country to determine whether the UN should provide assistance. It considers whether the basic conditions for a legitimate and truly democratic process are present, estimates the degree of support for electoral assistance, reviews legal provisions relevant to the electoral process, and assesses the overall context and conditions for the planned election (Report to the General Assembly, 1994e).

Seven types of assistance are available. The first and most complex is the *organization and conduct of elections* (as effected in Cambodia). Since such operations require substantial financial, human, and material resources, as well as a longer lead time, they are unlikely to be used very often. A second type is the *supervision of an electoral process*. This approach has usually been undertaken as part of a peacekeeping operation in the context of decolonization (such as in Namibia) and requires the UN to certify that all stages of the electoral process are in order—to assure the legitimacy of the outcome. The third type is *verification of an electoral process* (as carried out in Angola, El Salvador, Haiti, Nicaragua, Mozambique, and South Africa), where the UN is asked to verify the freedom and fairness of particular aspects of an electoral process, which is conducted by the national election authority. Because of their complexity and expense, all three forms of assistance are carried out with mandates from either the Security Council or General Assembly.

A fourth version, and one that is being used with increasing frequency, is the *coordination of international observers* (as carried out in Malawi and Ethiopia). A small secretariat provided by the UN acts as an umbrella framework to coordinate observers from a range of organizations. It provides observers with protocol, logistic, and observational support, to ensure consistent and rational coverage of the election. A fifth formula, used for the first time in Mexico, is *support for national observers*. This approach is intended to emphasize long-term national capacity-building and the strengthening of national institutions. Assistance is provided in areas such as observation methodology, logistics, strategic planning, and the conduct of quick counts, and is most useful for countries with a relatively well-developed democratic culture. A sixth kind of assistance (used in the Russian Federation and Ukraine) involves the dispatch of a small team (or in some cases, one person) to follow an election process and report back to the Secretary-General. This is referred to simply as *observation,* and is largely symbolic, with its practical impact on the electoral process being negligible. The final type is *technical assistance*. This includes advice to electoral authorities, design or restructuring of electoral systems, computerization of electoral components (such as registration rolls or vote tabulation), civic and voter education, advice on the drafting of electoral laws, constitutional reform, training of poll workers, boundary delimitation, design and preparation of national identity card systems, election organization and budget preparation, advice on election security, or procurement of election material (such as ballots, ballot envelopes, ballot boxes, or indelible ink). To sum up, the establishment of the Electoral Assistance Division has provided a much-needed service to member states wishing to carry out multiparty elections.

Possible Next Steps

Since the end of the cold war, progress has been made in the areas of peacemaking through the increased use of good offices under the auspices of the Secretary-General and the personal representatives as well as the International Court of Justice. Progress has also been made in the area of offering assistance in human rights and electoral assistance. This now needs to be systematically built upon. Some possible next steps will be briefly outlined below.

Preventive Diplomacy

As discussed above, the UN has not found a satisfactory means of providing preventive diplomacy. The appointment of special or personal representatives on a per case basis is the model currently used for most of its peacemaking activities, and exceptionally for preventive diplomacy. Such a model, however, is useful only *after* specific cases have been identified and the parties have agreed to avail themselves of third-party assistance. Thus, it cannot substitute for a more comprehensive and permanent preventive diplomacy capacity, whose function would be to encourage members to avail themselves of its services to assist in more timely *early* prevention.

It will be argued that a more useful approach would be to assign skilled senior staff on a full-time basis to preventive diplomacy and place them "on the ground" in the region. Observing problems firsthand in the field provides a much richer understanding of the situation in its cultural, historical, and political context than reading a newspaper report or talking to one of the parties when they visit UN Headquarters in New York City. Developing relationships with the disputing parties, understanding their interests, gaining their trust, and nudging them in the direction of negotiation or mediation are difficult to carry out by telephone and fax from New York.

Indeed, the last two secretaries-general have proposed establishing offices within individual countries, which would follow developments and provide early warning of impending problems, as well as an "on the ground" presence for diplomatic initiatives. Although these proposals were significantly different from one another, they were both opposed by a number of member states, who feared that having UN political offices or embassies in their countries could lead to an erosion of their sovereignty.

What is required, therefore, is a proposal that can overcome these objections and be able to provide a *dispute-resolution service,* which is acceptable to member states. A proposal for establishing UN Regional Centers for Sustainable Peace will be discussed in chapter 13. The advantage of regional centers is that they would be regionally based, and should thus be less expensive to implement and more acceptable than a permanent presence within each state. Their regional focus would allow for more effective coordination with regional organizations and, where possible, such centers could even be mounted as a joint venture between the UN and regional organizations. Regional centers could bring together the functions of tracking disputes with the functions of offering dispute resolution assistance. Thus, regional centers, as an extension of the Department of Political Affairs, would mean that both information collection and analysis and early action would be handled by the same part of the organization. By being a permanent structure, they would also provide an ongoing involvement and continuity from one intervention to the next, which would assist in promoting institutional learning and skill.

The International Court of Justice

Until recently, much of the debate about improving the International Court of Justice as an option for dispute settlement has focused on how to expand its jurisdiction. However, the increased use of the Court (which has occurred naturally with the end of the cold war) has highlighted the need to streamline its procedures so that it can operate more efficiently. The ability to hear more than one case at a time and the increased use of smaller ad hoc chambers could assist in this regard.

In terms of enhancing its general dispute settlement functions, the authority to seek an advisory opinion could also be extended to the Secretary-General. This authority could be granted by the General Assembly, and would allow the Secretary-General (in the process of carrying out good offices) to submit the legal aspects of a case at an early stage for an opinion of the Court. It would assist in preventive diplomacy by providing not only an objective opinion, but also a cooling off period, while the Court deliberated. To work in this way, however, the Court would have to develop "fast-track procedures." The Commission on Global Governance

(1995) has also suggested that fast-track procedures might encourage the Security Council to use the Court more often for advisory opinions.

The Court continues to play an important role in the international system through modeling a *process of reason,* whereby disputes can be settled through recourse to international law. However, because it is limited to interstate disputes, it cannot offer assistance with intrastate problems.

Human Rights

Establishing appropriate mechanisms for the monitoring and protecting of human rights has also been a difficult task for the UN, since human rights became yet another battleground of the cold war, with considerable time spent on airing and debating ideological differences between East and West. Because of the varying views on the topic, the UN's human rights bodies were often forced to take a minimalist approach. Ambivalence about human rights also resulted in the whole area being badly underfunded, with less than 1 percent of the UN regular budget currently being allocated for human rights. Nonetheless, with the end of the cold war, several of the human rights bodies have been freed, at least in part, to pursue their mandates more vigorously, and some recent progress in adopting more satisfactory procedures has been made, as noted in the above discussion.

It is clear, nonetheless, that the whole domain of human rights needs much more attention. Of overriding importance is the need to *prevent* human rights abuses. An improved and enlarged program for technical assistance in human rights would be useful in this regard. It might also be helpful to relate the human rights and political sections of the organization more closely. Even now, there is very little contact between the two. The presence of human rights experts as part of regional centers could provide a much-needed link between the Department of Political Affairs and the Center for Human Rights and allow preventive diplomacy teams to have ready access to human rights expertise and vice versa. With regard to both prevention and protection, the appointment of a High Commissioner for Human Rights is a major step forward. The use of human rights observers and field operations and offices may turn out to be another important approach.

The years 1995 to 2004 represent the United Nations Decade for Human Rights Education as well as the International Decade of the World's Indigenous People, and 1998 is the fiftieth anniversary of the Universal Declaration. These offer further opportunity for the international community to strengthen and support work in this vital field.

The Report of the United States Commission on Improving the Effectiveness of the United Nations (1994) has also called for the establishment of an international human rights court, to hear human rights cases. It suggested that such a court could be modeled after the European and Inter-American human rights courts, to have jurisdiction over human rights treaties, although its authority could not be invoked until all domestic remedies had been exhausted.

Summary

One of the major factors still interfering with the UN's ability to function effectively in the area of prevention is its *crisis orientation*. By focusing most of its energies on this end of the continuum, it often intervenes at a time when it is *least* likely to be effective. Its limited resources are then sucked into a few situations that seem to closely resemble black holes. Efforts to prevent tomorrow's crises are neglected as the organization struggles to cope with today's tragedies. As a result, conflicts that might have been prevented then emerge to occupy the organization's resources and distract it further from prevention. Thus, a major shift in emphasis toward prevention will be needed if the organization is to become more effective. Chapters 13 and 14 will outline some ways in which this could be done.

6

The Council of Europe

Security Issues in Europe

EVEN BEFORE THE RUBBLE had been cleared from World War II, the United States and Western Europe on one side of the divide and the Soviet Union and Eastern Europe on the other quickly faced off in a new and potentially deadly conflict. Although the cold war was fought in every region, it was probably chilliest in Europe, where the two blocs stood face to face, poised for either a limited or all-out confrontation—with the ever-growing fear that either could lead to nuclear annihilation. In response to this threat, NATO and the Warsaw Pact were created as a different kind of regional arrangement than those that will be discussed in this book, their mandate being military readiness for just such a nightmare scenario.

Simultaneously, other regional arrangements, such as the European Community (now the European Union) and the Council of Europe, evolved with more cooperative aims—to put an end to the divisions that had twice devastated the continent in the first half of the century. Today, after fifty years of endeavor, their success is evident in the neighborly relations among the countries of Western Europe, and the high standard of living and freedom enjoyed by most of their citizens.

In the Soviet Union, the headlong rush to compete with the West in the arms race and the eventual failure of planned economies led to progressive economic and political decline. The growing disparity between the standards of living and freedoms enjoyed in the West and those in the East did not escape the notice of either the leadership or the people. Under President Mikhail Gorbachev, a liberalization in thinking emerged, which provided a wide enough gap that the floodgates of peaceful protest were opened. The communist regimes of Eastern Europe were confronted with a wave of discontent so far reaching that their mandate to govern was undercut. In response to similar pressures, the Soviet Union itself disintegrated as a political entity, the Berlin Wall was torn down, and the peoples of Eastern Europe embraced the twin aspirations of democratic governance and a market economy. The resulting euphoria was, however, short-lived, as the consequences of such massive change played themselves out—with only a limited moderating influence from the international community, which was simply unprepared for this development.

The adjustment to independence, democratization, and market reform proved difficult for the states of Eastern and Central Europe and the former Soviet Union, causing unexpected shifts in the distribution of economic and political power. In some cases, changes in the status quo led to the formation of new minorities and new dominant groups. Also, a number of ethnic groups were mobilized to pursue their aspirations for political access or autonomy. In short, new sets of interests arose that needed to be reconciled and accommodated in the political, legal, and economic structures of these states.

Only two years after the fall of the Berlin Wall, Yugoslavia disintegrated, but much less peacefully than the Soviet Union, and the international community became entangled in picking up the pieces and sorting out the complex relationships and territorial claims of the parties. The hope that the Russian Federation would develop a new identity without major trauma evaporated when the separatist movement in its Chechen Republic provoked a devastating military response. On top of this were a range of other problems, from accommodation of Russian populations in the Baltics to separatist movements in Abkhazia, Ossetia, Tajikistan, Moldova, and Nagorno-Karabakh. Fears persist concerning the political and economic stability of some of the former Soviet republics and their future interactions with one another. Finally, the ultimate shape of relations between some of the countries in the Commonwealth of Independent States and the West is still unclear, leaving many governments in Eastern Europe feeling less than confident.

Western Europe is not without its own problems. It has had its share of intractable conflicts, such as in Cyprus and Northern Ireland. Various grievances still exist for the 29 minorities in Western Europe that Gurr identifies as at risk, and while many of these grievances have been largely expressed through protest, rather than rebellion, the problems are far from solved. Much institutional and individual discrimination remains, not only for minority groups, but also for immigrants, whose population growth now represents one birth in ten in Europe and who face growing xenophobia.

Finally, some problems linger on both sides of the East-West divide.

Many states still maintain large conventional, and in some instances, nuclear forces, which, although no longer explicitly brandished as threats, are maintained as expressions of implicit power and coercive control. While perhaps comforting to a few, they are of concern to many, who do not always see these states in the same benign light that they see themselves.

Clearly, the various regional organizations of Europe have their work cut out for them. Like their counterparts in other regions, they have been struggling to adapt to the realities of the new era, and they have produced a surge of innovation to cope with the need to manage the complex process of global change. European regional organizations, however, have two significant advantages over others. First, there are several of them, so they can be interlocking. In other words, they can specialize in certain areas according to their natural advantages; and, in areas where they overlap, they can work together, extending their reach. Second, they are far better funded and staffed than their counterparts in other regions, which simply allows them to do more (the Council of Europe's annual budget, for example, is $161 million). Two of Europe's regional organizations, the Council of Europe and the Organization for Security and Cooperation in Europe, are especially active in conflict prevention and will be reviewed below.

The Role of the Council of Europe in Promoting Sustainable Peace

With ten founding members, the Council of Europe was established in 1949 to promote intergovernmental and parliamentary cooperation. It was set up in response to Europe's traumatic experience with the Nazi regime, and its main aim was to secure democracy in Europe and to prevent the recurrence of gross violations of human rights.

The Council of Europe was designed to cover all of Europe, but the onset of the cold war turned the council (during its first 40 years) into a Western European organization. It became one of the main organizations responsible for the gradual development of shared norms and values throughout Western Europe and the steady movement toward the institutionalization of democratic processes in all aspects of Western European society. With its emphasis on democracy and human rights, however, the Council of Europe was viewed with great suspicion by the leaders of the Soviet bloc.

After the collapse of the Soviet Union, the newly democratic states of Eastern and Central Europe were eager to develop their democratic credentials and join the regional architecture that their Western neighbors had established for security and prosperity. In response, the council's Parliamentary Assembly was quick to welcome the parliaments of Central and

Eastern Europe, granting Special Guest Status to several of these governments as early as 1989. As Pinto (1995) notes:

> Four decades of Communist rule (and more than seven for most states of the
> former Soviet Union) had not exactly prepared these countries to qualify for
> admission to the Council of Europe with its strong requirements in the realm
> of human rights, political pluralism and rule of law. In all cases, democratic
> states, institutions and behaviours had to be rebuilt from scratch. Confronted
> with this new political context, the Council had to choose. It could either
> stand back and bide its time waiting for each country to attain "spontane-
> ously" the proper level of democratic maturity to qualify for admission. Or it
> could actively intervene by responding to the requests of the states themselves
> who sought help in their transition to democracy. The Council chose the
> latter course.

Since then, 16 Central and Eastern European states have become full
members of the council (Hungary, Poland, Bulgaria, Estonia, Lithuania,
Slovenia, the Czech Republic, Slovakia, Romania, Latvia, Albania, Moldova, the Russian Federation, the Republic of Croatia, the Former Yugoslav Republic of Macedonia, and Ukraine), bringing the council's
membership to 40 (Council of Europe, 1997). A number of other applica-
tions are pending. The Russian Federation's application was suspended in
1995, due to the government's actions in Chechnya, but since making
peace with Chechnya it has become a full member.

Thus, the dramatic change in the strategic environment gave the Council of Europe a new life and mission. As Pinto (1995) again comments,
"With the fall of the Berlin Wall, the Council of Europe was finally free to
attain its 'natural' pan-European scope. It is thus not an overstatement to
say that the revolutions of 1989 did not throw the Council into an existen-
tial crisis (as it did some regional arrangements) but instead brought it
back to life." The council now sees one of its major goals as the spreading
of democratic values and practices to Central and Eastern Europe.

The Council's Multilayered Structure

Unlike other regional organizations, the Council of Europe requires
states to achieve certain standards of democracy and human rights before
they can become members. To fulfill the requirement, a state must show
that it has

- institutions and a legal system in line with the basic principles of democracy, the rule of law, and respect for human rights
- a parliament chosen by free and fair elections based on universal suffrage

- guaranteed freedom of expression, including a free press
- a system for the protection of national minorities
- a record of observance of the principles of international law

The Council of Europe's structures reflect the democratic institutions of its member states. It operates through the Committee of Ministers, which consists of the ministers of foreign affairs from each member state, who meet twice a year but are represented at biweekly or special meetings by permanent representatives. The Committee of Ministers is the main organ of political dialogue and intergovernmental cooperation, which considers the action required to further the aims of the Council of Europe, including the conclusion of conventions or agreements and the adoption by governments of a common policy with regard to particular matters. In some cases, the conclusions of the committee may constitute recommendations to members in the form of declarations or resolutions on political questions.

The Parliamentary Assembly is composed of members appointed by national parliaments from among their own members (with representation of all major national political parties). The number of parliamentarians that each state is permitted is based on the size of its population (and ranges from 2 to 18). The Parliamentary Assembly is, therefore, the most widely based European assembly (in contrast to the European Parliament, which is composed of the directly elected representatives of the member countries of the European Union). The assembly, which meets four times a year, is a deliberative body with no legislative powers. It is a major driving force within the Council of Europe and its recommendations to the Committee of Ministers are often a starting point for action.

The Council of Europe also works to promote democracy at the local level. The Congress of Local and Regional Authorities of Europe was established in 1994 and is composed of elected local and regional representatives from member states. It is divided into two chambers—the Chamber of the Regions and the Chamber of Local Authorities. In addition to adopting resolutions, which it submits to the Committee of Ministers, it also organizes hearings, conferences, and seminars on topics relating to local and regional authorities.

Across a range of areas, the Council of Europe works closely with nongovernmental organizations, which it regards as important contributors to the democratic process. Over 350 NGOs have consultative status with the council—with two-thirds of them being human rights groups. They are invited to participate three times a year in meetings convened during the Parliamentary Assembly to discuss recent developments or matters of concern in the human rights field.

A secretary-general and large secretariat serve the council and carry out many of its programs. Through all of these structures, as well as through its various secretariat bodies, the Council of Europe has been extremely active in the promotion of both democracy and human rights. Indeed, the council sees these two issues as so intimately related that it is difficult to separate them or to neatly divide its programs into one category or the other. It has been involved in the development of human rights instruments, in helping member states introduce human rights protection into their laws and institutions, in promoting human rights and democratic practices through educational programs, and in protecting and enforcing human rights standards through the work of its quasi-judicial and judicial bodies. Each of these activities will be reviewed briefly below.

The Council's Role in the Promotion of Democracy and Human Rights

Setting Standards

The European Convention on Human Rights was concluded in Rome in 1950, and came into force in 1953. Krüger and Strasser (1994) note that "the European Convention marked a major breakthrough in the development of international law in that it was the first ever treaty creating binding obligations for states in the area of human rights." A report from the Council of Europe (1995c) comments that the convention has matured into the most effective human rights treaty in existence due to the common values and political will of its members. The enforcement mechanisms of the European Convention will be discussed later in this chapter.

Other major conventions, such as the European Social Charter (which came into force in 1961 and is currently being modified), the European Convention for the Prevention of Torture and Inhumane or Degrading Treatment or Punishment, the European Charter of Local Self-Government, the Convention on the Participation of Foreigners in Public Life at the Local Level, and the European Outline Convention on Transfrontier Cooperation between Territorial Communities or Authorities are also important milestones in the development of standards for human rights and democracy in Europe.

Two conventions will greatly strengthen the Council of Europe's standards with regard to minority protection. These are the European Charter for Regional or Minority Languages, which was opened for signature on 2 October 1992, and the Framework Convention for the Protection of National Minorities, which was opened for signature on 1 February 1995. These two conventions, which were designed to transform political commitments into legal obligations, are probably the most comprehensive international documents of their kind and the Framework Convention is the first legally binding multilateral instrument devoted to the protection of national minorities in general.

These conventions are open to voluntary accession by members, as well as nonmembers of the council who have been invited by the Committee of Ministers to accede. Once they enter into force, state parties will have to report at regular intervals to the secretary-general and the committee on the legislative and other measures they have taken to effect the principles established by the conventions. An advisory committee, composed of individuals with recognized expertise in the protection of national minorities, will report to the committee on the adequacy of the measures adopted. These reports will be public and the information will be compiled for dissemination by the council. The conventions will constitute the European reference point for the updating of national legislation and for the settlement of bilateral disputes.

Advisory Services and Technical Assistance

Since 1989, the council's major focus has been on helping Central and Eastern European states develop into full-fledged democracies. To this end, in 1990 the council set up the Cooperation and Assistance Programs with Central and Eastern European Countries for both members and nonmembers of the organization. The three goals were (1) to promote their gradual integration into the Council of Europe's programs, institutions, and structures through participation in conferences, colloquia, and intergovernmental committees; (2) to foster the dissemination of information, political dialogue, and mutual understanding through roundtable discussions in fields of special interest, including seminars about the council, translation of documents into local languages, training schemes, and the creation of Information and Documentation Units; (3) to promote pluralist democracy, human rights, and the rule of law through expert missions on the inclusion of human rights provisions in draft constitutions and other legal texts, workshops on the European Convention on Human Rights, and legislative assistance in drawing up the reform of legislation.

More than any other regional organization, the council's structure has allowed it to work at all levels of society. As Pinto notes:

> Democracy can only exist when its values and reflexes become deeply embedded at all levels of the state and above all within society itself, from the smallest provincial prison guard to the loftiest supreme court justice, from individual citizens to their elected representatives, from lawyers and teachers to civil servants who run the administrations of state. Furthermore, democracy can only exist if the powers of the state are counterbalanced and con-

stantly monitored by non-governmental organizations working on behalf of the common good, and above all, by independent media.

Under the umbrella of the Cooperation and Assistance Programs, the council has set up two general programs, one for member states and another for states with guest status, to organize seminars, traineeships, travel grants, and exchanges of expert missions that may be East-West, West-East, or East-East. Eligible for participation are national and local leaders within the political system, civil servants and administrators, judges and lawyers, youth leaders, leaders of NGOs and other voluntary associations, journalists, and specialists in various fields relevant to Council of Europe activities. A third program was established to train judges, prosecutors, lawyers, notaries, and prison administrators in the running of a democratic state respectful of human rights and the rule of law. In conjunction with the Congress of Local and Regional Authorities, the council also set up the Local Democracy Program to foster the development of grassroots democracy and to train local leaders, elected officials, and administrators in the area of local politics and finance. Pinto explains the council's methodology as follows:

> Council cooperation programmes are always set up at the request of the states themselves, who define their needs, and ask for technical advice which they are always free to adapt and even to reject (with the proviso that certain rejection of fundamental democratic principles would make the country ineligible for admission within the Council). There is no "neo-colonial" attitude on the part of the Council when it proposes its democratic training or acts as a broker between training programmes provided by older member states on behalf of the new members or "guests." The Council does not "sell" any given type of democratic model, for its member states incarnate many possible variations. At most, the Council can suggest that one national model might be more relevant than another for a given country as it embarks on fundamental legal and constitutional reforms. But the final choice in all these domains remains exclusively within the purview of the states themselves. This is why Council of Europe programmes are flexible and evolve constantly to meet the changing needs of the states that request assistance.

Examples of the activities of these programs include traineeships at the European Court and Commission in Strasbourg, as well as study visits to the more established democracies. For example, Albanians have been sent to Hungary, Austria, and Italy to study constitutional provisions for minority rights in those countries. Latvians have been advised on how to draft legislation on laws of citizenship and the rights of aliens, and Romanians, on the creation of the institution of ombudsman. In the Former Yugoslav Republic of Macedonia, the council was asked to provide technical assistance on supervising a new census of the population. The council organized extensive seminars for midlevel Hungarian administrators on human rights protection. Seminars on the compatibility between human rights requirements and domestic law were held for Bulgarian and Polish lawyers and Czech judges. Estonian prison wardens have been sent to Scotland, and Albanian prison wardens to Italy to observe procedures.

With regard to minority rights and the protection of minority languages, the council cosponsored, with the Hungarian Office of National Minorities, a conference on government and minorities with the participation of all governmental structures dealing with minority questions in the states of Central and Eastern Europe.

The council also assists with the legal prerequisites of the democratic state. This has taken the form of advice and seminars on reform of the penal code and prosecution system; new civil codes; prison reform; the status and role of the judge in a democratic society; or topics such as habeas corpus, bail, and European prison rules. The council has also undertaken an extensive program in promoting tolerance and intercultural learning among police, prison and immigration officers, social workers, and the schools.

The Local Democracy Program has also provided meetings on the role and responsibility of local authorities, which cover issues such as how to modify their relationship to the state authorities and how to raise and manage local finance. Staff members have helped to revise and draft legislation on local elections and have assisted in monitoring them. As well, a manual for newly elected local representatives has been prepared and distributed. An extensive program is under way with the Russian Federation to analyze how to promote better relations between its federal authorities.

In cooperation with various professional media organizations, the council offers advice on the legal dimensions of publishing and broadcasting and has helped to draft a regulatory legal framework for the media in Croatia. It sponsored seminars on the role of the media during electoral campaigns in Estonia and on the creation of local and regional radio stations in Poland. It holds special seminars on human rights for journalists and assists them in attending important international conferences on this topic.

In cooperation with Western European nongovernmental organizations, the council has held extensive seminars with Eastern European NGOs on their role in a democratic state. The council plans to become involved in helping these organizations with networking within their own country, as well as in networking with international NGOs.

The Human Rights Information Center provides an information service to a large mailing list of individuals and institutions and it is establishing databases for the council's human rights mechanisms. The council's Human Rights Library is the best in the world and has set up satellite depository libraries in a number of European countries. Translation and printing of the most important council documents for East and Central European countries are under way, and the council has opened Information and Documentation Centers in Bulgaria, the Czech Republic, Hungary, Lithuania, Poland, Romania, the Russian Federation, and Slovakia, as well as sending complete collections of human rights documents to a number of other libraries in Central Europe.

Alarmed by the upsurge in racism, xenophobia, and antisemitism, the 1993 meeting of the council's Heads of State and Government adopted a Declaration and Plan of Action, which provided for the European Youth Campaign against Racism, Xenophobia, Anti-Semitism and Intolerance. It was launched on International Human Rights Day in 1994 and includes training courses, high-profile events, seminars, and the production of educational materials.

In addition to advisory and technical services, the council has been active in promoting confidence-building measures. Pilot projects have been organized at the grassroots level aimed at improving relations between dominant and minority groups. While a large part of the Council of Europe's overall agenda can be conceived of as confidence building, since it promotes mutual understanding and tolerance and a respect for the cultures of others, much of its work is at the intergovernmental level. It was decided, therefore, that the pilot projects would help expand the organization's confidence-building activities at the community level (Report of the Council of Europe, 1995b). An important aspect of these projects is that they are conducted in partnership with NGOs. Examples include a bilingual Estonian/Russian television station in Estonia and a project in the Slovak and Czech Republics to develop positive relations between the dominant population and the Romas through shared activities, such as joint construction of homes for the most deprived, creation of leisure centers for intercultural activities, introduction of experimental curricula in primary schools, and other activities designed to build better understanding between communities.

When totaled, the Council of Europe's many initiatives entail an almost bewildering number of individual projects. In 1994 alone, for example, the council organized or sponsored 240 seminars and workshops; 50 expert missions; 50 expert legal opinions; 140 study visits; and 85 training courses—in Bulgaria, the Czech Republic, Estonia, Hungary, Latvia, Lithuania, Poland, Romania, the Slovak Republic, Slovenia, Albania, Belarus, Croatia, Moldova, the Russian Federation, the Former Yugoslav Republic of Macedonia, and Ukraine.

Making the council's work more challenging, these programs cannot remain static, but must continually evolve and adapt:

Council programmes must take into account the organic development of each country as it embarks on its major political, judicial and social transformations. It goes without saying that the political co-operation of Poland and Hungary needed in 1990 as they undertook their democratic change is not the same as that needed today, nor can the advice given to them initially be transposed automatically in such countries as Moldova and Albania as they tackle their own democratic challenges. Each country evolves in its own manner and at different speeds; consequently programmes of cooperation must be increasingly custom-tailored. (Pinto, 1995)

The Council's Monitoring Role

The council carries out its monitoring functions in several ways. The first kind of monitoring begins when a state petitions to join the council. A special body, called the European Commission for Democracy through Law, is asked to verify that the state's constitution conforms with the provisions of the European Convention on Human Rights. If the document does not properly enshrine political pluralism, respect for human rights, and the rule of law, the experts charged with examining the legislation make suggestions for change.

Once a member state has acceded to the European Convention (now a condition of membership), it is asked to report periodically on the measures taken to comply. The first report is due one year after the entry into force of the charter for that party, with additional reports due at three-year intervals. These reports are examined by the Committee of Experts (with recognized competence in human rights) appointed by the Committee of Ministers. Other entities that are legally established within a state, such as NGOs, may also file reports with the committee. After consulting the state concerned, the Committee of Experts prepares a report, which it submits to the Committee of Ministers (which can be accompanied by comments from the state party). These reports, which may contain recommendations and proposals to the state for change, can be made public by the Committee of Ministers.

Following the Declaration and Plan of Action on Racism, Xenophobia, Anti-Semitism and Intolerance, governments were asked to reexamine their legislation and to reinforce and implement preventive measures in these areas. To assist them, the European Commission Against Racism and Intolerance was established to review member states' legislation, policy, and other measures and to propose further action at local, national, and regional levels. As well, the commission is mandated to formulate general policy recommendations to member states and to study international legal instruments to see how they can be reinforced.

Finally, a potentially important preventive diplomacy process was established in a declaration issued at the end of 1994. The Committee of Ministers decided that it should be able to monitor compliance with commitments accepted by member states on an ad hoc basis with regard to any matter concerning the situation of democracy, human rights, and the rule of law in any member state, which is referred to it by another member state, the secretary-general, or the Parliamentary Assembly. The declaration empowers the Committee of Ministers "to take account of all relevant information available from different sources" and "consider in a constructive manner" what should be done, "encouraging Member States, through dialogue and co-operation to take all appropriate steps to conform with the principles of the Organization's Statute." In cases requiring specific action, it may decide to "request the Secretary-General to make contacts, collect information and furnish advice; issue an opinion or recommendations; forward a communication to the Parliamentary Assembly; or take any other decision within its statutory powers" (Council of Europe, 1995a). This gives both the committee and the secretary-general wide latitude in working with member states on matters substantially in their internal jurisdiction and, as such, provides a more advanced acceptance of this principle than in any other region. Inclusion of the Parliamentary Assembly as one of the parties that can bring a problem to the attention of the committee also expands the usual range of sources from which such a concern can emanate. It remains to be seen whether this preventive approach will be effective, but it clearly holds promise.

Promoting Human Rights through Enforcement

The European Convention on Human Rights has three supervisory organs—the European Commission of Human Rights, the European Court of Human Rights, and the Committee of Ministers. Cases may come to the commission in two ways: a state may bring a case against another state (which happens rarely) or *any* individual may bring a complaint against a state. Although the convention contains an optional clause for both the commission and the court with regard to individual complaints, the council decided in 1989 to make acceptance of compulsory jurisdiction a political condition for admission of new member states. (By that time, all existing members had already accepted the convention's jurisdiction.) *This represents an important precedent in terms of states as a group agreeing to accept compulsory jurisdiction* and could serve as an important model for other regions and indeed for the member states of the United Nations in their acceptance of the jurisdiction of the International Court of Justice.

Thus, the European system has an important advantage over any other region. Obligations are now universally *binding,* and the Council of Europe has a kind of soft *enforcement power* to back up the commission, since its recommendations are reinforced by the threat of suspension from membership in the council, if a state is found to be noncompliant. Indeed, the council has already demonstrated its willingness to use this power in such cases.

The European Commission of Human Rights

The European Commission of Human Rights is composed of one commissioner from each member state. Although nominated by governments and elected for renewable six-year terms by the Parliamentary Assembly, commissioners act in an independent capacity and do not represent their governments.

When complaints are received by the commission, a panel of three commissioners reviews them for their admissibility under the European Convention. At this point, approximately 90 percent of complaints are rejected as inadmissible (Council of Europe, 1995c). When complaints are found to be admissible, the commission seeks to obtain a friendly settlement between the parties. Over 10 percent of accepted cases have resulted in friendly settlements in which there is financial compensation or a change in the law of the state concerned (Council of Europe, 1995c). If such an outcome is not achieved, the commission requests that further information be provided, either in writing or in an oral hearing, so that it can establish the facts and express an opinion as to whether there has been a violation of human rights. Once a report is written, cases are either forwarded to the Committee of Ministers for binding recommendations to the state, or they are brought before the Court of Human Rights. Where there is applicable case law, cases are normally handled by the Committee of Ministers. If they are more complicated, they are dealt with by the court.

Since its inception in 1954, the European Commission of Human Rights has registered approximately 25,000 complaints. Of these, over 1,500 have been found admissible and examined as to their merits (Council of Europe, 1995c).

The European Court of Human Rights

The European Court of Human Rights, which is not yet a permanent court, has its seat in Strasbourg and, as a rule, sits once a month. Like the commission, each member of the Council of Europe has a judge on the court, who is appointed through the Parliamentary Assembly to a nine-year, renewable term. Barring exceptional circumstances, the court sits in chambers of nine judges, including, ex officio, the president or vice president of the court and the judge who is a national of the state party involved in the case. If the national judge does not wish to be involved, the state concerned can select an ad hoc judge. In extraordinary cases, a Grand Chamber of 19 judges may sit or, very occasionally, a plenary of the court can be convened.

Cases may be submitted to the Court by either the commission or a state. Since October 1994, with the entry into force of Protocol No. 9 to the convention, a person, group of individuals, or governmental organization can bring a case directly to the court, if it has been lodged with the commission and found to be admissible and if the attempt to reach a friendly accommodation has failed. When a case bypasses a commission investigation, a panel of three judges (including the judge from the state concerned) may, by unanimous decision, reject the case, at which point it passes to the Committee of Ministers for review.

When the commission brings a case to the court (by far the most common occurrence), it submits its report and related documents. The court can then invite the state party and/or the applicant to provide written comment on the commission's report. Following the review of written memorials and other documents, the court usually holds a public hearing. Subsequently, a decision is taken by majority vote and, if a breach is found, the court may award damages. Judges may annex their concurring or dissenting opinions to the judgment, which is usually delivered in public by the president of the court. There is no provision for appeal. The Committee of Ministers is then responsible for supervising the implementation of the court's judgments.

The European Court of Human Rights has heard 784 cases since its creation in 1959 (Council of Europe, personal communication, 1997). As a result, the commission and the court have developed a considerable body of case law, which now forms the backbone of European law and practice.

The Role of the Committee of Ministers in Enforcing Human Rights

In cases that do not go to the court, the Committee of Ministers is asked to decide by a two-thirds majority whether there has been a breach of the convention. However, this procedure has been criticized, since the ministers are representatives of member states and, thus, not independent. This is one of the reasons that a decision has been taken to change the framework of the convention's mechanisms, as will be discussed below.

Much more important, however, is the Committee of Ministers' function as the supervisor in the implementation of judgments by the court. A case ends only after a resolution is passed by the committee, declaring that a state party has complied with the ruling. The Committee of Ministers' supervisory role in the execution of the court's judgment has been considered to be one of the main features that accounts for the effectiveness of the European Convention on Human Rights. Member states, for example, have often even changed their legislation to avoid future violations. This mechanism, therefore, has contributed to what has been called a "European public order in the field of human rights" (Council of Europe, 1995c).

The Future European Court of Human Rights

With a rapidly expanding case load (due in part to an ever-increasing number of member states), the work of the commission and the court has been falling progressively behind. It now takes an average of over five years from the time a case is lodged until a final decision is reached. The current system is also complicated and time-consuming. Therefore, in 1994, a decision was made to add an amending protocol (Protocol No. 11) to the convention. This protocol, which will enter into force one year after all states party to the convention have ratified it, provides for the establishment of a full-time single permanent court in Strasbourg to replace the old commission and court. As of February 1997, 30 member states had ratified the protocol (Council of Europe, 1997). It is expected that the end of 1998 is the earliest date by which such a court could begin to function, and it may take longer (Bratza and O'Boyle, 1997).

It is anticipated that this reform will streamline the system. The right of individual application will now be mandatory and the court will also have jurisdiction over all interstate cases. Cases will be screened by a three-judge committee and unfounded cases will be declared inadmissible. The court will normally sit as a seven-judge chamber except in exceptional cases where, for the most important issues, it may sit as a Grand Chamber of 17 judges. The Committee of Ministers will no longer have jurisdiction to decide on the merits of a case. It will, however, continue to act to enforce the court's judgments (Council of Europe, 1997; Bratza and O'Boyle, 1997).

Cooperation with the UN

Since its inception, the Council of Europe has worked in areas similar to the UN, but its Parliamentary Assembly has acknowledged that closer and more formal cooperation is needed, especially with the UN's human rights bodies. To date, most cooperation has been informal, such as the exchange of information between directors and desk officers of the two organizations or consultation with the UN on some of the council's assistance to countries of Central and Eastern Europe. Staff of the council often attend meetings of the UN Commission on Human Rights and staff from the UN Center for Human Rights sometimes attend relevant meetings in

Strasbourg. Nonetheless, closer cooperation, especially in relation to the provision of technical and advisory assistance in human rights would appear to offer advantages to both organizations (just as the council's cooperation with the OSCE's Office of Democratic Institutions and Human Rights has yielded positive results).

Summary

Like the other regional organizations to be reviewed here, the Council of Europe has had to reshape its identity and programming to fit new geopolitical realities. It has done so rapidly and, in the process, been revitalized as an institution.

Compared to other regional organizations, the Council of Europe focuses much more narrowly on democracy, human rights, and the rule of law. Indeed, it can be said that the council's *primary function is the prevention of conflict through the promotion of good governance at all levels*. It attempts to do this by establishing a club of democratic states, which attaches certain preconditions to entry. This conditionality on membership is unique, and occasional suspensions have given additional weight to the recognition and seal of approval that goes with membership. The provision that states cannot qualify for associate membership in the European Union without first obtaining full membership in the Council of Europe is a powerful incentive, since the economic advantages of the European Union are obviously attractive to many states. Fearing a reemergence of Russian expansionism, Eastern European states are also motivated to become integrated into the Western European community for security and identity, as well as economic reasons.

The Council of Europe has been proactive in helping states meet its criteria for membership, providing an extensive range of programs to assist them in achieving constitutional and legal reform, and implementing those reforms in the everyday practice of governance. While many regional organizations operate largely at the intergovernmental level and work primarily through their executives and ministries of foreign affairs, the Council of Europe brings together groups from all segments of society, including parliamentarians, regional and local government officials, and NGOs. This broader-based level of representation and approach not only makes it a more democratic institution, but also allows it to reach into all levels of democratic society, as expressed earlier—"from the smallest provincial prison guard to the loftiest supreme court justice." The council also continues to push forward the boundaries of its work into new and vital areas of human rights protection, such as racism, xenophobia, antisemitism, protection of minority rights, and migrant issues.

Finally, the council operates by developing common norms and standards through multilateral decision making. It then acts to socialize governments and peoples in these standards through education; accountability (reporting, monitoring, feedback, and recommendations); exposure to successful and unsuccessful models; recognition, acceptance, and participation of those governments who do comply; and censure and temporary expulsion for those who stray. Indeed, this kind of socialization process can be a powerful one. The Council of Europe's good governance program provides a useful model for long-term structural reform that could be adopted elsewhere—if resources were available. Of course, most regional organizations would be unwilling to adopt the council's formal criteria for membership. However, the provision of technical assistance, as carried out by the council, would go a long way toward promoting sustainable peace.

7

The Organization for Security and Cooperation in Europe

Security Issues in Europe and the First Phase of the CSCE Process

A T THE HEIGHT OF THE cold war, another kind of regional arrangement began to evolve in the larger European scene, in the form of the Conference on Security and Cooperation in Europe (CSCE)—now renamed the Organization for Security and Cooperation in Europe (OSCE). It grew from a 1954 Soviet call for a pan-European security conference, which Moscow hoped would legitimize and stabilize the post–World War II divisions and ultimately lead to an acceptance of the permanent division of Germany. For these reasons, the idea was rejected by the West, which had a different agenda. It wanted negotiations on conventional force reductions in Europe, at a time when Central Europe was the most militarized area in the world, with the Soviets having conventional superiority.

Not until the early 1970s, following a five-year "communiqué dialogue" between NATO and the Warsaw Pact to develop a common understanding for a conference project, did the United States and the Soviet Union finally agree to both agendas—at the signing of the SALT-I Treaty in Moscow in May 1972. There were to be negotiations on Mutual and Balanced Force Reductions, which ultimately took place in Vienna from 1973 to 1989 (developing, after they floundered, into the more successful Conventional Forces in Europe Talks). Simultaneously, the Conference on Security and Cooperation in Europe was to be organized. In 1972, it began meeting in

Helsinki and Geneva, and concluded with the 1975 signing of the Helsinki
Final Act. This act set up the framework for follow-up conferences of the
CSCE, which continue even now.

If the Council of Europe can be seen as an example of an organization
devoted to the development of good governance, as proposed in the previous chapter, the Conference on Security and Cooperation in Europe can
be said to have been devoted from its inception to preventive diplomacy.
The CSCE was established to find common ground through a process of
dialogue, norm-setting, and consensus. Like its smaller cousin, ASEAN
(which will be discussed in chapter 10), it was designed as a *process*, with
an informal structure that could provide flexibility. Although the founders
of this process were scorned by their hard-line colleagues in both the West
and the East, their efforts have had far-reaching consequences. As Wilhelm
Höynck (1995b), the former OSCE secretary-general, points out:

> The Final Act codified a political basis for normalization of relations on the
> continent, establishing in particular principles guiding the behaviour of states
> toward each other. Among these principles one was of particular significance:
> respect for human rights and fundamental freedoms. Its substance was mod-
> est and essentially a repetition of existing obligations, the notion of "democ-
> racy" was not to be found in the whole Final Act. . . . But this very general
> human rights provision provided a basis and a driving force for change by
> linking it with overall cooperation. Thus, the Final Act affirmed that the re-
> spect for human rights and fundamental freedoms is an essential factor for the
> peace, justice and well-being, necessary to ensure the development of friendly
> relations and cooperation.

Essentially, the Helsinki Final Act established a standard for East and
West, and began a process that contributed to a liberalization in thinking
in the former Soviet Union. The first breakthrough in a practical sense
came from negotiations to lower Soviet visa fees and to reduce delays in
processing travel documents, which led to people on both sides being able
to meet. The Helsinki Final Act created somewhat freer access to information—by limiting the jamming of radio broadcasts in Eastern Europe and
helping to reduce control over speech and print. These concessions were
made in exchange for greater economic opportunities in order to obtain
Western capital and technology transfers. But the development of business
relationships and the flow of economic and commercial information had
unforeseen side effects, as the inefficiency of the Soviet system was increasingly obvious. At the first follow-up meeting in Belgrade, when the West
"exposed Soviet hypocrisy evidenced in human-rights violations," the
process was nearly brought to collapse. But "the insistence lent a new credibility to the Helsinki Commitments. The signal was understood—the
Final Act had to be taken seriously" (Höynck, 1995b).

Support from the West emboldened those in the Soviet Union and Eastern Europe who were concerned with human rights, encouraging the formation of grassroots organizations, such as Helsinki Watch and Charter 77, which later became springboards for the democracy movement. By establishing a network of political channels, the CSCE was able to build continuously on the changes going on in the socialist system. In part as a result of these links, the collapse of communist societies was not accompanied by violent convulsions (Höynck, 1995b).

From the beginning, the CSCE process adopted a broad agenda for military and political, economic and environmental, and humanitarian and human rights issues in its well-known three "basket" approach. In the "security basket," for example, the Helsinki Final Act introduced the idea of confidence-building measures—arrangements for increased transparency and predictability of military activities. Over time, these expanded into a significant system of exchanges of information on defense planning and armed forces, risk reduction, military contacts, notification and observation of military activities, verification and evaluation of agreed measures, and constraints on activities of armed forces, as well as arms control measures, which are still in force.

Thus, the OSCE of today was not initially established as an international organization, but rather grew out of a 20-year-long series of conferences and meetings. (It is interesting to note that because of this process-oriented history, the term "membership" has never been used. Those involved are referred to as "participating states.") The legacy of that course of development is a modus operandi grounded in consensus.

The end of the East-West divide created a major identity crisis for an organization dedicated to bridging this schism. The CSCE's flexibility, however, quickly demonstrated its value.

The Second Phase: The Development of the OSCE

In response to the dramatic changes of 1989–1990, the CSCE convened in Paris for its 1990 summit and adopted the Charter of Paris for a New Europe. The charter and its supplementary documents created, for the first time, permanent structures within the CSCE. Biennial follow-up meetings were planned at the level of heads of participating states or governments. The Council of Foreign Ministers was to meet regularly—at least once a year—as the central forum for political consultations within the CSCE process, to prepare for the summit meetings and prioritize activities for the coming year; and the Committee of Senior Officials (subsequently renamed the Senior Council) was formed, which would bring together senior diplomats several times a year to serve as the executive body for the

Council of Foreign Ministers, carrying out its decisions, reviewing current issues, and considering future work. The Committee of Senior Officials was also given overall responsibility for the management of conflicts.

The charter also established an embryonic secretariat, initially located in Prague, but later moved to Vienna. (The secretariat was purposefully decentralized to prevent it from gaining too much power or becoming too bureaucratic and inflexible.) In Warsaw, the Office for Free Elections (now the Office for Democratic Institutions and Human Rights) was set up, and Vienna became the headquarters for the Conflict Prevention Center (which, despite its name, is largely involved in military confidence-building measures, although it now also provides support and logistics to OSCE missions). The center was to have a decision-making Consultative Committee, later reinvented as the Permanent Council, representing all participating states. The Permanent Council now has a significant role in day-to-day conflict prevention and management.

The CSCE's first attempts at conflict management, however, were largely frustrating. Its efforts in the former Yugoslavia, like those of so many other organizations, made little headway, despite the CSCE's recently adopted "consensus-minus-one" rule. Its newly established mechanism for the compulsory use of third parties, the Valetta Mechanism, which had been painstakingly worked out in Malta (and which will be discussed later in this chapter) was not used.

At the second Helsinki Summit in 1992, agreement was reached on strengthening the organization's weaker mechanisms. A High Commissioner on National Minorities was appointed to enhance the CSCE's operational capacity and to respond quickly to emerging conflicts. A secretary-general was also appointed, although he was given few explicit powers. Subsequently, an expanded role was given to the chairman-in-office; a Permanent Council replaced the Consultative Committee; and the idea of long-term missions was endorsed. The Parliamentary Assembly of representatives from national parliaments also began annual meetings in 1992.

Today, the OSCE has declared itself to be a regional arrangement under Chapter VIII of the UN Charter. It has 53 participating states and wide geographical spread, referred to as "from Vancouver to Vladivostock." As such, it is the only forum that brings together all of the states of Europe (with the exception of Andorra and Serbia/Montenegro, the latter having been suspended from participation in 1992), the United States and Canada, and Central Asia. Höynck (1995b) summarizes the OSCE's two-stage evolution as follows: "Before 1990, the CSCE was a conference and its task was to introduce dynamic elements into a frozen status quo based on confrontation and deterrence. Since 1990, the CSCE has been transformed step by step into an organization whose task is to manage a difficult period of transition by making practical contributions to the creation of new stability, based on common interests and values."

Currently OSCE priorities are to consolidate common values and build civil societies; to prevent local conflicts, restore stability, and bring peace to war-torn areas; to overcome real and perceived security deficits; and to avoid the creation of new divisions by promoting a cooperative system of security. Zaagman (1995b) notes that "the OSCE group of states includes both the politically, militarily and economically greatest power in the world, the United States of America, and the largest and militarily still most daunting European power, the Russian Federation. One could even argue that one of the key, albeit implicit tasks of the OSCE, is to keep Russia positively involved in Europe—and vice versa."

The Role of the OSCE in Promoting Sustainable Peace

Once charged with the responsibility, the OSCE soon became "the most creative organization in the world in the field of preventive diplomacy" (United States Institute of Peace, 1994a). Indeed, there have been so many proposals and innovative mechanisms that not all of them have been logically integrated into the system. Those that are most functional will be reviewed below, along with the latest mechanism, the Court of Conciliation and Arbitration (and its predecessor—the Valetta Mechanism), the utility of which remains to be seen.

The Permanent Council

The Permanent Council, composed of ambassadors from all participating states with representation in Vienna, currently meets weekly as a permanent forum for political dialogue and decision making. As such, it is now the OSCE's most important operational forum for conflict prevention. It is chaired by the representative of the chairman-in-office. The Permanent Council's meetings provide an opportunity for frank and open dialogue on any political issue. Members of the Council are encouraged to discuss small incidents or problems at an early stage, including internal situations in other states. Items may be put on the agenda by any participating state or by the chairman-in-office, who often prepares discussion papers on a given problem. A regular agenda item called "current issues" allows any matter of concern to be raised. In some cases, however, individual delegations ask the chairman-in-office to have prior discussion with the relevant participating state before an issue is placed on the agenda. The Permanent Council also issues statements, when it feels that it is useful to do so.

The Chairman-in-Office

The chairman-in-office (CIO), whose term is one year, is the foreign minister of the state holding the chairmanship of the OSCE. Along with the Permanent Council, the CIO is the prime mover in translating the process of dialogue into action. When a problem comes to the attention of the CIO, he or she has a range of options. The issue can be referred to the Permanent Council or the High Commissioner on National Minorities. Alternatively, a personal representative or an ad hoc steering committee can be appointed to carry out fact-finding or mediation, or the CIO can become involved in providing good offices. The chairman-in-office, however, has a demanding role, since this person simultaneously bears the full-time responsibilities of being the foreign minister of his/her state.

The mechanism of personal representatives has been used a number of times in recent years, such as when the Hungarian ambassador (as a personal representative of the Hungarian chairman-in-office) visited Moscow and the Northern Caucasus after violence erupted in Chechnya. He was able to use OSCE agreements, such as the Budapest Declaration and the Code of Conduct on Politico-Military Aspects of Security, to persuade the Russian authorities to allow an OSCE mission presence in Chechnya (Kovacs, 1995). The OSCE has also employed what are known as Ad Hoc Steering Committees to carry out long-term peacemaking. They are composed of senior diplomats from participating states. The Minsk Group, for example, has worked for several years in an attempt to find a settlement to the seemingly intractable conflict in Nagorno-Karabakh.

Chigas and her colleagues argue that the role of the chairman-in-office, as the "political executive," is a significant innovation in the realm of international organizations and that it has been an important factor in the OSCE's success.

> The CIO has also served as a link between the OSCE as an international organization and the OSCE participating States in a way that maximizes the likelihood that any action taken by the OSCE has the political support and resources needed to make it effective. Unlike the Secretary-General of the United Nations, who is accountable only to the Security Council but independent of it, the CIO is not only accountable to the political structure but is a representative of it and, moreover, has a vested interest in it. The CIO is the embodiment of the political process; a Foreign Minister, based in a state's capital, with direct access to political decision-makers in capitals, acting as chair, facilitator, and implementor of a political process, but without any formal independence from it. There is little risk that the CIO will try to set up a competing authority to the OSCE's political bodies or act contrary to their interests. On the contrary, the CIO provides a credible link to political capi-

tals, and often plays the role of catalyzing the political process and mobilizing resources for OSCE action. (Chigas et al., 1995)

The one-year term of the chairman-in-office and the fact that he or she is so closely tied to the Permanent Council may give participating states confidence in the process, but it also creates some problems with continuity, even with the Troika arrangement, whereby the incoming and outgoing chairmen-in-office meet frequently for consultations.

The High Commissioner on National Minorities

Probably the OSCE's most powerful instrument for preventive diplomacy is the High Commissioner on National Minorities, established in December 1992. Rather than being a general ombudsman for minorities, as the title may imply, the High Commissioner is charged solely with conflict prevention. The official mandate calls for the High Commissioner to carry out fact-finding, to issue "early warning notices" to the Permanent Council and then to ask the council for authority to carry out early action. Max van der Stoel, the only person to hold the position to date, has established an excellent precedent for the office through the development of a successful methodology (and although somewhat different from the role originally envisaged, participating states seem to have agreed with his interpretation of the mandate). Indeed, the High Commissioner has never issued an early warning notice or formally taken a problem to the Permanent Council, since he feels that doing so could exacerbate a situation. Instead, he has acted as an informal fact finder and adviser/facilitator, promoting moderation and dialogue among the parties and making recommendations to the governments involved. Typically, he begins his work with on-site visits, meeting with representatives from all sides, including senior government officials, such as the president, prime minister, and relevant ministers; the opposition parties; representatives of minority groups; heads of NGOs; and sometimes even parties in neighboring states. Thereby, he attempts to gain an understanding of the concerns of all parties. At the same time, he seeks to develop a relationship with the major parties, so that he can engage them in a cooperative problem-solving process. Once he feels that he has a full grasp of the situation, he normally writes a letter to the government involved, acknowledging and legitimizing the different perspectives and concerns of all sides, providing relevant data, and reminding the parties of the legal obligations and international norms and responsibilities that apply. His letter may also highlight the consequences of following or not following certain actions. Finally, he provides new ideas and perspectives, along with a nonobligatory set of recommendations, usually in the form of specific proposals for changes in government policy or legislation regarding minorities. Copies of his letters are provided to the Permanent Council. The High Commissioner then follows up with frequent contact with the parties to discuss his recommendations and to lobby for their implementation. Also, he may offer further suggestions regarding any problems that develop during the implementation process.

The substance of the High Commissioner's efforts can best be understood from looking at a sample of his work. In visits to Kazakhstan and Kyrgyzstan, he presented recommendations to the governments of these countries on issues related to citizenship. In Kazakhstan, he provided recommendations on the use of the Russian language, ethnic balance among public officials, and mechanisms for addressing complaints regarding ethnic discrimination. In Estonia, he focused on the implementation of legislation on citizenship and aliens. He recommended extending the deadline for the registration of noncitizens and the simplification of the registration process. In addition, he dealt with the question of travel documents for noncitizens and helped obtain international assistance for an Estonian-language training system. In Hungary and Slovakia, he worked with a team of experts to study the situation of the Slovak minority in Hungary and the Hungarian minority in Slovakia. Implementation of Slovakia's recently adopted minority law was discussed, as was the question of minority representation in parliament. After several visits to Crimea, the High Commissioner proposed sending a team of experts to examine and make recommendations on the constitutional and economic relationship between Ukraine and its Crimean province. He also suggested that state organs should make greater use of minority languages, alongside the official Ukrainian language. In Romania, he recommended that the government take action to combat expressions of ethnic hatred and investigate and prosecute perpetrators of violent attacks on ethnic groups, particularly the Roma. Although this represents only a small part of the High Commissioner's activities, it gives an indication of the way in which he seeks to address the kinds of grievances discussed in chapter 3.

In addition to his substantive recommendations, the High Commissioner often suggests an ongoing dialogue between the parties, to help them resolve not only the problem at hand, but also future ones. To this end, roundtable discussions were proposed and implemented in Romania, Slovakia, Estonia, and Macedonia and an ombudsman was established in Lithuania. The Special Office for Minority Questions was set up in Albania and the National Commission on Ethnic and Language Questions in Latvia and Estonia.

In summary, the High Commissioner's role, as it has evolved, is one of *providing conflict prevention via advice on how to deescalate tension and carry out structural reform, including how to establish an ongoing process of dialogue*

for tackling the root causes of conflict within society. As Chigas and her colleagues (1995) suggest, the recommendations are not an end in themselves, but instead are meant to provide a framework within which the
government and minority groups can start to address their problems constructively in an ongoing manner.

It is noteworthy that the High Commissioner's approach overcomes an
obstacle often raised as a reason why it is difficult for representatives of
international organizations to become involved in preventive diplomacy
within states. Often governments refuse to sit down and negotiate with
the leaders of communal groups for fear that doing so will confer recognition and status on them and correspondingly increase their demands.
Rather than attempting to act as a formal mediator between disputing
parties, the High Commissioner simply provides an advisory service to
governments. Nevertheless, the High Commissioner establishes an informal dialogue with these groups, which has been generally acceptable to
participating states. In this process, governments do not have to engage in
formal negotiations; they are simply asked to consider adopting the technical advice in dispute resolution that is provided. Finally, the High Commissioner is backed up by socialization from participating states, since
most governments wish to be seen to be living up to their commitments
within the OSCE community.

Virtually all of the High Commissioner's diplomacy is conducted *quietly*. His position is that of a unique *independent authority* within the OSCE
system, not directly representing the governments of the participating
states. Indeed, if the chairman-in-office has an advantage over the UN Secretary-General in being more closely linked to governments, the High
Commissioner could be said to have the advantage of being *less* closely
linked. His office, for example, is located in The Hague, intentionally distant from Vienna, where the Permanent Council meets. His independence
of mandate and reporting gives him the freedom to act largely as he sees
fit. Of course, as the High Commissioner himself notes, he must maintain
the general confidence of all participating governments if he is to succeed.
To ensure that this is the case, he engages in informal consultations with
the chairman-in-office and individual delegations, and avoids formal petitions to the Permanent Council, as the original mandate proposed. This
wide-ranging latitude and flexibility to work closely with the political parts
of the organization, when required—or more independently, as needed—
may be one of the High Commissioner's greatest assets in carrying out
preventive diplomacy.

The success of this model demonstrates that *even having one person* of
knowledge, stature, and skill carrying out full-time preventive diplomacy
on a daily basis is cost-effective. In the first three years, the High Commissioner was involved in preventive diplomacy efforts in Latvia, Estonia,

Hungary, Romania, Slovakia, Macedonia, Ukraine, Russia, Greece, Kazakhstan, Kyrgyzstan, Moldova, and Albania. On the whole, governments have received his recommendations well and acted on his proposals.

Finally, the High Commissioner on National Minorities *operates the world's most active preventive diplomacy mechanism with a staff of only six advisors and a budget of just over a million dollars* (OSCE, 1997).

Long-Term Missions

The OSCE has also instituted a program of long-term preventive diplomacy missions. These missions are established with a mandate from the Permanent Council and, through the chairman-in-office, report weekly or biweekly on the situation on the ground, as well as on their own activities. There have been ten long-term missions—four preventive diplomacy missions (in Latvia, Estonia, Ukraine, and Macedonia) and six missions in situations where conflict had already erupted (Kosovo, Georgia, Tajikistan, Moldova, Sarajevo, and Chechnya). The mission to Kosovo, Sandjak, and Vojvodina, however, was terminated when the Serbian government asked it to leave. Of particular interest was the OSCE's "Assistance Mission" in Chechnya, which was negotiated with the Russian authorities, as mentioned above.

OSCE long-term missions are usually small (its mission to Bosnia-Herzegovina is an exception; it is not called a long-term mission, but simply a "mission," and since its aim is not preventive diplomacy, it will not be discussed here), averaging around eight staff members per mission. Some involve only civilians, while others are composed of both civilians and military personnel. Their minimum mandate is six months, but most have lasted much longer. In the course of their development, these missions have often been complementary to the work of the High Commissioner. By providing a permanent presence on the ground, they are able to provide more accurate and objective information to the organization than the High Commissioner. This ongoing analysis allows the Permanent Council and other OSCE bodies to improve the quality and timeliness of their decision making.

Normally, missions establish a small office in the country's capital city. This serves as a base for staff to travel widely to gather information, monitor developments, and reduce tension. Missions also provide information to the parties. Through their ability to move easily between the parties, they can provide a communications link, reducing suspicion and fear and helping all sides understand one another better. Long-term missions can offer objective factual information, as well as information to minorities about rights and procedures.

Like the High Commissioner, they also provide advice and assistance to governments in formulating legislation or regulations in areas such as constitutional law, citizenship law, minority rights, and the establishment of councils for interethnic dialogue. In some countries, they have established an open door policy for members of minority communities who wish to complain about government discrimination. By listening to individual cases, and bringing these to the attention of the authorities, they have helped to alleviate tension and been able to assess where governments need to change their practice.

Long-term missions, however, are subject to the political consent of the state and so must walk a fine line. If they become viewed as simply an advocate for the minority population, the mission may be terminated by the government, but if they do not raise sensitive issues, they will not be able to facilitate dialogue and reduce tensions (Chigas et al., 1995).

The general consensus is that long-term missions have been successful, with preventive diplomacy missions being better able to effect change than those that were dispatched after conflict had already broken out. To refine practice through the sharing of information and discussion of problems, an annual Heads of Mission Meeting is organized, a noteworthy innovation among international organizations.

In explaining why the High Commissioner and OSCE Long-term Missions have been so successful, Chigas and her colleagues (1995) argue that it is the presence of both coercive and mediative functions but also their separation that have created a cooperative, problem-solving role for the High Commissioner and the missions as "unambiguous facilitators for positive action."

> If a government follows HCNM or mission recommendations, it is less likely to be accused of giving in or backing down to unfair pressure. The HCNM's and missions' lack of authority to bind or judge allows them to offer the parties a face-saving manner to take de-escalatory actions. At the same time, the pressure generated by publicity, shame, and bilateral activity by influential countries is always present. It is, however, kept in the background, allowing the OSCE to create "friendly" rather than coercive pressure on the parties to cooperate with the HCNM or the missions. The HCNM and the missions remain untainted by the more coercive strategies. *They* do not possess or exercise any coercive authority, and pressure that may be applied is not tied directly to their activities. The OSCE's political organs, for their part, have also refrained from interfering with or linking their discussions of substance of the disputes, or their more coercive activities, to the High Commissioner or the missions. (Chigas et al., 1995)

It is interesting to note that, at the Budapest review meeting, a proposal to schedule regular reviews of government compliance with recommendations by the High Commissioner failed because of concerns that this kind of action would make governments less cooperative and open with the High Commissioner (Chigas et al., 1995). The importance of this issue of keeping noncoercive and coercive procedures separate will be highlighted further in chapter 12.

The Office for Democratic Institutions and Human Rights

The Office for Democratic Institutions and Human Rights (ODIHR) evolved from the Office of Free Elections, established in Warsaw in 1992. Currently, it is charged with assisting participating states in the implementation of human rights, democratic societies, and the rule of law (the "human dimension," in OSCE parlance). Among the ODIHR's tasks is the implementation of provisions of the Copenhagen Document of 1990, one of the first agreements to enshrine minority rights in international law. The Copenhagen Document also provides the most extensive and coherent statement of principle available on free and fair elections and has been hailed as a veritable European charter on democracy. Glover (1995a) notes that the ODIHR's main task is translating "the grand principles set out in the OSCE documents into concrete realities and turning the universal standards into specific programmes."

The first step involves educating the governments and people of participating states about their OSCE commitments. Much like the Council of Europe, the ODIHR organizes large and small seminars on a range of topics. The ODIHR also translates and publishes OSCE commitments into local languages.

Also like the Council of Europe, the ODIHR has set up a Programme for Coordinated Support for Recently Admitted Participating States to provide diplomatic, academic, legal, and administrative expertise and training through seminars and meetings. For states in transition to democracy, the ODIHR provides assistance in analyzing constitutions, drafting laws, and organizing training programs for jurists, the judiciary, lawyers, journalists, and the public. Its seminars range across a wide variety of topics, such as the role of the constitutional court, the changing role of the judiciary, drafting human rights legislation, human rights and the judiciary, freedom of association, management in the print media, promoting tolerance, local democracy, and migrant workers. As well, workshops are organized to help new NGOs establish themselves as viable groups (ODIHR, CSCE/OSCE Newsletters, 1994–96).

The ODIHR also provides expert advice on democratic institution-building. For example, upon request from the OSCE Mission to Tajikistan, it sent that country's draft constitution to the Council of Europe's European Commission for Democracy Through Law (since Tajikistan is not a member of the COE and therefore would not normally have access to its advice) and to several leading world constitutional experts for comment. These comments were subsequently transmitted to the Tajik authorities. An ODIHR Expert Working Group on the Georgian Constitution was formed and visited Tbilisi at the request of the Georgian Constitutional Commission to evaluate drafts of the proposed constitution. A roundtable meeting was later held to help reconcile different drafts. Sixty Armenian Supreme Court judges, parliamentarians, and attorneys discussed judicial modernization and Armenia's draft constitution during a conference cosponsored by the Armenian Ministry of Foreign Affairs and the ODIHR. The office also sometimes sends experts to act as observers at controversial trials, for example those of members of the Albanian Greek minority in Tirana, or of Kurds in Ankara.

Having begun its life as the Office for Free Elections, the ODIHR continues to participate in election monitoring and assistance. In countries where elections are about to take place, it has begun organizing international roundtables on electoral law and practice to instruct local officials on how to monitor elections. Often, it plays a coordinating role for OSCE monitors from participating states. After an election, it holds debriefings with monitors and issues a report to the electorate and politicians concerning compliance with relevant OSCE commitments (Glover, 1995a).

Following a joint seminar with the High Commissioner on National Minorities and the Council of Europe, the ODIHR also assumed a coordinating role regarding the problems of the Roma. The office was tasked with the collection and dissemination of information on the implementation of commitments to these communities, and the facilitation of contacts between participating states, international organizations, and NGOs.

Another new role for the ODIHR involves alerting the political organs of the OSCE when problems arise in the area referred to as the human dimension. The preamble to the 1991 Moscow Document states that "commitments undertaken in the field of the human dimension of the CSCE are matters of direct and legitimate concern to all participating states and do not belong to the internal affairs of the state concerned." This concept was taken further in the Budapest Document, which authorizes the chairman-in-office to raise human rights issues in the Permanent Council on the basis of information from the ODIHR or from the High Commissioner on National Minorities. As Glover (1995a) notes, this provides an opportunity for NGOs to provide the ODIHR with information about human rights violations and for the ODIHR to bring such matters to the Permanent Council. She cautions, however, that such discussions will have to be handled carefully, since none of the OSCE institutions want to adopt the role of policemen. Nonetheless, she argues that as an institution that is concerned about the human dimension, this opportunity must be seized.

The ODIHR's work across a huge region is carried out with ten professional staff members (thirty-five staff members, in all) and a budget of $3.9 million.

The Dispute Settlement Mechanism or the Valetta Mechanism

In 1991 the CSCE adopted the Valetta Mechanism, which, at the time, was considered to be a breakthrough for dispute settlement. The opening clauses of the agreement remind participating states of their obligations to prevent disputes from arising, or failing that, to settle them peacefully by addressing them at an early stage. The most important thrust of the mechanism is its provision that, if they are unable to reach an agreement through negotiation or to agree on a dispute settlement procedure, parties are obligated to accept *"the mandatory involvement of a third party"* (Report of the CSCE Meeting of Experts on Peaceful Settlement of Disputes, 1991a).

The Valetta Mechanism provided the rules of procedure for establishing an OSCE Dispute Settlement Mechanism. A register of qualified third parties was to be maintained by a Nominating Institution (with up to four experts nominated by each participating state). Disputing parties were to agree on the selection of one or more of these third parties as their preferred dispute settlement mechanism. If such agreement could not be reached, the Senior Official of the Nominating Institution was to select the third parties, in consultation with the disputing parties. The third parties were then to work informally and flexibly to find either a procedural or substantive solution. If this effort were not successful in a reasonable time period, either disputing party could bring the matter to the attention of the Senior Council. Further, within three months after notifying the other, either disputing party could request that the third parties provide general or specific comment or advice, which all parties would then be obliged, in good faith, to consider. Finally, by mutual agreement, the parties could request an expert assessment of the issues related to the dispute, or accept the mechanism's recommendations as binding. In other words, parties could use this third party mechanism in mediation, conciliation, or arbitration mode. Exceptions to the Valetta Mechanism were allowed if either party considered that the dispute raised issues concerning its territorial integrity or national defense.

Despite early hopes, use of the Valetta Mechanism has been a disappointment. Limited to interstate disputes in an era in which intrastate problems are more prevalent, and falling victim to the reluctance of governments to become involved in a process they cannot fully control, the mechanism has never been used.

The New Court of Conciliation and Arbitration

Taking this approach one step further, the Convention on Conciliation and Arbitration within the OSCE was opened for signature in Stockholm on 15 December 1992, and as of June 1995 had been signed by 34 states, and ratified by 16. It entered into force on 5 December 1994. The convention establishes the Court of Conciliation and Arbitration, which has opened in Geneva.

The convention provides disputing parties with an option of a conciliation procedure, which is nonbinding and recommendatory, or an arbitration procedure, which is binding. Like the Valetta Mechanism, the competence of the court is limited to *interstate* problems, but proponents contend that there is still a wide range of issues that the court can cover, including small as well as large disputes, thus offering a kind of preventive approach for interstate disputes to complement the organization's existing intrastate instruments.

The court is composed of both conciliators and arbitrators. Each state party to the convention appoints two conciliators and one arbitrator (as well as one alternate) for six-year renewable terms. These conciliators and arbitrators form a group of experts from which Conciliation Commissions or Arbitration Tribunals are to be selected. The Bureau of the Court, which oversees this process, consists of five members elected by the group of conciliators and arbitrators (with at least two of each represented). The first Bureau of the Court was elected in May 1995.

The Conciliation Procedure

Requests for conciliation are to be accepted by the court in cases where states are parties to the convention, or at least one is a state party and the others are OSCE participating states, so long as all parties agree. Each party may select one conciliator to sit on the Conciliation Commission. After consultation with the parties, the Bureau of the Court selects the remainder of the conciliators.

Conciliation proceedings are confidential and all parties have a right to be heard. Again, in consultation with the parties, the Conciliation Commission determines its own procedures. The mandate of the Commission is simply to assist parties in finding a settlement in accordance with international law and their CSCE/OSCE commitments (Convention on Conciliation and Arbitration within the CSCE, 1992a). The rules of the court also obligate parties to "refrain from any action which may aggravate the

situation or further impede or prevent the settlement of the dispute." The
commission may also suggest interim measures that they could take to
prevent the dispute from being aggravated or its settlement made more
difficult.

If, during the course of the proceedings, the parties reach a mutually
acceptable settlement, they are to record and sign the terms of the settlement and the commission then forwards the document to the OSCE Senior Council. If a settlement is not forthcoming, the commission draws
up a final report containing the commission's proposals for the peaceful
settlement of the dispute (based on a majority opinion). Following the
report, the parties have 30 days to inform the commission as to whether
they are willing to accept the proposed settlement. The report and its acceptance or nonacceptance is then forwarded to the Senior Council.

The Arbitration Procedure

As with the conciliation procedure, requests for arbitration will be accepted by the court in cases where states are parties to the convention, or
at least one is a state party and the others are OSCE participating states,
so long as all parties agree. The arbitrator appointed by each state to the
court automatically becomes an ex officio member of the ensuing Arbitration Tribunal and the Bureau of the Court is authorized to appoint the
remainder of the arbitrators. Appointed arbitrators must, however, equal
at least one more than the ex officio members. The arbitration procedure
is intended to conform to the principles of a fair trial and consists of written and oral pleadings held in camera. Also, the tribunal has fact-finding
and investigatory powers, which it can use, if necessary. The tribunal may
issue interim orders to the parties "to avoid aggravation of the dispute,
greater difficulty in reaching a solution, or the possibility of a future award
of the Tribunal becoming unenforceable." When decided, the award of the
Arbitral Tribunal states the basis upon which the decision was made, and
dissenting opinions can be attached. The award is final and not subject to
appeal (except when a previously unknown fact is brought to light that
materially alters a case). The award is published and communicated to the
parties and to the OSCE Senior Council.

The Provision for Directed Conciliation

Of particular interest is the Provision for Directed Conciliation, which
states that the Council of Ministers or the Senior Council may direct "any
two participating States to seek conciliation to assist them in resolving a
dispute that they have not been able to settle within a reasonable period of
time." This provision, therefore, allows the OSCE to *prescribe* a type of

dispute settlement to disputing parties. However, the exceptions in the Valetta Mechanism also apply to the court. Naturally, this limits to some extent the applicability of the procedure.

It remains to be seen if and to what degree this new court will be used. Its advocates maintain that its conciliation procedures, in particular, allow for considerable control by the parties over the process, making the court an attractive alternative for dispute resolution. If a few parties can be persuaded to bring their disputes to the court, they argue, the effectiveness of its procedures will be demonstrated and its use will grow.

Cooperation with the UN

At times, cooperation between the OSCE and the UN has been less than ideal. Attempts by both organizations to improve the situation have led to a considerable amelioration of the problem, but there remains further scope for progress.

On 28 October 1992, the UN General Assembly adopted a resolution entitled "Cooperation between the United Nations and the Conference on Security and Cooperation in Europe," stressing the need for increased cooperation. The Framework for Cooperation and Coordination between the UN and the CSCE was signed on 26 May 1993, in which both organizations agreed to regular consultations and exchange of information to foster international security and to avoid overlap and duplication. On 22 October 1993, the General Assembly invited the CSCE to participate in the work of the UN by granting it Observer Status. In 1994 and 1995, representatives of the OSCE attended the meeting convened in New York by the UN Secretary-General to promote dialogue between the UN and regional organizations; and the UN Secretary-General has subsequently attended OSCE Senior Council meetings and summits, and has maintained regular contact with the chairman-in-office. Senior staff members from the UN Department of Political Affairs and the OSCE secretariat are also frequently in touch with one another.

While the two organizations work well together in some situations, problems have occurred in the field when the two had similar mandates. At times, field missions have appeared to act competitively rather than cooperatively (Kemp, 1995). Since some of these problems derived from insufficient clarification regarding the division of labor, it was decided to divide responsibilities, with one organization taking the lead on each matter of common interest and the other playing a supporting role. For example, it was agreed the UN would take primary responsibility for Tajikistan and Abkhazia, while the OSCE would have preeminence in South Ossetia, Nagorno-Karabakh, and Moldova. (Kemp, however, notes that the division of the two problems in Georgia is a "bizarre arrangement that seemed to imply that the two areas were not part of the same problem.")

The 1995 Report of the Secretary-General on Cooperation between the United Nations and the Organization for Security and Cooperation in Europe states that specific efforts have been made to improve contacts and cooperation in the field, at the negotiating table and between the respective headquarters. These steps have resulted in better coordination with the aim of making better use of the resources of the international community. Examples include UN logistical support for the OSCE mission in Sarajevo; a division of roles in Tajikistan (with the UN taking the leading role regarding peacemaking and the OSCE taking the leading role regarding human rights and the building of democratic institutions); and the UN sitting in as an observer in the meetings of the Minsk Group.

As a further attempt to clarify the division of responsibility, a proposal to institute a policy of "OSCE First" was brought to the 1994 Budapest Summit. This concept entailed the OSCE taking primary responsibility for managing all disputes in its region, transferring this burden to the UN only when it assessed its own efforts as having failed. This idea, however, met with political resistance from a number of sources (Kemp, 1995). Although burden-sharing is certainly an important issue, the idea that participating states might be discouraged from taking their disputes to *any* forum they wish does not seem in keeping with either Article 33 of the UN Charter, which suggests that choice of the dispute settlement method is up to member states, or Chapter VIII of the UN Charter.

To further enhance cooperation at the sensitive political level, it has been suggested that a senior UN staff member from the Department of Political Affairs be placed at the OSCE secretariat in Vienna, to sit in on Permanent Council meetings, to be in daily contact with OSCE staff, and to manage coordination between the two organizations. (As will be seen in chapter 9, a similar arrangement has been suggested for the OAU.) Given the OSCE's active role in preventive diplomacy and peacemaking, this would appear to be a useful idea. Another proposal has called for the inclusion of at least one member of each organization on missions deployed by the other, to keep both organizations informed about the situation on the ground and to assist in the sharing of resources.

Summary and Possible Next Steps

As discussed above, the OSCE has developed in two distinct phases, both of which have been remarkably successful. In the first phase, its activities promoted East-West dialogue and confidence building, which helped bring about not only a peaceful end to the cold war but also a revolution in favor of human rights and participatory democracy. In its second phase, it reshaped itself to help participating states meet the challenges of reemergent ethnic conflict and the transition to democracy.

Although the OSCE has been acclaimed for its innovation in implementing preventive diplomacy, it is undergoing another identity crisis, as it tries to determine how it can best fit into the regional security architecture of Europe and as it struggles to shape its policy regarding CIS peacekeeping operations. Moreover, the mission in Bosnia-Herzegovina has overwhelmed its capacity and some believe has detracted from its advantage as specializing in preventive diplomacy. Some states have argued that the organization should adopt a collective security rather than cooperative security identity. Speaking for those against the OSCE changing its focus, Zaagman (1995a) argues that: "We should not saddle the organization with a burden it is not equipped to carry." Among other limitations is the OSCE budget—$49 million for 1997 (OSCE Budget Office, 1997).

Related to this is the debate over whether the organization should retain its consensus approach to decision-making. Zaagman maintains that the consensus rule is only a problem if the OSCE decides to choose a more coercive approach. Chigas et al. (1995) argue further that consensus is the *soul* of the organization. They note that it

> sets a tone of persuasion rather than coercion and ensures that governments have a significant say in the formation of policies that affect them. Consensus decision-making not only makes it difficult to refuse to engage in the process, but its inclusiveness can encourage conformity and "buy in," thereby deterring noncompliance with the resulting norms and decisions, even though they are not binding. In fact, within the OSCE process, states withhold their consensus only on those very few items on which they feel so strongly that they are willing to "cash in" political credibility and capital that might have been used to obtain support for future policies and, in the extreme case, risk isolation. The essentially political process creates a tremendous amount of "peer pressure" to conform—not become the spoiler—and in this way acts as an effective and valuable instrument of preventive diplomacy and conflict resolution.

This debate aside, there are a number of things that the organization could do to reinforce its role in preventive diplomacy. The first involves strengthening the mechanisms that have already served it well. Zaagman (1995a) suggests that "focusing on conflict prevention sets an objective which is ambitious enough in itself but very well suited to the particular 'comparative advantages' which the OSCE possesses . . . Institutionally there is much in place which only needs to be made to work better." He adds that "it is a fact, however, that the cooperative possibilities are insufficiently understood and in general underutilized."

A related problem is that the OSCE, in its rush to develop appropriate mechanisms for such a dynamic and unpredictable era, has developed a number of parallel procedures that have not always related to each other in a logical fashion. Thus, some rational integration is needed. One idea might be to tie these mechanisms more effectively to the role of the Permanent Council. For example, the emergency mechanism for discussing unusual military activities or military activities of a hazardous nature, at short notice, could, at least in part, be integrated into its agenda, as could the human dimension emergency mechanisms and the peaceful settlement of disputes mechanisms, discussed earlier.

Moreover, the roles of both the chairman-in-office and the secretary-general are underdeveloped and underutilized in terms of their good offices potential. The secretary-general has operated largely as a political adviser to the CIO, and in an administrative and public relations capacity. In contrast, as will be seen in the next two chapters, both the OAS and OAU have taken a decision to give their secretaries-general a more important role. The OSCE would be likely to benefit from following their lead. A German-Dutch proposal to this effect was submitted to the Budapest Summit, suggesting that the secretary-general should be authorized to refer to the decision-making bodies any matter, which, in his opinion, might threaten peace and security in the OSCE region (that is, a similar provision to Article 99 of the UN Charter). However, this was not accepted.

Austria and Hungary have proposed that the OSCE establish an Adviser on Issues of Stability and Security who would have a mandate for quiet preventive diplomacy modeled on that of the High Commissioner, but in areas not related to minorities. Once again, this proposal was rejected, although it, too, could significantly extend the preventive diplomacy capacity of the OSCE (and in fact is somewhat similar to the proposals to be made in chapter 13). Currently, this role is assigned to the chairman-in-office, but as a full-time foreign minister of his/her country, the CIO does not always have sufficient time to fulfill it properly.

Since the demands on the High Commissioner on National Minorities are large, the position needs an increased capacity in terms of both resources and staff support. Demands for his services are already overwhelming. Strengthening his senior support staff, in particular, would be useful.

Additionally, OSCE missions need to be provided with more professionally trained and experienced staff who can meet the challenge of such difficult tasks. Lawyers skilled in drafting legislation, as well as those with training in facilitation and conflict resolution, should be among those regularly assigned to such missions. Currently, participating states provide mission staff on a secondment basis, some of whom are quite junior and inexperienced. States should be encouraged to offer experienced staff whose skills are tailored to the particular mission.

With regard to the ODIHR, Zaagman (1995a) notes that many states remain unaware of the programs that the organization offers. Further, not all participating states have supplied the office with their national inventory of expertise. NGOs, national parliaments and the OSCE Parliamentary Assembly should be urged to make their inventories available for publication and distribution by the ODIHR.

Members of the Parliamentary Assembly could also work more effectively in the area of conflict prevention. At home, they could play a greater role in ensuring that their states live up to OSCE commitments by helping to introduce and pass the necessary legislation. Parliamentarians could also do more to promote public and state understanding of the role of the OSCE. Finally, although some parliamentarians already participate in OSCE election monitoring, parliamentarians could play an even greater role in this area.

Finally, the OSCE has not operated very effectively in its relationship with NGOs. It has been argued that, in particular, the organization should tap the knowledge and expertise of those NGOs operating in the conflict resolution field (Gutlove and Thompson, 1995; Zaagman, 1995a). Seminars to examine the issue have been sponsored by both the OSCE and by NGOs, with these discussions culminating in a statement at the 1994 Budapest Summit calling for increased utilization of NGOs by the OSCE. In response to this dialogue, the secretary-general prepared a Study on Enhancement of NGO Participation, after over 600 NGOs were asked to comment on their views about improving OSCE/NGO cooperation. Some of the more interesting recommendations from this study include the appointment of an NGO liaison to participating states; the appointment of an NGO liaison to the Vienna secretariat; a yearly meeting to be hosted by the Permanent Council and NGOs for a broad exchange of information; briefings with NGOs by the Permanent Council on specific points on its agenda; an opportunity for NGOs to disseminate written contributions, petitions, and communications to participating states; due consideration by the ODIHR of NGO information regarding the monitoring of the human dimension; the use of NGO expertise in supplying missions with background studies; NGO training of OSCE mission members; regular meetings of NGOs in the conflict prevention field with the High Commissioner and the ODIHR; and regular contact between relevant NGOs and missions.

In conclusion, although there are many things that the OSCE can do to improve its effectiveness, its progress in developing a capacity for preventive diplomacy and peacemaking provides an example of what can be done in a short time, with limited resources but with a critical mass of "political will," consensus, and access to appropriate human resources. Most analysts suggest that the key to its success has been its cooperative approach to problems. Zaagman (1995a) notes that

> As far as the recognition of the legitimacy of international interference in the internal developments of states is concerned, the OSCE is the leading international actor in the world . . . but it is cooperation which lies at the heart of the exercise of common responsibility of OSCE states, or as it is sometimes called "the cooperative implementation of OSCE commitments." . . . Durable solutions are only possible if there is a sufficient measure of consent from the parties directly involved. At the same time, in view of the great and many challenges of today the participating states should assist each other and request each other's assistance. It is in the light of this crucial aspect of cooperation that we should look upon the process of increasing OSCE intrusiveness in the affairs of participating states.

As will be discussed in more detail later, a number of the regional organizations reviewed in this book appear to be moving in this direction. Thus, it would be a regressive step for the organization with the highest profile in cooperative security to retreat to a collective security approach, especially since the OSCE is the only intergovernmental body that is engaged in comprehensive conflict prevention in Europe (or anywhere else). The way forward should be to build on this unique strength and to develop a model of sustainable peace that can serve as an example to other organizations.

8

The Organization of American States

Security Issues in the Americas

M ANY OF THE SECURITY ISSUES in the Americas have been present for a long time, but perceptions of them have gradually changed. During the cold war, there was a preoccupation with the possibility of extra-hemispheric aggression and a concomitant fear of communist regimes and movements developing within the region. While the promotion of democracy was seen as an ideal (eventually enshrined in the OAS Charter in 1985), military juntas and other authoritarian, nondemocratic regimes dominated many governments throughout this period, and human rights abuses were frequent and even massive in some countries. These dangers to peace and security were often tolerated or ignored, due to the concentration on the extrahemispheric threat. The Commission on Inter-American Dialogue (1994), an independent Washington, D.C. think tank that works closely with the OAS, states that "democracy and the rule of law were subordinated to the aim of containing communism."

Today, by contrast, civilian and constitutionally legitimate governments are in place in nearly every Latin American country. As the commission notes:

> This development provides the necessary (but not always sufficient) foundation for the full protection of human rights. Massive violations have been curtailed, and there has been a sea change in outlook, reflected by greater legitimacy for human rights ideals and the democratic model. Such a shift has been reinforced by the end of the Cold War, which has helped reduce the

pronounced ideological polarization that had fueled the region's political violence for the past three decades. (Commission on Inter-American Dialogue, 1994)

As can be seen in table 3.2, over the past few years, the Americas have had one of the lowest levels of overt armed conflict of any region in the world. However, even with the growth of democracy, major threats to peace and security remain. Drug trafficking and organized crime have created new forms of violence that undermine the democratic state. Problems of excessive military authority, human rights violations, and the exclusion of large sectors of the population continue to plague much of the continent (Chernick, 1996). Uneven economic and social development between and within countries, extreme poverty, and transnational migrations all continue to be serious problems. Indigenous peoples and "tribal peoples" (as those brought as slaves from Africa are called in the Draft Inter-American Declaration on the Rights of Indigenous Peoples) have, in particular, been systematically disadvantaged and discriminated against over many years and are increasingly demanding political access, as well as economic and cultural rights.

Further, although a number of the region's territorial disputes have been resolved (for example, between El Salvador and Honduras on the Fonseca Gulf and between Argentina and Chile on the Beagle Channel), the military confrontation between Ecuador and Peru demonstrates that these issues still pose a risk to peace and security in the hemisphere.

The Role of the OAS in Promoting Sustainable Peace

The Organization of American States is the oldest regional organization, originating at the first International Conference of American Republics, held in Washington, D.C. in 1889–90. This meeting approved the establishment of the International Union of American Republics, which evolved, after World War II, into the Organization of American States. The OAS now has 35 members, including all sovereign states of the Western Hemisphere (although the Cuban government has been excluded from participation since 1962).

The Charter of the OAS, which was signed in 1948, entered into force in December 1951. It was later amended by the Protocol of Buenos Aires in 1967 (which entered into force in 1970) and the Protocol of Cartagena de Indias in 1985 (which entered into force in 1988). The charter proclaims the following purposes for the organization:

- to strengthen the peace and security of the continent
- to promote and consolidate representative democracy, with due respect for the principle of nonintervention

- to prevent possible causes of difficulties and to ensure the pacific settlement of disputes that may arise among the member states
- to provide for common action on the part of those states in the event of aggression
- to seek the solution of political, juridical, and economic problems that may arise among them
- to promote by cooperative action, their economic, social, and cultural development
- to achieve an effective limitation of conventional weapons that will make it possible to devote the largest amount of resources to the economic and social development of member states

Although the OAS Charter contains many references to the need for individual member states to be involved in promoting democracy, human rights, social justice, and development, its focus in terms of peaceful settlement of disputes, like the UN Charter, is primarily on interstate disputes. (In 1948, the American Treaty on Pacific Settlement, known as the Pact of Bogota, was also approved for this purpose, but it was ratified by only 14 states and was never employed.) Articles 23, 24, and 26 of the charter state that:

> All international disputes between member States shall be submitted to the peaceful procedures set forth in the Charter. . . . The following are peaceful procedures: direct negotiation, good offices, mediation, investigation and conciliation, judicial settlement, arbitration, and those which the parties to the dispute may especially agree upon at any time. . . . A special treaty will establish adequate means for the settlement of disputes and will determine pertinent procedures for each means such that no dispute between American States may remain without definitive settlement within a reasonable period of time.

In terms of intrastate conflict, the OAS Charter contains numerous references to the noninterference in the internal affairs of member states.

Since 1985, however, the organization has made a series of constitutional changes that are unprecedented in other regional organizations and that not only allow, but actually mandate, the organization to become involved in the internal affairs of a member state when there is a threat to a democratically elected government. In 1985, the following phrase was added to the charter: "Representative democracy is an indispensable condition for the stability, peace and development of the region." In 1991, the Santiago Commitment was made, in which member states declared *their inescapable commitment* to democracy. As well, the approval of Resolution 1080 in Santiago called for the convening of foreign ministers in the event of a coup or other interruption to a legitimately elected government and authorized them to take "any decisions deemed appropriate" in accordance with the charter and international law. In 1992, the General Assembly approved the Protocol of Washington, allowing it, by a two-thirds vote, to suspend the participation of any regime that comes to power by deposing a democratic government. These developments mark a real turning point in the organization's history, in which domestic political circumstances (the interruption of a democratic government) can become the grounds for collective action.

Finally, the Declaration of Managua, approved in 1993, puts forward the concept of *"ethical and effective governance"* and it calls on member states to "modernize domestic administrative and political structures and systems; improve public administration; protect minorities and political opposition groups; achieve national reconciliation and consolidate a democratic culture; meet basic human needs; safeguard human rights; and ensure the subordination of armed forces to legitimately constituted civilian authority." It states further that the OAS must "prevent and anticipate the very causes of problems that work against democratic rule." As such, the Organization of American States as an institution goes beyond any other regional organization and beyond the United Nations in its declaration of support for and defense of democracy. Of course, these declarations do not necessarily reflect deeper behavioral realities, and a gulf still exists between institutional rhetoric and political action.

Like many other regional organizations, the OAS has not yet developed a specific mechanism for, and, indeed, practices very little, preventive diplomacy per se. It does, however, engage in a number of activities that help to reduce intrastate tensions, through the promotion of democracy, the defense of democracy, the development of human rights standards, and the protection of human rights. Moreover, it has, in a few cases, played a role in peacemaking. The following briefly summarizes current OAS practices and mechanisms in these areas.

Preventive Diplomacy and Peacemaking

Meeting at the level of foreign ministers, the General Assembly is the supreme organ of the OAS, and has, as one of its principal powers assigned to it by the charter, the ability to "consider any matter relating to friendly relations among the American States." Indeed, the General Assembly does consider and pass resolutions on a range of issues related to peace and security. But the fact that it meets for only a few days once a year means that it cannot effectively carry out peacemaking and preventive diplomacy functions, apart from endorsing the actions of other parts of the organization.

Thus, it is the Permanent Council (composed of ambassadors), which meets in Washington every second week, as well as in special meetings, that is more likely to be able to respond on an ongoing basis to security problems within the hemisphere. If a situation is especially grave, the Permanent Council can convoke a meeting of Consultation of Ministers of Foreign Affairs.

For the most part, all three of these forums for peace and security issues pass resolutions condemning or commending member states for their actions. Their primary function, in terms of peaceful resolution of disputes, is, therefore, one of socialization, in which norms are shaped and governments are encouraged to conform by the social sanction or approval of peers. In a few instances, more substantive actions have been taken. In the case of Haiti, for example, a mission was sent and economic sanctions were imposed.

The 1985 Amendment to the Charter contained a provision that entitled the secretary-general to bring to the attention of the General Assembly or the Permanent Council any situation that, in his judgment, could affect the security of the hemisphere. Like Article 99 of the UN Charter, it has been used very sparingly, and only in situations that were extremely serious. It has, however, been interpreted as an informal authority for the secretary-general to offer his good offices. The secretary-general did so in the border dispute between Ecuador and Peru, as well as in the constitutional crisis in Ecuador, where the secretary-general sought to bring together the country's president, the president of Congress, and the chief justice to work out a constitutional solution.

The Permanent Council can also legitimize the peacemaking efforts of others, as it did in the Ecuador-Peru problem, when it recognized the overtures by Argentina, Brazil, Chile, and the United States as the guarantors of the 1942 Protocol of Rio de Janeiro and expressed confidence that such assistance would bring an end to the conflict. The practice of appointing special representatives or envoys has not been common within the OAS, the only instance being the appointment to Haiti of a special representative, who was also appointed as the special representative for the UN.

Protection of Human Rights

Next to the Council of Europe, the OAS has the most well-developed and active human rights machinery of any regional organization (and, indeed, some of its instruments were modeled after those of the COE). It consists of an Inter-American Commission on Human Rights, which is now an organ of the OAS, and an Inter-American Court of Human Rights, which is an autonomous judicial institution created by the American Convention on Human Rights but linked to the Commission. Although the system is still evolving, its work has already made an impact on the hemisphere and, no doubt, will be developed further.

The Inter-American Commission on Human Rights

The Inter-American Commission was established in 1959 and began its work in 1960, long before it had the legal foundation of the American Convention on Human Rights, which entered into force in 1978. The commission represents all members states of the OAS and its principal function is to promote the observance and protection of human rights and to serve as a consultative organ for the organization. Its mandate includes monitoring, handling petitions, and educational and training activities.

Composed of seven commissioners, selected in their personal capacity from nominees presented by governments, the commission receives written complaints from victims, other individuals, or NGOs. The ability of nonvictims to introduce petitions is important, since victims may be unaware of international protection mechanisms or prevented from presenting a petition. The ability of individuals to submit petitions against their own governments is also an important provision. In addition, states can present complaints, but seldom do so.

The commission publishes and distributes a booklet, which explains, in easy-to-understand language, how to file a complaint. Approximately 1,500 individual complaints are received each year, of which about one-third become formal cases. When a petition is received, it is evaluated, and if deemed admissible (that is, if all local remedies have been exhausted), the commission conducts fact finding, receives evidence and testimony, and seeks a friendly settlement between the petitioner and the accused state. If a friendly settlement cannot be obtained, the commission examines the evidence and prepares a report, noting the facts and offering its conclusions, as well as any proposals or recommendations it may have. The state concerned is then asked to remedy the situation within a given time frame. When the time has expired, the commission decides whether the state has taken suitable measures and whether to publish the report. The commission can also forward its report to the General Assembly for further discussion. In cases where the state is a party to the American Convention on Human Rights and has accepted the court's jurisdiction, the commission can also refer the case to the court. However, even if the state involved has not accepted the court's jurisdiction, the commission may call upon it to do so for that particular case.

Precautionary Measures

One of the most effective means of responding to individual or NGO complaints against state bodies, in cases that are serious and where all local remedies have been exhausted, is for the commission to issue an urgent request to governments (sometimes within 24 hours of receiving a complaint) to ensure the protection of a given individual or group. Unlike provisional measures, which will be described below, precautionary measures can be used with any member state of the OAS. They request a government to take all necessary measures to protect the human rights of the individual or group in question. A streamlined procedure of consultation with two commissioners—the commissioner responsible for the given country and the president of the commission—allows the secretariat of the commission to act quickly.

Although the procedure is usually confidential in the first instance, the commission has the option of publicizing its request if a given government fails to respond. In a few cases, when it was felt that publicity would be helpful, the commission has issued press communiqués, for example, when judges in the Appellate Court in Guatemala were threatened. Precautionary measures are used frequently, an average of 200 times a year, with generally good results.

Provisional Measures from the Court

Another option, although one that is used much less frequently, is for the commission to request that the Inter-American Court of Human Rights issue provisional measures. While these measures have the advantage of having the strength and publicity of the court behind them, they typically take much longer to effect than precautionary measures. They require a strong case with sufficient evidence, and can be used only in cases where states have agreed to the jurisdiction of the court. In a few instances, the commission has gone to the court to seek provisional measures when precautionary measures were disregarded by a state. To minimize the time required, a fast-track procedure has now been devised, whereby the president of the court consults with two vice presidents about whether to issue provisional measures and hold a hearing.

On-site Visits and an Informal Mediation Role

The commission can and does make on-site fact-finding visits to study the situation in given countries firsthand. Examples include on-site visits to Haiti (prior to the return of President Aristide), which subsequently informed the General Assembly of the deterioration of the human rights situation there; an on-site visit to the Bahamas regarding Haitian refugees; and visits to Guatemala and Ecuador to examine prisons and assess the conditions in which indigenous communities live.

On-site visits also provide an opportunity for the commission to play an informal role in mediation between governments and ethnic groups whose human rights are being violated. In the case of what was called the "Communities of Peoples in Resistance in Guatemala," for example, a few of the commissioners and secretariat staff were able, through visits, to bring about a formal agreement, which was signed by both parties and which helped to significantly ameliorate the problem of the 50,000 indigenous people who had been in hiding for a decade.

Publication of Cases in the Annual Report

Analyses and findings of two kinds of cases are published in the annual report—individual cases, in which both states and individual perpetrators are named, and more general "special country" or "special situation" cases. These reports go to the General Assembly for discussion and/or resolutions. Thus, the commission has both a legal and political function. General Assembly censure is usually unwelcome and may prompt desired changes in practice within member states by exposing situations, thereby marshaling moral outrage. Argentina, Paraguay, Uruguay, Peru, Brazil, Nicaragua, Panama, and many other states have, at one time or another, been subjects of Special Country Reports. An account of the forced relocation of the Misquito Indians represents the kind of situation taken up in a Special Situation Report.

Some OAS actions of this type have been of historic importance, such as the delegitimation of the Somoza regime, when, following a 1979 commission report and a UN resolution, the OAS condemned the human rights violations of the Nicaraguan government. In another instance, the continuing commission reports of human rights abuses in Haiti (four reports in four years) added to the momentum for action in that country by the international community.

Development of International Instruments

The commission is also responsible for the development of new declarations on human rights. The commission has presented a Draft of the Inter-American Declaration on the Rights of Indigenous Peoples. This document relates both to peoples "who embody historical continuity with societies which existed prior to the conquest and settlement of their territories by Europeans," as well as "peoples brought involuntarily to the New World who freed themselves and re-established the cultures from which they had been torn." The document calls for full observance of human rights; the right of indigenous peoples "to collective action, to their culture, to profess and practice their spiritual beliefs and to use their languages." It prohibits states from taking any action that forces indigenous people to assimilate and prohibits any policy or practice involving discrimination, destruction of a culture, or extermination of any ethnic group, while recognizing that special guarantees against discrimination may have to be instituted. Further, the document states that, in respect of property of which they have been dispossessed, indigenous peoples are entitled to restitution or compensation in accordance with international law.

In summary, the Inter-American Commission on Human Rights is a versatile body that has had to work in difficult circumstances, especially in the 1970s and 1980s, but that has gained credibility and authority through its actions and played an important role not only in the protection of human rights in the hemisphere, but also in the development of greater awareness of human rights standards. Given its current caseload, however, the commission is understaffed and, as a result, is unable to process cases as quickly as it should for more effective operation. Its unique relationship with the Inter-American Court of Human Rights also provides it with a legal backup and is an important source of both legal and moral persuasion.

The Inter-American Court of Human Rights

Established by the American Convention on Human Rights, the Inter-American Court of Human Rights is made up of seven judges, elected by the state parties to the convention. It meets twice a year at its seat in San Jose, Costa Rica, to hear both advisory and contentious cases, and can also meet in special sessions, as required. Only state parties to the convention and the Inter-American Commission on Human Rights have the right to submit a case to the court. However, a case must first go to the commission, which is obligated to appear in all contentious cases. In deciding which cases it wishes to bring before the court, the commission typically attempts to choose strong cases in which the plaintiff can win, thereby serving as a deterrent to similar abuses. Once a case is taken up by the court, the parties can also be represented by agents, who may have the assistance of advocates, advisors, or any person of their choice.

Cases are decided by a simple majority, and the president of the court may break a tie. A rationale for the judgment of the court is provided, and any dissenting judge can register his/her opinion as well. If the court finds a violation of a right or freedom protected by the convention, it can rule that the injured party be ensured the enjoyment of that right or freedom, that the measure or situation that caused the breach of such right or freedom be remedied, and that fair compensation be paid to the injured party.

Any member state of the OAS, as well as OAS organs, can consult the court for an advisory opinion regarding the interpretation of the convention or of other treaties concerned with the protection of human rights. Similarly, the court's opinion can be sought regarding the compatibility of domestic laws with the OAS's human rights instruments.

The court reports each year to the General Assembly, and if a state has not complied with its judgments, the court can make pertinent recommendations to the assembly. To date, however, the court has not earned the same reputation as the commission, in part because it is not a full-time body and therefore has been unable to hear many cases. Moreover, the political process involved in the selection of judges has led to the appointment of at least one judge who was considered to be inappropriate in terms of human rights credentials, undermining the court's credibility.

Promotion of Democracy

The Unit for the Promotion of Democracy was set up in 1990, following the Protocol of Cartagena de Indias, which established the promotion of democracy as one of the "major aims of the organization." The unit was created to provide advisory services and direct technical assistance to member states. Until recently, the unit's major focus has been on providing electoral monitoring, typically through small electoral observation missions and technical assistance.

The unit now plans to extend its activities into the consolidation of democracy, aided by a recent doubling of its budget (although this still remains at only $2 million). Targeting the more vulnerable democracies and the poorer countries in the hemisphere, the unit will focus on strengthening and developing electoral institutions and procedures, including election monitoring, legislative institutions (for example, parliaments), and education about democracy. A Documentation and Information Center is planned, which will develop a database on democracy for member states to consult. It is to include a compilation of constitutions, election codes, information on legislatures, electoral institutions, election monitoring missions, unit projects, and so on.

Due to its newness and relative lack of funds, the Unit for the Promotion of Democracy has, to date, been understaffed and underdeveloped. Moreover, since it can only carry out tasks agreed to by member states, its further development will, in part, depend on what they ask (or allow) it to do. Nonetheless, if it can marshal the right expertise and formulate and carry out a strategic program, it could make a significant contribution to the development of good governance in the region.

Defense of Democracy

In a hemisphere where military coups have been a regular occurrence, the Santiago Commitment to Democracy and Renewal of the Inter-American System, as well as Resolution 1080, both of which were adopted in 1991, were important steps toward giving priority to democratic principles and helping to stabilize democratic governments. In particular, Resolution 1080 was a milestone in terms of a mandate for an intergovernmental organization to be able to respond to at least one category of intrastate problems. It instructs the secretary-general

> to call for the immediate convocation of a meeting of the Permanent Council in the event of any occurrences giving rise to the sudden or irregular interruption of the democratic political institutional process or of the legitimate exercise of power by the democratically elected government in any of the Organization's Member States, in order, within the framework of the Charter, to examine the situation, decide on and convene an *ad hoc* meeting of the Ministers of Foreign Affairs, or a special session of the General Assembly, all of which must take place within a ten-day period.

The ad hoc meeting of ministers of foreign affairs or the special session of the General Assembly is "to look into the events collectively and adopt any decisions deemed appropriate, in accordance with the Charter and international law." Since 1991, the foreign ministers have met and taken action of this sort in regard to Haiti, Peru, and Guatemala. The OAS has, however, opted for largely cooperative security rather than collective security measures in such cases.

Cooperation with the UN

In 1948, the OAS became the first observer in the United Nations General Assembly. Cooperation between the two organizations, however, has not always gone smoothly. Institutional jealousies and difficulties in coordinating field operations, such as electoral monitoring, have occasionally created tension. At an operational level, the OAS/UN mission in Haiti provided an opportunity for the two organizations to overcome some of these problems by mounting their first joint mission. While there were the usual problems of coordination, the mission was generally viewed as a success in terms of regional cooperation.

Over the past several years, annual meetings have been held between senior secretariat officials from the relevant parts of the OAS and the UN. These have been well attended by representatives of the two systems and have led to a new, more meaningful dialogue. At the third such meeting, in April 1995, the OAS and the UN signed a cooperative agreement between their two secretariats, in which they pledged to hold consultations regularly, invite each others' representatives to meetings where observers are allowed and where the matters are of special interest, and to exchange information and documentation in the public domain to the fullest extent possible on matters of common interest (Cooperation Agreement between the Secretariat of the United Nations and the General Secretariat of the Organization of American States, 1995).

More specifically, the Working Group on Preventive Diplomacy recommended (1) greater information-sharing in order to improve the early warning and the preventive diplomacy capabilities, and (2) the bringing together of representatives of the two organizations with representatives of the academic community in an informal forum to discuss the concept, functions, and tools of preventive diplomacy. It was suggested that an independent research organization might best organize such a meeting (Report of the Third General Meeting between Representatives of the United Nations System and the Organization of American States, 1995c).

Another Working Group on Democracy and Human Rights recommended joint subregional and regional conferences to build consensus and divide responsibilities on issues related to improving governance in the region, strengthening UN and OAS cooperation in the area of advisory services and technical assistance in human rights and the promotion of democracy. It was suggested that this kind of cooperation could be extended to relevant NGOs, such as the Inter-American Institute of Human Rights. Closer cooperation between the Inter-American Commission on Human Rights and the UN Commission on Human Rights and the UN's treaty-based bodies was also proposed, for example, exchanging information and reports, and building a roster of specialized resource persons for short-term missions and technical assistance.

Summary and Possible Next Steps

A number of proposals for strengthening the Inter-American system of human rights, democracy, and the rule of law have been put forward recently. The historic 1994 meeting of the democratically elected Heads of State and Government of the American Nations, called the Summit of the Americas, established the Partnership for Development and Prosperity in the Americas, based on a commitment "to democratic practices, economic integration and social justice." Underscoring the OAS role as the principal hemispheric body for the defense of democratic values and institutions, this agreement spells out a comprehensive Plan of Action and sets forth a timetable for implementation. In response, the secretary-general published a document entitled *A New Vision of the OAS*, outlining the steps necessary for such implementation.

As well, the General Assembly has instructed the Permanent Council, through its Special Committee on Hemispheric Security, to conduct studies and to develop proposals to identify, classify, and systematize the areas of competence and the functions of various institutions involved in hemispheric security issues. It also instructed the Permanent Council to examine issues related to confidence building, the peaceful settlement of disputes, and conflict prevention.

Finally, the Inter-American Dialogue set up a commission, which has published a special report containing a number of excellent recommendations (Commission on Inter-American Dialogue, 1994). Some of the next steps suggested by these and other proposals for reform are set out below. With regard to the development of preventive diplomacy and peacemaking, the Commission on Inter-American Dialogue (1994) has recommended that, since the tasks of defending democracy in the hemisphere—in effect, crisis prevention and management—are seen as preeminently political, the secretary-general should be given "the support and flexibility to manage these tasks and to recruit adequate staff to carry them out with determination and vigor." In addition, the commission proposed that:

> To prevent crises, the Secretary-General and his staff should play an effective leadership role in anticipating and responding quickly to threats to democratic governments throughout the hemisphere. The Secretary-General should provide a "menu" of services that can be utilized by the Permanent Council, the Meeting of Foreign Ministers, and OAS member states to deal with troubling and thorny political situations. These should include fact-finding missions, and mediation efforts designed to promote negotiation between parties in conflict.

> To resolve crises, the Secretary-General and his staff should be prepared to engage in, and support, negotiations and other conflict resolution methods, as appropriately authorized. *A cadre of hemispheric experts, trained in conflict resolution techniques, should be organized. In the event that Resolution 1080 is invoked—as in the cases of Haiti, Peru, and Guatemala—the Secretary-General should be able to provide the Meeting of Foreign Ministers with support and resources, for fact-finding, reconciliation and mediation* (emphasis added).

> The Secretary-General should have primary responsibility for organizing electoral observation missions. He should work through the Executive Coordinator of the UPD in drawing on qualified Unit staff to participate in such missions. He should also prepared to issue a judgment on the integrity of the election, and recommend appropriate action to the General Assembly and Permanent Council in the event that electoral fraud and irregularities are uncovered.

> The Secretary-General, in coordination with the director of the UPD, should *avail himself of the expertise of relevant scholars, universities, research institutions,*

and think tanks throughout the hemisphere. An informed "network" of contacts with such entities would enable the Secretary-General (and the Permanent Council) to request information and analysis on given problems or situations related to the defense of democracy (emphasis added).

Were these recommendations to be adopted, it would constitute a big step forward for the OAS and would cover much of the same ground as the proposal for Regional Centers for Sustainable Peace to be discussed in chapter 13.

With regard to improving the Inter-American system for human rights, considerable progress could be made if all member states ratified the full range of Inter-American human rights instruments and accepted the jurisdiction of the court. Indeed, as the Commission of the Inter-American Dialogue (1994) has commented: "Nothing would strengthen the Inter-American system of human rights more."

To make them more effective, both the Inter-American Commission on Human Rights and the Inter-American Court of Human Rights should be instituted as full-time bodies and be provided with additional secretariat staff. Currently, both are part-time bodies (meeting two or three times per year). The spread of democratic ideals and the success of the commission's work has, however, meant that the number of cases being brought before it is growing. At the same time, governments have become more serious about litigating. Consequently, resources have become inadequate for the expeditious examination of the increasing volume of complex cases. In particular, the commission needs staff who can enhance its ability to investigate cases and who can make more frequent and extensive on-site visits and organize a database for its cases and evidence.

The commission and the court could operate in a more complementary manner, with the commission submitting some of its cases to the court for review of its findings, rather than having the court retry each case. In this manner, the court could serve as an appellate tribunal (Commission on Inter-American Dialogue, 1994).

Since many serious human rights abuses take place during declared states of emergency, a mechanism is needed, such as a Permanent Standing Committee of the General Assembly, to investigate emergencies at an early stage, to assist in harmonizing the emergency provisions of the convention with domestic legislation, and to publicize the human rights situation in the country involved (Grossman, 1989).

Since individuals and NGOs involved in human rights work are often the target of governments that engage in human rights violations, a special rapporteur could be appointed by the commission to provide information regarding the treatment of human rights activists by their governments (Grossman, 1989).

Support is also needed for improving and strengthening national systems to protect, promote, and defend human rights. In particular, work is needed to guarantee universal access to justice and to reform institutions to provide a climate of respect for human rights. The Plan of Action from the Summit of the Americas called upon the OAS to increase dialogue and enhance coordination on human rights. To this end, the secretary-general has stated his intention to ask the Permanent Council to convene a meeting of all the hemisphere's major actors in the human rights field. Further, the OAS, with support from the Inter-American Defense Board and the Inter-American Defense College, plans a study to consider which countries can provide appropriate models in the training of law enforcement officers, and the OAS plans to subsequently provide expert assistance in helping member states review and redesign their programs (Gaviria, 1995b).

In conclusion, the OAS has responded in its own unique ways to the changes in the geopolitical environment that followed in the wake of the cold war. Its emphasis on democratization (stronger than that of any regional organization outside Europe) is an important step toward preventing conflict within states. The organization's stand in defense of democracy is particularly important in a climate where civilian and military sectors are still deeply divided regarding their respective roles in society. To effect change, however, these commitments will need to be followed up with corresponding action. The consolidation of a democratic culture and institutions is a vital step in extending full civil, political, social, and cultural rights to all peoples, including indigenous and tribal peoples. Achieving these goals will require considerable technical assistance and other support from the international community. Perhaps even more important will be economic development and a better distribution of resources within societies, so that the injustices and grievances caused by poverty can be alleviated. The Plan of Action of the Summit of the Americas contains a number of recommendations in this regard that can serve as a blueprint for the future. It will also require a change in norms and attitudes, as well as in the behavior of the region's elite, and will probably only be achieved through the emergence of good leadership. Thérien, Fortmann, and Gosselin (1996) warn, however, that "The convergence of political and economic attitudes in the Americas, albeit real, should not be blown out of proportion. In particular, a significant gap still separates the OAS diplomatic discourse on the promotion of democracy and economic development from hard reality. If this gap were to endure, the recent advances of inter-American multilateralism could be quickly lost."

Another factor constraining the development of mechanisms for preventive diplomacy within the OAS is the historical fear of U.S. domination in the hemisphere, which, in the past, has been responded to with the jealous guarding of sovereignty and strong advocacy of the nonintervention principle. Adding to this concern is the fact that the United States is the main financial contributor to the OAS, providing two-thirds of its $91 million annual budget. On the other hand, offsetting these fears is the increasing sense of common interest accompanying the growth of democratic governments in the region, recent changes in U.S. policy, and Canada's having joined the organization. Nonetheless, these concerns remain an impediment that is probably best overcome, in the case of preventive diplomacy, by framing preventive efforts in the light of the organization's most important priorities, that is, democratization and the promotion of human rights.

9

The Organization of African Unity

Security Issues in Africa

O F ALL REGIONS, Africa has had the highest number of conflicts in recent years and has borne a terrible burden of warfare (Wallensteen and Sollenberg, 1996). It is estimated that, in the 1980s, two to three million people lost their lives in wars and 150 million (about 27 percent of Africa's population outside Egypt, covering one-third of the continent's land area) were living in countries seriously affected by war (Smock and Gregorian, 1993). With major conflicts in Somalia, Liberia, Sierra Leone, Sudan, Angola, Burundi, Rwanda, the Democratic Republic of the Congo, the Congo, and elsewhere in the 1990s, the toll in this decade has been equally and appallingly high. Africa has the largest number of refugees and internally displaced persons of any region in the world—approximately 6 million refugees and 20 million internally displaced persons (United Nations High Commissioner for Refugees, 1995). Otunnu (1992) notes that:

> There is a "curse" stalking the African continent. Entire societies are being decimated in internecine wars. Millions of ordinary Africans have been destroyed and sometimes states have become so fragile that they can no longer carry out effectively even the most basic functions expected of them. Indeed, some states have simply collapsed in the wake of these conflicts, and more countries could potentially be exposed to the same fate. Not only have these conflicts inflicted devastating domestic costs—a colossal loss in human lives, a huge drain on meager resources and diversion of attention from the development agenda, and the destruction of essential infrastructure—but they have also had broad implications: destabilizing effects on neighboring countries,

massive and sudden refugee movement across borders, and humiliating damage to Africa's collective image.

Gurr's study has shown that there are far more minorities at risk in Africa, south of the Sahara, than in any other region. Minorities also represent a larger share of the population (see table 3.3). Many of these problems stem from the 1884–85 Berlin Conference, where most of the boundaries of Africa were drawn by colonial powers without regard for, or knowledge of, existing African political or cultural boundaries. Instead, they were configured to encompass territory already occupied by colonial states (in order to avoid a European war over Africa) or drawn according to certain "logical" extensions between the borders of occupied lands (Scarritt, 1993; Stedman, 1996). As a result, groups with no affinity to one another were combined and others were arbitrarily divided among different states, creating a potential both for intrastate and interstate conflict (Ocaya-Lakidi, 1992).

The colonial state structures that were superimposed on traditional African societies were usually kept in place by military force. The "development" brought by colonial administrations was fostered unevenly within countries, leading to inequities in the relative economic, social, and political outcomes of the ethnic and regional groups inhabiting the same countries (Ocaya-Lakidi, 1992). With its policy of "divide and rule," colonialism also created the conditions for many of today's ethnic enmities, by pitting one group against another, or simply by favoring some over others.

After World War II, the many political, economic and social grievances that had persisted for so long, coupled with the desire for self-determination, resulted in an anticolonial movement throughout the continent. Where colonial powers were unresponsive to these aspirations, they boiled over into violent confrontations—first with the colonial power and subsequently, in some cases, between groups within the new state (Bakwesegha, 1995). As colonial powers had divested local communities and ethnic groups of much of their indigenous autonomy and replaced them with a degree of centralized authority, once control of these central institutions was relinquished by the colonial powers, the struggle for control at the center became inevitable.

In the search for leadership, colonial neglect of education "posed nearly intractable problems for Africa's new states" (Stedman, 1996). Stedman notes that there were less than 20 college graduates in Zaire at independence. When the Portuguese left Angola, there were no African civil servants and when Mozambique became independent, there were only three African doctors and one lawyer, and 90 percent of the population was illiterate. In the absence of appropriate training for governance, universal education or a democratic culture, the best leaders did not always rise to the top, and civil society protections were not in place to correct such mistakes. Moreover, nationalists, who had promised to rectify the inequities after independence, often lacked the financial or organizational resources to do so when they came to power.

As a result, the new states were often extremely weak, causing leaders to fear and resist change, sometimes through one-party rule. As the new elites in some parts of the continent sought to harness economic power through the nationalization of industries, the state became the largest employer and a pattern of "patrimonial politics" was established. Under these conditions, groups organized to obtain access to state largesse and "national interests were subordinated to the interests of politicians and their supporters, who viewed public office as private property" (Stedman, 1996). Moreover, the circumstances surrounding presidential power—where success could bring extraordinary prestige and financial wealth and loss could result in disgrace or even death—meant that, once in office, some African leaders tended to hold onto it at all costs (OAU/IPA Consultation, 1993). Ocaya-Lakidi (1992) comments that African leaders began strengthening the state apparatus vis-à-vis the people:

> The security organs in particular were used for suppression and repression. Leaders increasingly based political support on narrow sectarian considerations, neglected the well-being of the national economy and drained it of resources for personal use, and failed to forge national unity. . . . Corruption, favoritism, lack of political transparency and lack of accountability became the order of the day. The state became "privatized" and served the selfish interests of a minority, not the general good. As governments became more distant from the people, the latter no longer felt that they were full participants. The stage was thus set where groups suffering an injustice or believing that they were wronged felt they had no recourse but to come into sharp confrontation with the state, given the absence of any possibility of democratic redress.

Moreover, external intervention on the continent continued as the superpowers, former colonial powers, and even regional actors, became involved in supporting one faction or group against another, often providing political support, large quantities of weapons, or in a few cases, mercenaries. This fueled already existing problems and too often fanned the flames of violent conflict.

Further, patrimonial politics had "devastating economic consequences," since existing resources were used to buy political support and the production of wealth was neglected, causing investment to dry up and leading to massive borrowing as economies declined. When the world's financial institutions began to impose strict conditions in the 1980s, some leaders were forced to cut state employment, liberalize price controls, sell state businesses, and reduce state regulation of markets, undercutting their patrimonial base and bringing about an additional wave of economic and political chaos (Stedman, 1996).

Deteriorating economic conditions, in turn, created new grievances, which have had their political repercussions. Thus, a vicious cycle has evolved in which scarcity and unproductive economic policies heighten competition for resources and fuel intergroup conflict, which, in turn, creates worsening economic conditions. Today, 33 of the world's 48 least-developed countries are in Africa. Moreover, Africa is the only region in the world to have suffered from a continuous economic downturn since 1980. Africa's share of total world exports has dropped, flows of official development assistance have fallen in real terms, and external debt (which Secretary-General Boutros Boutros-Ghali termed "the millstone around the neck of Africa") increased from $48 billion in 1978 to $297 billion in 1993, a figure nearly equivalent to the continent's combined gross domestic product (Panel of High-level Personalities on African Development, 1995; UNDP Report, 1994). In summarizing the problems, Berhe-Tesfu (1995) notes:

> Africa entered the 1990s with a poor, marginalized, primarily rapidly increasing subsistence farming population, an environmental crisis, tremendous socio-cultural diversity, a destroyed infrastructure, a history of natural and man-made disasters . . . decades of centrally planned economies . . . a century of political disenfranchisement, and a new mixed economic system under structural adjustment programs, and at a time of donor fatigue.

In spite of Africa's many problems, however, it is important not to give in to what is sometimes called "Afro-pessimism." The resilience and innovation of African culture has shown itself to be profound, and with appropriate management (something the continent has seldom seen, with its legacy of colonial mismanagement) and *real* help from the international community (as opposed to additional exploitation or paternalism), Africa could find solutions to its problems and a better life for its peoples. The recent demise of apartheid and peaceful transition to democracy in South Africa mark the end of the colonial era and demonstrate the power of good leadership, persistent regional and international pressure, and patient negotiation. The end to wars in Namibia and Mozambique provides hope for other trouble spots, such as Angola and Liberia.

Moreover, it is important not to adopt an undifferentiated view of Africa, since the political, economic, and cultural situations of each of its states are unique. Stedman (1996) laments the fact that the major humanitarian problems on the continent have taken attention and resources away from assisting African countries that are trying to develop good governance, and he argues that this neglect will simply create more humanitarian crises. This highlights the need to support those states that are taking steps in the right direction, in order to encourage their progress and to demonstrate to others that change is possible.

The Panel of High-Level Personalities on African Development (1995) has suggested that the democratization process may be the key to achieving peace, security, and stability in the region. In 1992 Salim Salim, the secretary-general of the OAU, stated that it is important

> to insist to all policy-makers that *the new agenda for the resolution of internal conflict must address the fundamentals of governance*. For while classical negotiations can bring an end to internal hostilities, it is only genuine political reform, economic development and providing greater opportunity for all our people, which will act as an insurance against instability and conflict. Building democracy will require the building of institutions of democracy to oversee the political process. For, it is through building a culture of democracy that it will be possible to establish a firm basis for national unity and concord.

In *An Agenda for Democratization*, Boutros Boutros-Ghali (1996) argues that democracy should be seen as a "practical necessity" for development since nondemocratic states generate conditions that are "inimicable" to development, including politicized military rule, a weak middle class, a population constrained to silence, prohibitions on travel, censorship, restrictions on the practice of religion or imposition of religious obligations, and pervasive or institutionalized corruption. He states that "the reality is that no state can long remain just or free, and thus also have the potential to pursue a successful and sustainable development strategy, if its citizens are prohibited from participating actively and substantially in its political processes and economic, social and cultural development."

Rapid democratization, however, has not always been the answer. It has sometimes generated, rather than mitigated, violent conflict. Johnston and Nkiwane (1993) conclude that:

> The lesson of recent years is that, in the democratization process, the prevailing social and political context must be taken into account. The transition to democracy must be managed carefully, both internally (by domestic officials and political actors) as well as continent-wide. Without a conscious and evolutionary process of building democratic structures, the period of transition can be destabilizing.

For a poorly funded and under-resourced regional organization, such as the Organization of African Unity, the prevention of conflict and the promotion of good governance is, indeed, a tall order. Nonetheless, the OAU has begun to take steps toward this goal, as will be discussed below. Whether it is able to achieve some modicum of success will depend on factors such as a critical mass of like-minded African states, the support of the international community, and wise leadership within the organization. But it would be naive to expect the OAU to be able to tackle these massive problems on its own. It is in the interest of the whole international community to join in the effort to create the conditions for sustainable peace in Africa. This will require a new partnership between North and South. Some first steps toward this objective will be proposed in chapter 14.

The Role of the OAU in Promoting Sustainable Peace

The OAU was founded in 1963 in Addis Ababa with 32 members states and is currently composed of 53 members. All states on the continent are members, with the exception of Morocco. Early deliberations about how the organization should evolve included an ideological dispute between those who wanted a political union of African states and those who preferred a loose form of association, based on functional cooperation. The result was an organization whose principles amounted to a compromise between unity and independence, although the balance was weighed on the side of independence (Amoo, 1993). Indeed, it is perhaps not surprising that states that had recently become independent, after years of external domination, should fiercely guard that independence and strongly defend their sovereignty and the principle of noninterference in their internal affairs. This response (which has been echoed in other regional organizations and in the UN) did, however, cause the organization's conflict management capacity to be weakened. As Secretary-General Salim Salim (1992) notes:

> Traditionally, a strong view has been held that conflicts within states fall within the exclusive competence of the states concerned. Arising from this basic assertion was the equally strong view that it was not the business of the OAU to pronounce itself on these conflicts and that the organization certainly had no mandate to seek its involvement in resolving problems of this nature. In consequence, the organization has had to stand by in apparent helplessness as many of these conflicts have torn countries apart, caused millions of deaths, destroyed infrastructure and property, created millions of refugees and displaced persons and caused immense hurt and suffering to innocent men, women and children.

Nevertheless, the OAU charter supported the principle of peaceful settlement of disputes through negotiation, mediation, conciliation, or arbitration and, to this end, established the Commission of Mediation, Conciliation and Arbitration. The protocol for the commission, however, made its jurisdiction optional and its mandate was limited to disputes *between* member states. Further, the commission's report could only be published with the consent of the parties. Due to these and other limitations, the Commission of Mediation, Conciliation and Arbitration has never been used.

The Role of the Assembly of Heads of State and Government and Its Ad Hoc Committees in Conflict Management

In the absence of a functioning conflict resolution mechanism, the Assembly of Heads of State and Government took responsibility for this role, primarily by creating ad hoc committees of "wise men" from member states. The first committee of this type was formed in 1963 to respond to the situation between Algeria and Morocco.

To activate this procedure, an aggrieved party had to lodge a complaint against a member state with the assembly. If the complaint was accepted and inscribed on the assembly's agenda, a debate was held in closed plenary session. Normally, this concluded with a resolution that represented the general consensus of the assembly and laid down the principles upon which an ad hoc committee's more intensive search for a negotiated settlement was based.

Amoo (1993) notes that the assembly's ruling on legitimacy had a positive impact on regional stability by narrowing the area of uncertainty in a dispute, creating a predictable conflict environment through precedent and consistency, and defining the bargaining space. The latter was done by delineating relevant principles and identifying (often by implication) the "aggressor" and the "defender," as well as by articulating the legitimacy of the status quo or the demand to change it.

Moreover, the assembly's regular meeting provided an opportunity for heads of states in conflict to meet without loss of face, and also for other member states or groups of members to act as intermediaries. The fraternal atmosphere at summit meetings also helped parties find accommodation in the spirit of African solidarity and unity.

Nonetheless, there were a number of problems with this method. The OAU Assembly faced a problem similar to that of the Security Council or the General Assembly of the UN. It was not an adequate forum for mediation:

> Mediation by plenary resolution is conceptually a zero-sum process, whose outcome would favor the position of one party over the other. Conflicting

parties strive to influence the organizational consensus of the voting majority; the OAU thus becomes a battleground and a prize in the dispute. . . . With organizational and regional interests, norms and values to uphold, the OAU becomes a mediator as well as a negotiating party with its own motives and objectives. Further, in any particular conflict situation that attracts regional intervention, member states invariably have their own separate and often conflicting agendas. (Amoo, 1993)

The ad hoc committee procedure was also not ideal for intensive and ongoing third-party mediation. Convening the committee was dependent on the schedules of busy foreign ministers and heads of state, and a rotating chairmanship entailed a rotating secretariat. Both of these factors undermined continuity and institutional memory and reduced opportunity for the parties to involve the mediators in time-consuming tactics of limit-testing. Finally, in some cases, the selection of member states' representatives intensified "the dynamics of regional politics in the mediation process" (Amoo, 1993). As Amoo concludes:

In spite of its demonstrated commitment and acknowledged salience, the OAU has had mixed results from mediating in regional conflicts. In fact, the overwhelming body of informed opinion and scholarship contends that the OAU's interventions in regional conflicts have been largely ineffective. The OAU is indeed confronted with a paradox. It has salience and commitment as a mediator, but it has failed to develop appropriate machinery and processes for efficient intervention. . . . Its almost total abdication of mediation responsibility in internal (domestic) conflicts has condemned it to numerous charges of impotence.

Moreover, the secretary-general did not have a mandate from the organization for assuming a preventive diplomacy or peacemaking role and, in the few past instances where the incumbent attempted such activities, there was considerable political fallout.

The New OAU Mechanism for Conflict Prevention, Management, and Resolution

In the post–cold war period, with the West's preoccupation with political and economic problems in Eastern Europe and the former Soviet Union and the concurrent scaling down of superpower interest in African conflicts, the OAU began seriously reappraising its role. At its 1990 summit, the organization issued a landmark declaration—known as the Declaration on the Political and Socio-Economic Situation in Africa and the Fundamental Changes Taking Place in the World—in which African leaders committed themselves to "the further democratization of our societies and to the consolidation of democratic institutions in our countries." As well, they expressed their determination to work together toward the speedy and peaceful settlement of all conflicts on the continent. According to the consensus that emerged, Africans should, as much as possible, rely on their *own* resources and traditions in resolving regional conflict.

The 1990 declaration was a watershed in terms of collective appreciation of the value of open political systems as an essential part of assuring national peace and economic development. It meant that the organization accepted that the issue of governance should not be ignored, as it had been in the past, on the pretext of being exclusively within the domain of the sovereign rights of states (Adeniji, 1993). Links were also made between peace and stability, and between economic development and the reduction of expenditure on defense and security.

Following the declaration, in June/July 1992, the OAU secretary-general submitted to the 56th Ordinary Session of the Council of Ministers and the 28th Ordinary Session of the Assembly of Heads of State and Government in Dakar, a document entitled "Report of the Secretary-General on Conflicts in Africa: Proposals for an OAU Mechanism for Conflict Prevention, Management and Resolution," which outlined a number of options for such a mechanism. The assembly then adopted, in principle, the ideas in the report.

At its July 1993 meeting, the secretary-general submitted to the 58th Ordinary Session of the Council of Ministers and the 29th Ordinary Session of the Assembly of Heads of State and Government in Cairo, a further report, which covered all aspects of the Mechanism, including ideas for its institutional and operational details and financing. The assembly then adopted its Declaration on the Establishing Within the OAU of a Mechanism for Conflict Prevention, Management and Resolution. This declaration noted that:

> The Mechanism will have as a primary objective, the anticipation and prevention of conflicts. In circumstances where conflicts have occurred, it will be its responsibility to undertake peace-making and peace-building functions in order to facilitate the resolution of conflicts. In this respect, civilian and military missions of observation and monitoring of limited scope and duration may be mounted and deployed. In setting these objectives, we are fully convinced that prompt and decisive action in these spheres will, in the first instance, prevent the emergence of conflict, and where they do inevitably occur, stop them from degenerating into intense or generalized conflicts. Emphasis on anticipatory and preventive measures, and concerted action in peace-making and peace-building will obviate the need to resort to the complex and resource-demanding peace-keeping operations, which our countries will find difficult to finance. (OAU Declaration, 1993b)

The Mechanism was set up with a Central Organ to provide overall direction and coordination. The Central Organ consists of the state members of the Bureau of the Assembly of Heads of State and Government, who are elected annually from each of five subregions. At the Cairo meeting, where the Central Organ was elected, the number of representatives from each subregion was raised to two, when it was determined that by "expanding the pie" in this manner, disputes over representation could be avoided. It was decided further that both the outgoing chairperson and, where known, the incoming chairperson, should be considered members of the Central Organ. Finally, the OAU secretary-general is expected to attend meetings of the Central Organ.

The Central Organ is scheduled to meet at OAU Headquarters once a year at the level of heads of state and government, twice a year at the ministerial level, and once a month at the ambassadorial level. However, it can also be convened at any time at the request of the secretary-general or any member state of the OAU, and it is currently meeting at the ambassadorial level on a weekly (and sometimes daily) basis. The Central Organ reports to the Assembly of Heads of State and Government.

Importantly, the Mechanism also empowers the secretary-general, under the authority of the Central Organ, and in consultation with the parties, to "deploy efforts and take all appropriate initiatives to prevent, manage and resolve conflict." The establishing declaration calls upon the organization to build the capacity of the general secretariat to a level commensurate with the magnitude of this task. It also notes that the secretary-general may wish to resort to eminent African personalities or others in sending special envoys or special representatives, and in dispatching fact-finding missions to conflict areas. The importance of close cooperation between the Mechanism and other African regional and subregional organizations and neighboring countries, as well as the United Nations, is also stressed.

To fund the activities of the Mechanism, an OAU Peace Fund was established, with five percent of the organization's annual budget of $30 million being designated for this purpose. Voluntary contributions are also accepted from member states and, with the consent of the secretary-general, from sources outside Africa. According to Bakwesegha (1996), the fund has attracted a total contribution of $11,901,092 but since 1993 has spent $12,220,736, leaving it with a current deficit.

In summary, the new OAU Mechanism is potentially an important breakthrough in the prevention and management of conflict, since it establishes a regular forum where conflicts can be discussed by a representative group of member states, as well as a mechanism for empowering the secretary-general and the secretariat to become active in conflict prevention and resolution.

According to its proponents, because of the secretary-general's preference for a quiet diplomacy approach, the new Mechanism has been more active than widely realized. Through the use of good offices by the secretary-general, eminent persons, special envoys, representatives of the secretary-general, and missions from the secretariat, the OAU has been active in the Congo, Gabon, Sierra Leone, Somalia, Rwanda, Burundi, Sudan, Nigeria, Cameroon, Niger, Guinea, Lesotho, and the Comoros (Bakwesegha, 1996; Ibok, 1996). As Bakwesegha (1996) concludes: "Today's OAU Mechanism for Conflict Prevention, Management and Resolution should be seen and understood as the launching pad of a long-run process in the course of which the OAU will use experiences gained in countries like Burundi, Rwanda, Liberia, Angola, Mozambique, the Congo and South Africa to redefine the Mechanism and dovetail its structure to match the present realities in Africa." He cautions, however, that too much time is still allocated to dealing with the effects of conflict rather than to preventing tensions from growing into full-blown confrontation (Bakwesegha, 1995). As mentioned previously, the problem of crisis management overwhelming preventive activities is a common one.

Nongovernmental Organizations and the OAU Mechanism

The International Peace Academy, a nongovernmental organization located in New York, has acted as a catalyst for change and consensus building by bringing together African diplomats and academics in four OAU/IPA Consultations (with financial support from Carnegie Corporation of New York, the Ford Foundation, and the John D. and Catherine T. MacArthur Foundation). The first of these took place in Arusha in March 1992 and provided the impetus for the secretary-general to propose the new Mechanism a few months later in Dakar. The second consultation was held in Addis Ababa in May 1993. It provided ideas for input into the secretary-general's second report to the Cairo meeting, discussed above. In 1994, a third consultation was convened, and as of August 1995, an "OAU/IPA Taskforce on Peacemaking and Peacekeeping in Africa" was established to make practical suggestions for operationalizing the Mechanism, and mapping out how the OAU can develop its relationship with other actors toward this goal. The report from this task force is nearly finalized and will be forthcoming. A fourth consultation was held in Cape Town in June 1996 entitled "Civil Society and Conflict Management in Africa." Finally, in early 1997 the IPA held a meeting of scholars who have worked on Africa to explore ways in which they could contribute to the conflict management work of the OAU. This example of fruitful interaction between an NGO think tank and a regional organization provides another model of the rich cross-fertilization that can occur when a range of knowledgeable actors is brought together to focus on an important task.

Notably, the first OAU/IPA Consultation in 1992 pointed out the need for basic research both on the causes of conflict in Africa and on models of governance that would be appropriate for preventing it. A summary of the consultation stated:

> Since there are still considerable gaps in basic knowledge about the sources, causes, nature, and forms of internal conflicts in Africa, a great deal of basic research needs to be done. Seminars, symposia, consultations, and other fora need to be organized to seriously consider these subjects, with independent non-governmental actors having an important role to play in this regard. The OAU should promote and tap into networks of Africa-concerned research establishments for the same purpose. Independent research institutions that focus specifically on the problem of conflicts in Africa and that provide much-needed data for the more action-oriented organizations in this field are also needed. Africa's traditional methods of conflict resolution, which constitute a rich archive of practical experiences, need to be more fully tapped. (OAU/IPA Consultation, 1992)

Finally, there has been informal discussion on involving some of the major African research institutes as regional centers for early warning and analysis. Six locations were identified as possible sites for such a function, but the idea has not yet progressed beyond this point.

The Conflict Management Division in the OAU Secretariat

To support the Mechanism, an embryonic Conflict Management Division was set up within the OAU Secretariat in 1992. It is now in the first stages of establishing an early warning system, based upon a network of Africa-based governmental and nongovernmental institutions. The idea is to set up a Crisis Management Room, which would be staffed by a core of military officers and civilians who would receive, synthesize, and analyze relevant information and data and make recommendations to the secretary-general and the Central Organ on options for "early political action." Drawing on experts from OAU member states, subregional organizations, academic and research institutes, the UN and its specialized agencies, NGOs, and the media, the Conflict Management Division hosted a seminar in January 1996 to study how such an operation could be most effective.

The OAU secretariat is also setting up a database, which will store information on each of the organization's 53 member states, OAU involvement in election observation, the effects of conflict situations (for example, the flow of refugees and internally displaced persons), decisions of the Central

Organ relating to its work, and successful, as well as unsuccessful, conflict resolution initiatives in Africa (Bakwesegha, 1996). Further, the proposed database will include profiles of eminent personalities who could serve as special envoys or representatives of the secretary-general.

Another proposal calls for the division to be expanded to a department, headed by an assistant-secretary-general. This, it is argued, would lend it greater political weight and attract staff and resources more appropriate to its needs. Such a department could join in the creation of a Regional Center for Sustainable Peace, to be discussed later.

The Electoral Unit

Following the July 1990 decision of the OAU to reaffirm the right of each African state to decide which form of democratic government is most appropriate for itself, and the resurgence of interest in multiparty democracy, a small electoral unit was established within the Political Department. Subsequently, the OAU has monitored and observed presidential and parliamentary elections and referenda in 40 member states (Bakwesegha, 1996). Highlighting the link between this task and conflict prevention, Bakwesegha (1995) notes that the OAU has also been involved in election monitoring in order to assist member states in the peaceful management of change, and in the building of democratic cultures and institutions capable of diffusing tensions arising from rival political groups.

The African Commission on Human Rights

The African Commission on Human Rights was established under the auspices of the African Charter on Human and Peoples' Rights, which was adopted by the OAU in 1981 in an effort to prepare an African human rights instrument based upon African legal philosophy and responsible to African needs (Banjul Charter or Human and Peoples' Rights, 1981). It entered into force on 26 October 1986 and currently has been acceded to by 50 of the 53 member states.

During debate on the African charter, the possibility of establishing an African Court of Human Rights was also discussed, but as Peter (1993) points out:

> The idea was shelved primarily because strong doubts were expressed over the efficacy of such a Court, on account of the "unfriendly" attitude of most African people towards the idea of litigation. It was argued that most African people prefer conciliation or arbitration to litigation. Consequently, the experts resolved to establish a Commission with very limited powers as a watchdog over human rights violations on the continent. This Commission has proved to lack any bite, let alone a bark that is noticeable.

The commission is composed of 11 members who act in a personal capacity and who are chosen for their high reputation and competence in matters of human and peoples' rights. The OAU is charged with providing a secretariat to the commission. The mandate of the commission is to promote human rights, to ensure their protection, to interpret provisions of the Charter on Human and Peoples' Rights, and to perform any other tasks entrusted to it by the Assembly of Heads of State and Government (Banjul Charter on Human and Peoples' Rights, 1981).

The OAU commission was, however, given much weaker powers than its OAS counterpart, the Inter-American Commission on Human Rights. First, its brief applied only to state parties to the treaty, as opposed to all member states (as in the case of the OAS commission). While complaints can be made to the commission by either states or individuals, and powers of investigation are provided, the commission does not have the discretion to make its reports public without permission from the Assembly of Heads of State and Government. It must also refer cases that reveal "the existence of a series of serious or massive violations of human and peoples' rights" to the assembly, which may then request the commission to undertake in-depth studies, draw up factual reports, and make recommendations. The commission's latitude for action is also functionally restricted by a severe shortage of funds (Peter, 1993). This has made it unable to fulfill even its limited mandate.

Cooperation with the UN

The UN and OAU have worked together closely over the past few years in an effort to prevent or resolve conflicts in Angola, Burundi, Lesotho, Liberia, Mozambique, Rwanda, Sierra Leone, Somalia, and South Africa (Report of the Secretary-General on Cooperation Between the United Nations and the Organization of African Unity, 1995b) as well as in the Congo and the Democratic Republic of the Congo. This has involved close consultation at the highest levels between secretariats, cosponsorship of meetings with parties in conflict, and, in some cases, coordinated parallel missions.

The OAU has observer status in the UN General Assembly. Over the past twelve years, there has been an annual meeting between the secretariats of the OAU and the United Nations system. Moreover, the OAU attended the two meetings between the UN Secretary-General and regional organizations.

In the area of conflict prevention and management, the OAU has recently requested UN assistance in establishing its early warning system. It has also proposed that a coordinating body should be set up, so that, once that system is functioning, the two organizations can regularly exchange information (Report of the Secretary-General on Cooperation Between the United Nations and the Organization of African Unity, 1995b).

Joint OAU-UN fact-finding missions, with both an assessment and mediation mandate, are also being discussed and it has been suggested that a common list of eminent persons should be drawn up. Finally, improving communication and coordination by posting one or two UN staff from the Department of Political Affairs to OAU headquarters is being seriously considered. This would be the first instance of what could be an effective means of achieving closer cooperation in general between the UN and regional organizations.

The UN has also been asked to provide support for the OAU Electoral Unit in terms of logistics, information gathering, and assessment of elections. The two organizations are planning to develop common criteria for the verification of electoral processes and for debriefing and issuing statements related to electoral processes.

Altogether, there is considerable scope for the OAU and the UN to work together to enhance each other's capacity. In particular, the UN could offer its expertise in terms of past experience, while the OAU can offer its more intimate understanding and knowledge of the region.

Summary and Possible Next Steps

The evolving mechanisms at the OAU reflect the evolving political climate within the organization, where there has been a qualitative change in leadership. Indeed, those leaders who came to power through multiparty elections are less sympathetic to the ways of the past and more likely to challenge those governments not responding to the democratic trend. The spread of this socializing influence is already being felt in a lessening of concerns over the OAU playing a role in addressing certain types of intrastate problems.

The shift in thinking has also allowed the organization to adopt new and potentially more-effective procedures for conflict resolution. These include the empowering of the secretary-general to offer skilled mediation and the kind of structural support and advice that could bring about real change. The Central Organ could be used to marshal political support for these initiatives. As discussed in the chapter on the OSCE, this kind of complementarity between the secretariat and member states is essential for maximum effectiveness.

For the OAU secretary-general and the Central Organ to carry out their newly defined mandate, however, will require access to a reservoir of knowledge and skills. Assembling the skilled professionals and diplomats who can bring this expertise should be possible, given the impressive talent found both in Africa and in the diaspora, but it will require adequate financial resources to be properly realized.

It will also be important for the new Mechanism and the fledgling Conflict Management Division not to become too preoccupied with the concept of "early warning," to the detriment of "early action." Indeed, for those who are politically knowledgeable about the continent, it will probably not be difficult to predict where tomorrow's crises will emerge. What will be important is the development of the human resources with an appropriate level of knowledge and skill to provide assistance in early dispute resolution and good governance. Equally important will be the diplomatic skill to frame these issues in such a way that the political elite are able to accept this kind of assistance. This issue will be discussed in more detail later.

As mentioned earlier, the International Peace Academy has sponsored a series of consultations and has now formed a joint task force of high-level African leaders and scholars to continue consideration of the operational aspects of the Mechanism. Without doubt, this will provide innovative and useful ideas. While more contentious issues, such as peacekeeping, may require longer and wider consultation, it will be important to establish effective methods for providing assistance in preventive diplomacy and good governance as an urgent priority. One way to move the process forward would be to appoint a small but high-level and knowledgeable core staff within the OAU secretariat to begin carrying out the mandate of the Mechanism.

Some commentators feel that Africa could also benefit from its own adjudication process (Peter, 1993). Indeed, an African Court of Justice has not only been discussed, but has been included in the framework agreement for the African Economic Community that was signed in June 1991 at the OAU Meeting of African Heads of State. (Although established by a separate legal instrument, this community is intended to be an integral part of the OAU.) To date, however, there have been no moves to carry the idea further.

Proponents of an African Court of Justice contend that it is sorely needed to better protect human and peoples' rights, to settle boundary disputes, to combat the use of mercenaries, and to protect the environment from illegal shipments of toxic waste. Peter (1993) states that

> with political maturity, building sound institutional structures is vital to consolidating and guaranteeing democratic traditions. An African Court of Justice is one such vital institution. It makes little sense to establish a half-baked court as a show piece for the international community to see that there is democracy and fairness in Africa. All attempts should be made to ensure that whatever court is established, it will effectively serve the continent.

He acknowledges that such a process will not be easy and will be confounded by issues such as the differing and often conflicting legal regimes in Africa, the potential for a dispute over where the court should sit, resistance to the court's having a binding jurisdiction for those who are part of the community, financial and other resources, and, most of all, the traditional concern of states with "non-interference in their internal affairs." Indeed, were such a court set up, Peter suggests that it might be more effective if established as an autonomous institution within the OAU rather than under the African Economic Community. In the light of this debate, it is interesting to note that African countries have increasingly resorted to the International Court of Justice in recent years, and that the ICJ has recently played an important role in resolving the long-standing border dispute between Chad and Libya and in provisional measures in the *Case Concerning the Land and Maritime Boundary between Cameroon and Nigeria*.

While full implementation of the Mechanism and an African court might go some way to resolving and preventing conflicts on the continent, equally vital will be changes in attitudes and norms, as well as the acquisition of the knowledge and skill necessary for the establishment of civil societies. With adequate resources, the OAU could develop a strong program in this area. It could work with other institutions to provide advisory services and technical advice in good governance. Subregional organizations, research institutes, and NGOs also have a crucial role to play in this regard, as will be discussed more fully later. In Africa, in particular, there has been an explosion of nongovernmental organizations active in both cities and the countryside. These groups have deepened popular participation and given ordinary Africans a voice in shaping the policies that affect their lives. Development of their capacity and a close working relationship with one another and the OAU would be likely to enhance their effect.

Finally, with the changes in the OAU discussed above, the traditional concern about noninterference has begun to abate. Given the transition to various forms of democracy in many African states, it may be worth considering whether initiatives similar to the Santiago Commitment and Resolution 1080 might be of use in Africa.

The OAU and its leadership face awesome challenges and will need appropriate support from the international community. Along with assistance in capacity building, financial contributions to the Peace Fund by those international actors whose past actions contributed to Africa's problems, together with member states' own contributions, will be required for the organization to effectively tackle the widespread and complex problems before it. In both the short and the long term, such contributions are likely to be extremely cost-effective in reducing the need for much more costly peacekeeping, humanitarian, and refugee operations. It is incumbent on the rest of the world to assist in whatever ways are possible and acceptable, given Africans' understandable desire to set their own priorities and manage their own affairs.

10

The Association of Southeast Asian Nations

Security Issues in Asia

ALTHOUGH THE ASIA-PACIFIC region has been the location for some of the deadliest wars of this century, today it is experiencing an unprecedented period of peace (Afghanistan and Sri Lanka being notable exceptions). Parts of the region have been among the most rapidly expanding economies in the world, while other parts remain among the poorest.

The vastness of the Asia-Pacific region and the great diversity among states in territorial and demographic size make it difficult to grasp its multifaceted and complex security issues. Historical backgrounds, cultures, stages of economic development, and perceptions of security threats differ greatly from one state to another. Historical factors, such as the creation and clash of empires, colonialism, mass migration, and ideological differences, have all taken their toll and led to long struggles for self-determination, unresolved border problems, serious ethnic and religious cleavages, and competition over scarce resources.

The cold war resulted in a communist-noncommunist polarization of the region, which was further complicated by the Sino-Soviet rift. Some of these schisms have now been eased or erased, but others remain. Nonetheless, the states of the Asia-Pacific region no longer face the eminent danger of becoming embroiled in a major East-West confrontation.

Instead, there are new problems—and some old ones. The shifting power balance in East Asia between the United States, Japan, China, and

Russia is causing considerable uncertainty and concern. Both the Russian Federation and the United States have reduced their influence in the region, leaving a power vacuum, which some fear could be filled by regional "hegemones" such as India, China, or Japan. At the same time, historical suspicions and rivalries have resurfaced between China and Japan, Korea and Japan, Vietnam and China, and Russia and Japan. There is concern that these tensions could escalate, if change takes place too quickly. Some observers also worry that, if the U.S.-Japanese relationship were to sour, Japan could embark on a major program of rearmament that would trigger a new arms race in the region. Rapid Chinese military expansion also could provoke such an arms race. Other long-standing conflicts, such as those between India and Pakistan, the two Koreas, and China and Taiwan, remain tense and potentially explosive. The situation in Afghanistan, of course, remains a tragedy.

In terms of intrastate problems, Gurr's study identifies 57 minorities at risk in East and Southeast Asia and on the Indian subcontinent. He reports that there is no predominant "Asian pattern" of relations between minorities and dominant groups. The communist regimes of the People's Republic of China, Laos, and Vietnam, and the democratic and quasi-democratic regimes of India, Malaysia, the Philippines, Papua New Guinea, Thailand, and Bangladesh, have both sought some internal political accommodation, and in a few cases, governments have even designed complex strategies to try to equalize economic opportunities among multiethnic groups (for example, in Malaysia and India). But discriminatory practices remain common. More serious problems have occurred where governments have turned to traditionally authoritarian methods to forcibly assimilate communal minorities, as in Burma, Indonesia (in East Timor and Irian Jaya), Pakistan (in Baluchistan and Bengal), and Sri Lanka, or when regimes have turned to harsher methods when their attempts at accommodation have failed, as in the case of the Chinese in relation to the Tibetans, or the Indians in relation to the Nagas, the Kashmiris, and the Sikhs (Gurr, 1993).

Another problem facing the region is that, in spite of the considerable threats to security mentioned above, some states, including those with serious problems, do not come under the socializing influence of a regional organization. Apart from the South Pacific Forum (which will not be discussed here), the Association of Southeast Asian Nations (ASEAN) is the only regional organization with a security role. As will be discussed below, this role, while growing in importance, is but a small voice in such a vast region.

Security Issues in Southeast Asia

Like other regions, Southeast Asia has undergone dramatic changes in the post–cold war period. With a settlement of the conflicts in Vietnam and Cambodia, which had dominated the area for much of the second half of the century, tensions eased between its two halves: the anticommunist, pro-Western grouping of states, and communist Indochina. However, with the shift in regional balance, including the withdrawal of the U.S. military presence from the Philippines, ASEAN countries have become increasingly concerned about external threats to their security. As Buszynski (1993) sums up:

> During the Cold War, the ASEAN countries relied on the US military presence to address external threats to the region. Even avowedly non-aligned countries . . . regarded the U.S. military presence as a temporary balancing factor against communism. ASEAN security and defence policies were formulated on the basis of the US military presence. Countries . . . could concentrate resources and attention on internal security in the knowledge that regional security depended largely on the United States. Now, the ASEAN countries are compelled to focus on the range of contingencies that are embraced by the term "external security."

ASEAN countries have responded to the new situation, in part, by increasing military expenditure. As well, there has been a manifest change in attitude about U.S. presence in the region, with that presence being more welcome than it was previously. Finally, these concerns have led to a search for a new forum for security dialogue.

In spite of ASEAN's apparent success in preventing conflicts among its member states, significant dangers still exist, including resource competition and territorial disputes, notably in the South China Sea. There are also human security and transboundary problems, such as human rights violations; ethnic demands for political, cultural and economic rights; extreme poverty in some parts of the region; the illegal movement of peoples; terrorism; drug trafficking; multinational criminal syndicates; piracy; and environmental degradation. Aggregates of these problems exacerbate existing tensions and could lead to armed conflict within or between states.

A positive factor, however, is that a number of states in the region have experienced enormous economic growth, which has resulted in improvement in the lives of their people. The increase in ASEAN trade has made it the fourth largest trade group in the world, following the United States, the European Union, and Japan. Indeed, protecting this growth and prosperity has become a major impetus for some states to search for a peaceful environment in which they can develop further.

The Role of ASEAN in Promoting Sustainable Peace

The Association of Southeast Asian Nations currently has nine members: Brunei Darussalem, Burma (Myanmar), Indonesia, Laos, Malaysia, the

Philippines, Singapore, Thailand, and Vietnam. The organization prides itself on its flexibility and informality and its permanent structures are small—its secretariat has only around 30 professional staff members. As a consequence, its capacity for prevention resides almost entirely at the diplomatic level in the relations developed among its members, and between ASEAN members and those states in the wider region. At the moment, there is virtually no scope for the ASEAN secretariat to be involved in preventive action.

ASEAN was formed in 1967 with five members, at a time of considerable tension in the region. Two of its members, Malaysia and Indonesia, had just ended three years of war; the dispute between Malaysia and the Philippines over the North Borneo state of Sabah was heating up; and relations between Malaysia and Singapore were sensitive, due to Singapore's recent expulsion from the Malaysian Federation. This was against a backdrop of wider security issues, among them the perceived threat from communism and China, the desire for disengagement from the superpower rivalry, the wish to contain Indonesia's past expansionist policies, and the hope of solving insurgency problems through a policy of "collective internal security" (Askandar, 1994). In spite of these significant security concerns, ASEAN decided (perhaps in a uniquely Asian approach) to downplay its political role and focus instead on economic cooperation and development, as an area where it was more likely to achieve consensus and build positive relationships among its members.

Through its process of consultation, known as "musyawarah" (developed from an Indonesian village practice of consultation and consensus), and through its practice of "self-restraint," a sense of regional solidarity was gradually established, tensions were slowly eased, and the organization eventually moved to take on a more overt political role.

Developments in Preventive Diplomacy and Peacemaking

ASEAN took one of its first political actions in 1971, when (after considerable discussion) it passed the Kuala Lumpur Declaration, calling for the creation of the Zone of Peace, Freedom, and Neutrality (ZOPFAN). Although the declaration advocated neutrality, it was understood that this would be a long-term goal and that, in spite of ZOPFAN, some ASEAN members would maintain foreign bases on their soil (Askandar, 1994).

The Declaration of ASEAN Concord and the Treaty of Amity and Cooperation in Southeast Asia were agreed to in 1976 and were important steps forward for the organization, since political cooperation on regional and international matters was formally recognized for the first time. The treaty also established a mechanism for the pacific settlement of disputes *between* states. This mechanism was the High Council, which was to be a forum of representatives at the ministerial level, who would monitor conflict situations and, in certain circumstances, recommend ways of peacefully resolving them. The treaty provides that "in the event no solution is reached through direct negotiations, the High Council shall take cognizance of the dispute or the situation and . . . [may] offer its good offices, or upon agreement of the parties in dispute, constitute itself into a committee of mediation, inquiry or conciliation. When deemed necessary, the High Council shall recommend appropriate measures for the prevention of a deterioration of the dispute or the situation." In fact, the High Council has never been invoked, even in situations where it might have been helpful, such as in the case of Sabah, which remains a disputed territory. Saravanamuttu (1994) concludes, "the formal mechanisms of the Amity Treaty are window-dressing rather than true instrumentalities for conflict resolution. Nonetheless, the treaty should be taken as a statement of intent to resolve conflict peacefully, and as a non-aggression pact rather than as a legal-political structure to solve disputes."

Conflicts within states were not covered by the Treaty of Amity and Cooperation in Southeast Asia and, indeed, a number of noninterference clauses were the cornerstone of the treaty, including "mutual respect for the independence, sovereignty, equality, territorial integrity and national identity of all nations," "the right of every state to lead its national existence free from external interference, subversion or coercion," and "noninterference in the internal affairs of one another." Thus, so-called internal problems such as resistance in East Timor or the Moro rebellion in the Philippines have typically not been addressed by ASEAN.

Unrelated to the Treaty of Amity and Cooperation in Southeast Asia, ASEAN did, however, play an important peacemaking role in Cambodia. Its long-term efforts at both conflict containment and conflict termination, along with those of the United Nations and other regional and nonregional partners, finally brought about a peace agreement and the beginning of the rehabilitation of that country.

ASEAN has also worked in the background on the problem of multiple claims in the South China Sea, in which several of its members are claimants. Since 1990, Indonesia and Canada have cosponsored a series of "Workshops on the South China Sea" to provide a framework for dialogue, to explore a range of creative options for joint gain, and to lay the groundwork for potential talks in the future. These workshops provide a useful model for future preventive diplomacy initiatives. Progress has been made, although there have been some setbacks.

In 1992, ASEAN issued the Manila Declaration on the South China Sea. However, in 1995, tension again rose in the area. In response, ASEAN foreign ministers released a statement expressing their concern over the deteriorating situation and calling on all states to remain faithful to the declaration. In addition, ASEAN-China Senior Officials Consultation Meetings (which began in 1995) have provided a valuable opportunity for the ASEAN members with claims in the region to exchange views with their Chinese counterparts.

Beginning in 1978, ASEAN established a process of yearly ministerial-level meetings with its "dialogue partners," called the Post-Ministerial Conferences (PMC), because they follow the ASEAN ministerial meetings. Typically, these conferences involve a joint meeting between the members of ASEAN and the seven dialogue partners, followed by separate meetings, which are held between the ASEAN members and each of the dialogue partners in turn. During the cold war, it was thought that such dialogue would strengthen confidence, allow investment to continue and, thus, create a check on the revolutionary communist movements in ASEAN countries. The PMC also provided an important forum for ASEAN countries to obtain support from their dialogue partners on issues related to the war in Indochina. After the cold war, as ASEAN's agenda was revised in the face of rapid geopolitical and economic change, the PMC have assumed a new importance as the major arena for discussion of political problems and potential conflict in the region.

Wider Regional Engagement: The ASEAN Regional Forum

With the end of the cold war and the reemergence of the regional concerns and fears discussed above, it was felt that there was a critical need for a new multilateral forum for dialogue on political and security issues, which would include not only ASEAN members and their dialogue partners, but also Russia and China. The Australian, and subsequently the Canadian, dialogue partners proposed models for a kind of CSCA (Conference on Security and Cooperation in Asia), but ASEAN members rejected the idea as "too European." Nonetheless, these initiatives eventually led to a new concept, which has become instituted as the ASEAN Regional Forum (ARF). In Singapore in 1992, the Fourth ASEAN Summit Meeting of Heads of Government approved the Singapore Declaration, which established the framework for the ARF and definitively removed the taboo on open discussion of security issues. While the ARF had a similar role to the Post-Ministerial Conferences, the latter were not deemed a suitable forum for major security issues involving powers outside the PMC, since those states did not qualify under the PMC's terms of reference to be dialogue partners. Nevertheless, the Post-Ministerial Conferences were retained, as it was felt that they offered an important link with the dialogue partners and provided a place where dialogue between traditional friends would allow a level of comfort and frankness that might not be present in the ARF (Singh, 1994). The PMC meetings, therefore, follow the ARF meetings each year, which, in turn, follow the AMM (ASEAN Ministerial Meeting). Thus, the foreign ministers of the region regularly come together for approximately a week of consultations each year.

The ASEAN Regional Forum involves not only the nine ASEAN Member States (Brunei, Burma, Indonesia, Laos, Malaysia, the Philippines, Singapore, Thailand, and Vietnam); the seven dialogue partners (Australia, Canada, the European Union, Japan, New Zealand, South Korea, and the United States); but also two "consultative partners"—China and Russia. ASEAN is the "primary driving force" behind the forum, but to date, the ARF has no separate secretariat.

With its first meeting held in Bangkok in 1994, the ARF is still in the early stages of evolution. At the Bangkok meeting, the ARF endorsed ASEAN's Treaty of Amity and Cooperation in Southeast Asia as a code of conduct and as a diplomatic instrument for regional confidence building, preventive diplomacy, and political and security cooperation. Currently, discussions are being held on a modality for making the treaty open for accession or association by other states outside Southeast Asia. The first ARF also agreed to institutionalize the Meeting of Senior Officials for the ARF (ARF-SOM), as a kind of executive body that could be convened between ARF meetings and could provide support to and follow up on the decisions and actions of the ARF.

At its 1995 meeting in Brunei Darussalem, a three-stage evolutionary approach to the ARF's agenda was agreed upon, with stage one being the promotion of confidence building; stage two being the development of preventive diplomacy mechanisms; and stage three, the elaboration of approaches to conflict (Chairman's Summary, 1995b). The ARF process is concerned with identifying confidence-building measures that could be implemented (most of those proposed involve military transparency). To further the work of confidence building, an Inter-sessional Support Group on Confidence Building was established, with Indonesia and Japan as cochairs, as well as Inter-sessional Meetings on Cooperative Activities, with Singapore and Canada as co-chairs. As the ARF Concept Paper (ASEAN, 1995a) notes:

> There remains a residue of unresolved territorial and other disputes that could be sources of tension or conflict. If the ARF is to become, over time, a meaningful vehicle to enhance the peace and prosperity of the region, it will have to demonstrate that it is a relevant instrument to be used in the event that a crisis or problem emerges. The ARF meeting in Bangkok demonstrated this by taking a stand on the Korean issue at the very first meeting. This was a signal that the ARF is ready to address any challenge to the peace and security of the region.

At its 1995 meeting, the ministers expressed their positions on a number of the region's security problems. They raised concerns about the overlapping sovereignty claims in the South China Sea and urged all claimants to reaffirm their commitment to the ASEAN Declaration on the South China Sea and relevant international law, welcomed the U.S.-DPRK talks and urged the resumption of a dialogue between the ROK and the DPRK, expressed their support for Cambodia's efforts to achieve security and national stability, called upon countries planning to conduct further nuclear tests to bring an immediate end to such testing, and urged the conclusion of a Comprehensive Test Ban Treaty. As Singh (1994) summarizes:

> The establishment of the ARF was an extraordinary achievement, unprecedented in any part of the world. Unlike NATO and many other security organizations, the ARF has not been established in response to any threat or crisis. Rather, it has been established at a time when the Asia-Pacific region is enjoying an economic boom and its first real peace in well over half a century. *It was thus proactive rather than reactive; a signal exercise in preventive diplomacy* (emphasis added). It provides a vast region, one rapidly becoming the economic dynamo of the world, a means for discouraging armed conflict so that economic growth and cooperation can continue.

He notes further that the ARF should inhibit extreme action, strengthen impulses toward moderation and compromise, and lead to the adoption of confidence-building measures in the military arena. "Whether it will also lead to mechanisms to prevent or resolve conflicts is, at this stage, unknown" (Singh, 1994).

Track Two Activities within the Context of the ARF

One of the more innovative developments in the search for a wider security dialogue within ASEAN has been the involvement of research institutes and think tanks of the ARF countries in helping to define and shape the dialogue and in beginning the process of creating wider consensus. The Council for Security Cooperation in the Asian-Pacific Region (CSCAP), which was launched in Kuala Lumpur in June 1993, has been designated as the coordinator of this process. The result of a two-year project by ASEAN-ISIS, the Pacific Forum in Honolulu, the Seoul Forum for International Affairs, and the Japan Institute of International Affairs, CSCAP was created as an organization whose primary purpose was to hold meetings and workshops on topics of interest to ASEAN and thereby to offer policy analysis and proposals from a wider audience directly to the policymaking body. As the ARF Concept Paper (ASEAN, 1995a) explains:

Given the delicate nature of many of the subjects being considered by ARF, there is merit in moving the ARF process along two tracks. Track One activities will be carried out by ARF Governments. Track Two activities will be carried out by strategic institutes and non-governmental organizations in the region, such as ASEAN-ISIS and CSCAP. To be meaningful and relevant, the Track Two activities may focus, as much as possible, on the current concerns of the ARF. The synergy between the two tracks would contribute greatly to confidence-building measures in the region. Over time, these Track Two activities should result in the creation of a sense of community among participants of those activities.

The two-track approach was formally adopted at the second ARF meeting (Chairman's Report, 1995), where it was decided that the ARF should be apprised of all Track One and Track Two activities through the current chairman of the ARF, who will be the main link between Track One and Track Two.

The Track Two process has already begun to examine a variety of preventive diplomacy and conflict resolution mechanisms through workshops, which have included a seminar, "Building of Confidence and Trust in the Asia Pacific," held in Australia; a "Seminar on Peacekeeping: Challenges and Opportunities for the ASEAN Regional Forum," held in Brunei Darussalem; and a "Seminar on Preventive Diplomacy," held in the Republic of Korea.

Finally, it should be noted that the Indonesian and Canadian-sponsored series of workshops on the South China Sea, mentioned above, provide an excellent example of the kind of preventive diplomacy that the Track Two approach can offer.

Cooperation with the UN

In a 1992 declaration, the UN General Assembly recognized that the Treaty of Amity and Cooperation in Southeast Asia provided a strong foundation for regional cooperation. In 1993 and 1994, a series of three workshops (with funding from the Ford Foundation) were held for ASEAN and the UN in Thailand and Singapore to explore how the two organizations could cooperate more effectively (Viraphol and Pfenning, 1995). The UN Secretary-General has also begun periodic meetings with the ASEAN Permanent Representatives in New York to discuss issues of mutual concern. For ASEAN's part, it has been discussing how it can involve the UN in its work. One idea put forward is to invite the UN Secretary-General to send a representative as an observer to Post-Ministerial Conferences, Senior Officials' Meetings on Security Questions and the ASEAN Regional Forum, as well as to ASEAN's workshops (Viraphol and Pfenning, 1995). In an apparently contradictory move, however, a decision was made by the ASEAN-SOM at its January 1995 meeting *not* to seek observer status at the UN, since the "present arrangement has been found to be adequate to serve the needs of ASEAN" (Report of the Secretary General, 1995c).

Summary and Possible Next Steps

In brief, ASEAN is one of the smaller regional organizations, covering only nine of the Southeast Asian countries. Within the ASEAN context, *process* factors appear to be given at least equal weight to substance in terms of how conflict between states is to be prevented. The consensus norm (where voting is not permitted), the emphasis on dialogue and relationship building, as well as norms of self-restraint, are some of the factors that are credited with the general level of peace and prosperity in the region. With regard to internal problems within member states, a norm of silence prevails as a means of preserving interstate peace (as well as individual governments' freedom of action or inaction).

Unlike Europe, Latin America, and Africa, the Southeast Asian region has not placed democracy and human rights high on its agenda. Indeed, discussion of these issues is actively resisted by some governments, which do not see them as appropriate regional concerns (at least as advocated by the West). Camilleri (1994), however, calls for the development of an Asia-Pacific human rights regime, arguing that the regional institutionalization of human rights "respectful of cultural differences while at the same time wedded to universal norms" would do much to enhance good governance and prevent conflict within the region, as well as to reduce a source of conflict between regions.

With the dramatic changes in Southeast Asia, it now appears that ASEAN may eventually expand to include all countries of the region. Socializing and integrating new members, Vietnam, Laos, and Burma, into ASEAN and helping these countries to enhance prosperity and achieve a greater sense of security will, without doubt, dominate some of the organization's energy.

An equally great challenge will be to evolve the ARF into a stabilizing force for the entire Asia-Pacific region, and to build relationships throughout the region that will be able to change the many different security perceptions and fears, avoid a regional arms race, and construct the foundation for a lasting regional peace.

In conclusion, the ASEAN approach to the ARF is likely to evolve slowly, not moving "too fast for those who want to go slow and not too slow for those who want to go fast" (ASEAN, 1995c), first building consensus, relationships, and a sense of community before actively setting up formal mechanisms for conflict prevention. This, of course, is its own form of conflict prevention, but it remains to be seen whether the "ASEAN way" can work its magic before tensions can spiral out of control in some serious geopolitical crisis.

As Saravanamuttu (1994) concludes: "ASEAN's more progressive approach in the security-issue area with the launching of its two-track diplomacy augurs well for a movement away from state-centrism on questions of security. But even here, any security integration of a comprehensive sort, as exists in Europe, remains only a distant hope." While the new ARF is an important regional effort, the tensions in the entire Asia-Pacific region may overwhelm such a small organization, unless efforts to prevent conflict are strongly reinforced by the international community and its international organization—the United Nations.

11

The Developing Role of Nongovernmental Organizations

THE REMARKABLE GROWTH of nongovernmental organizations has received considerable comment in recent years, but the impact of this phenomenon on the international community and intergovernmental organizations is not yet fully understood (Weiss and Gordenker, 1996). Many authors extol the promise of this trend, including its potential for tapping into a broader base of ideas and approaches, its ability to bring serious problems to public awareness and exert pressure on governments to respond, its capacity for participation, and its ability to develop linkages across borders and issues. Others have warned, however, of the potential dangers inherent in multiple agendas and competition for limited funds from donors, the problem of coordinating so many diverse efforts, or the difficulties posed by the contaminating effects of self-serving and illegitimate organizations, which have arisen with little oversight or accountability.

Weiss and Gordenker (1996) note that assessing the role of NGOs requires a more systematic way to classify them, and they outline a framework of salient factors that should be considered, including organizational dimensions (such as geographic range, support base, personnel, financing, and legal relationships), governance dimensions (such as governmental contact and range of concerns), strategic dimensions (such as goal definition and tactical modes), and output dimensions. But, with more than 36,000 nongovernmental organizations working internationally, as well as the thousands of grassroots organizations springing up in various parts of the world (Boutros-Ghali, 1996), generalizations are, indeed, virtually impossible and assessment of impact still seems to require a case-by-case analysis.

At the international level, nongovernmental organizations have tended to work mainly in areas such as development, the environment, disarmament, humanitarian assistance, human rights, and the promotion of democracy. More recently, an increasing number of nongovernmental organizations have been active in the area of conflict prevention and resolution.

The older of these organizations often based their work on social or religious concerns (e.g., the Quakers). New organizations often have, however, developed in response to the study of peace and conflict resolution in academic and research settings (e.g., the Conflict Management Group, which derived as an offshoot of the Harvard Program on Negotiation). Even more recently, a few institutions have been created to provide independent policy analysis and advice to governments or intergovernmental organizations (e.g., the United States Institute of Peace).

To consider how these conflict resolution NGOs have begun to work with intergovernmental organizations, this chapter will focus narrowly on delineating some of the roles that they have begun to play. (See the *Human Rights Quarterly* for a sample of some of the human rights work by NGOs; see Diamond [1995] for a review of NGO work in the promotion of democracy.) Moreover, the activities of one NGO, the Carter Center, will be reviewed in greater detail, since it represents the blend of operative and structural approaches to conflict prevention outlined in this book, that is, offering assistance in dispute resolution, as well as in promoting good governance. The Carter Center was also chosen for more detailed examination because of its innovative use of "high-level councils"—an idea that will be proposed for inclusion in the structure of Regional Centers for Sustainable Peace.

The Role of Conflict Resolution NGOs in Promoting Sustainable Peace

Official diplomacy by governments or IGOs is normally referred to as Track One diplomacy. Track Two diplomacy refers to unofficial efforts at finding peace between conflicting parties. Ideally, the two tracks could and should complement one another. Although this is sometimes true, it has not always been the case. Increasingly, however, IGOs are recognizing the more effective NGOs and are beginning to find new ways to work with them.

NGOs as Third-Party Intermediaries

In some cases, NGOs have acted as the primary intermediary between conflicting parties, to try to help them arrive at a negotiated solution to their conflict. Probably the best-known recent example is the "Oslo Channel," as it has come to be called. In 1991, a series of "confidence building measures" and "academic contacts" were organized, leading to a joint Israeli-Palestinian Declaration of Principles. The declaration was initialed in Oslo on 19 August 1993 by the heads of the two negotiating teams in the presence of the then Foreign Minister Shimon Peres of Israel and Chairman Yasser Arafat. Since that time, the principles outlined in this document have formed the basis for the ongoing peace process in the Middle East.

This effort was jointly carried out by a nongovernmental research organization, the Norwegian Institute for Applied Social Science, and the Norwegian Ministry of Foreign Affairs (under two different foreign ministers, Thorvald Stoltenberg and Johan Jorgen Holst). A survey of living conditions in Gaza, the West Bank, and Arab Jerusalem provided the teams with the cover for its many visits to Tunis and Israel. As noted by Egeland (1995), "Our secret channel had several advantages. No news media, no time-consuming diplomatic protocol and no speeches for the 'gallery'. Negotiation teams could devote 90 percent of their time in Norway to actual peace negotiations. The many provocations and counter-provocations in the field never derailed the back-channel, as was the case with the front-channel in Washington."

The peace settlement in Mozambique offers another example. In this case, the Community of St. Egidio, a private voluntary Catholic organization with contacts in the Vatican, acted as a third-party intermediary with the support of a number of governments. In a fascinating account of the process, Hume (1994) details the series of relationships, contacts, aid, and assistance that members of the Community of St. Egidio established over a period of fourteen years with both parties in the conflict (Frelimo and Renamo), which ultimately led to its assumption of a central mediation role in 1990. After initial informal talks by Mozambican church members and leaders of neighboring governments stalled because the parties could not agree on the process (direct negotiations versus mediation) or the location for talks, the Community of St. Egidio in Rome hosted exploratory talks that subsequently turned into formal mediation, when the four "observers" (Italian parliamentarian, Mario Raffaelli; the Archbishop of Beira, Don Jaime Goncalves; the President of the Community of St. Egidio, Professor Andrea Riccardi; and a parish priest who was a member of the Community of St. Egidio, Don Matteo Zuppi) were asked to become "mediators." After two years of intermittent meetings, the talks, which had made significant progress, were expanded to include four observer governments and the United Nations, since implementation of the peace agreement was to involve the deployment of a UN peacekeeping force. After a summit of African leaders was called to confirm and reinforce the progress, the final agreement was signed a few months later (27 months after the first meeting) in a ceremony held in Rome. Of course, this was not the end of the mediation process—difficulties in implementation led to ongoing negotiation by the UN Special Representative, Aldo Ajello. Nonetheless, the peace that exists today in Mozambique and the country's progress toward a multiparty democracy came about as a result of an NGO's intermediary efforts, supported by the international community.

The Beagle Channel dispute between Argentina and Chile provides a third example. In 1978, Chile and Argentina were threatening war in this territorial dispute when the Vatican took on a role as mediator. The pope appointed a cardinal and team as intermediaries. Six years later, in a successful example of NGO preventive diplomacy, settlement was reached (Princen, 1987).

In the above situations, NGOs were seen as more acceptable or more suitable intermediaries than governments or even intergovernmental organizations. Nevertheless, in most such cases, governments and IGOs are active in the background, urging, encouraging, and supporting the work of the NGOs. Indeed, in many cases, it is the synergetic effect of these actors working together that produces the results.

NGOs and Problem-Solving Workshops

A related, though less direct, process of Track Two diplomacy, which has been called "problem-solving workshops" (among other names), was pioneered by a number of conflict researchers, such as John Burton at the Centre for the Analysis of Conflict at University College London, Herbert Kelman at Harvard University, and Leonard Doob at Yale University. This method was refined by others, such as Edward Azar at the University of Maryland, Ronald Fisher at the University of Saskatchewan, Christopher Mitchell at George Mason University, and Jay Rothman at the Hebrew University, to name a few.

In this approach, social scientists with expertise in group processes and conflict resolution bring together representatives of disputing parties (either officials in a nonofficial capacity or those who are influential and have an impact on the decision-making process) in a neutral setting (often an academic setting). Their role is not that of mediator, but that of facilitator. Workshops are designed to provide an analytical, problem-solving framework for assessing the conflict and exploring a wide range of potential solutions. The setting, norms, ground rules, agenda, and procedures are all designed to facilitate a different kind of interaction than the one that usually occurs between the parties and thus to change perceptions and produce new ideas. As Kelman (1990) notes, "Workshops have a dual purpose, which can be described as educational and political. They are designed to produce both changes in attitudes, perceptions and ideas for resolving the conflict among the individual participants in the workshop, and transfer these changes to the political arena—i.e., to the political debate and the decision making process within each community."

Although methodologies vary somewhat, problem-solving workshops have been constantly evaluated and refined over the years in many different settings and are now widely considered to be a useful tool, especially in prenegotiation. In describing the various ways that problem-solving workshops can contribute to prenegotiation, Kelman (1990) notes that

> workshops can help produce a more differentiated image of the enemy and help the participants discover potential negotiating partners on the other side. They can contribute to the development of cadres of individuals who have acquired experience in communicating with the other side and the conviction that such communication can be fruitful. They enable the parties to penetrate each other's perspective. They contribute to creating and maintaining a sense of possibility—a belief among the relevant parties that a peaceful solution is attainable and that negotiations toward such a solution are feasible. They contribute to the development of a deescalatory language, based on sensitivity to words that frighten and words that reassure the other party. They help in the identification of mutually reassuring actions and symbolic gestures, often in the form of acknowledgements—of the other's humanity, national identity, ties to the land, history of victimization, sense of injustice, genuine fears and conciliatory moves. They contribute to the development of shared visions of a desired future which help reduce the parties' fears of negotiations as a step into an unknown, dangerous realm. They may generate ideas about the shape of a positive-sum solution that meets the basic needs of both parties. They may also generate ideas about how to get from here to there—about a framework and set of principles for getting negotiations started. Ultimately, problem solving workshops contribute to a process of transformation of the relationship between enemies. (Kelman, 1990)

It should be noted that none of the practitioners of problem-solving workshops see them as a panacea. Most agree that the approach should be regarded as simply one tool for preparing the ground for more substantive negotiations. Workshops have now been used in such diverse situations as the Soviet-U.S. conflict, Lebanon, Sri Lanka, the Israeli-Palestinian conflict, Cyprus, the Falklands/Malvinas, and others. Although seldom used in preventing conflict, such workshops might provide an effective new tool for preventive diplomacy.

NGOs and the Development and Dissemination of Theory and Research

An important role, especially for academic and research-based organizations, has been the development and dissemination of conflict resolution knowledge and theory. If the international community is to better understand and manage conflict, the development and testing of adequate theory is vital, so that those who are tasked with helping to resolve conflicts can have a solid conceptual framework to guide them in this difficult task. A better understanding is needed of the causes of conflict, the interaction process that leads to conflict escalation and de-escalation, and the kinds of structural and substantive solutions that have been shown to be effective.

Considerable basic and applied research in this area is being carried out by scholars around the world in a number of settings. As well, a number of academic departments or institutes have developed to pursue this work and are making a significant contribution: for example, the Harvard Program on Negotiation, the Center for Conflict Analysis and Resolution at George Mason University, the Center for International Development and Conflict Management at the University of Maryland, the International Peace Research Institute in Norway, the Norwegian Institute of International Affairs, INCORE at the University of Ulster, and others.

As an indication of the growing knowledge, the literature in this field is burgeoning. The number of books on the subject has increased dramatically and several journals—the *Journal of Peace Research*, the *Negotiation Journal*, the *Journal of Conflict Resolution*, and *International Negotiation*—are devoted to the topic, while a number of other journals in international relations, international organizations, and the political and social sciences now regularly carry articles on this issue. In a parallel fashion, specialized organizations, such as the International Peace Research Association and the Academic Council for the United Nations provide an opportunity for peace research scholars to share and discuss their findings and the subsequent policy implications at their annual conferences. Professional organizations in the disciplines of political and social science also now regularly include such issues on their conference agendas, thus broadening the discourse, increasing its interdisciplinary basis, and attracting a wider audience of new scholars to this growing field.

Equally important is the sharing of knowledge and experience between academics and practitioners. As noted by Alexander George (1993), there has traditionally been a wide gap between those who study conflict prevention and resolution and those who practice it. While there is still a long way to go, efforts in both directions have begun to close the gap. The International Peace Academy has been a pioneer in bringing together scholars and practitioners from the UN through its many New York–based seminars and colloquia and through annual training programs, such as its Vienna Seminar. In 1993, the IPA joined the United Nations Institute for Training and Research to create the Fellowship Programme in Peacemaking and Preventive Diplomacy, designed to offer training and reflective learning to UN staff and diplomats in conflict prevention and resolution. This program not only draws upon the expertise of these two institutions, but also on that of the United Nations, regional organizations, and conflict prevention NGOs (such as the Conflict Management Group at Harvard, CDR Associates in Boulder, Colorado, as well as a wide range of academics and practitioners). The United States Institute of Peace, with its base in Washington, D.C., near the U.S. foreign policy establishment, has, through numerous conferences, seminars, and roundtables, been bringing together foreign policy practitioners and scholars to share information and jointly analyze problems. Also, USIP has an extensive publication program aimed at making the study of conflict prevention and resolution accessible and relevant to those in the policy-making field. Similar institutes are also evolving in a few other countries. Nonetheless, diplomats from most national governments and the secretariat staff of a number of regional organizations have had too little access to this kind of knowledge and experience and could profit from similar opportunities.

NGOs as Consultants to IGOs

Some regional organizations have also begun to use the consultative services of NGOs to assist them in devising more meaningful approaches to conflict analysis, prevention, and resolution. For example, the OSCE High Commissioner on National Minorities asked Harvard's Conflict Management Group to work with his staff in developing the methodology now used by his office. The OAU has relied on the International Peace Academy to organize "consultations," which draw upon a wide range of expert opinion within Africa, as a means of developing ideas and a consensus for its new Conflict Prevention, Management, and Resolution Mechanism. The Conflict Management Division of the OAU has been working closely with London-based International Alert, the African Center for the Constructive Resolution of Disputes (ACCORD) at the University of Durban in South Africa, and others to develop its early warning capacity. The Inter-American Dialogue has a close relationship with the OAS and holds seminars to help consider and develop OAS policy. The Council for Security Cooperation in the Asian Pacific Region (CSCAP) is working closely with ASEAN as part of its program to study issues of significance to its policy development, and to hold a series of seminars between scholars and officials from the foreign policy establishments of ASEAN and the ARF to provide them with expert guidance on developing policies and procedures at the Track One level. CSCAP's relationship with ASEAN and the ARF (as described in chapter 10) is an especially interesting one as it creates an official link between Track One policy and Track Two ideas and policy making. A similar link will be proposed for Regional Centers for Sustainable Peace.

NGOs as Evaluators of IGO Action

In recent years, a number of research institutions have begun to study case examples of efforts at conflict resolution in order to derive policy recommendations for improving practice. The International Peace Academy has conducted a number of research projects to examine UN peacemaking efforts and subsequently made recommendations. The United States Institute of Peace has studied not only UN efforts, but also other multilateral and bilateral attempts at conflict resolution.

A particularly remarkable study, in terms of its scope and partnership, is the 1996 report, "The International Response to Conflict and Genocide: Lessons from the Rwanda Experience." This five-volume work was put together within a few months by a consortium of 19 OECD-member bilateral donor agencies, the European Union, and the Development Assistance Commission Secretariat of the OECD; nine multilateral and UN agencies; the International Committee of the Red Cross and Red Crescent Movement; and five other international NGOs. Distinguished experts from Africa provided a critique of the report through participation in two panel discussions with the authors and selected resource persons.

Such activities, if carefully carried out, can offer valuable feedback to IGO secretariats and their member states. Of course, to be truly effective, it will be important for these efforts to be comprehensive and genuinely analytical, considering all the factors that impinge on decision making. Without a sincere effort that resonates with those involved, there is little likelihood that such lessons will be taken on board. Indeed, NGOs can quickly alienate IGOs, if they strike a critical tone that is not fully informed. Thus, constructive critiques that can bring about needed change are what is required.

NGO Involvement in IGO Peacebuilding Efforts

Some NGOs are beginning to work with IGOs at the grassroots level, attempting to bring about reconciliation between community groups. The OAS Program for the Prevention and Resolution of Local Conflicts provides an interesting example (although it involves postconflict peacebuilding). The program was established in response to a request from the government of Guatemala, which asked the OAS to assist in dealing with local conflicts that it anticipated between returning refugees and those who had stayed behind during the civil war. Disputes centered on property tenure and titles, as well as more generally on enemy-image perceptions, with the refugees being accused of "pro-guerrilla" sympathies, and those who had stayed at home being viewed as being "pro-army." Since the OAS did not have adequate capacity to carry out such a program, it asked selected NGOs for assistance. Three target locations were chosen, and OAS staff members in the field were asked to identify local people who were particularly well respected (such as priests). These individuals were then offered training in mediation by three NGOs (two international and one Guatemala-based group). When this stage of the program was over, participants formed local Units for the Prevention of Conflict. Each unit then convened the disputing parties, provided them with an elemental understanding of problem solving, and tried to assist them in finding acceptable solutions to their individual problems. This program has not yet been evaluated, but offers promise as a basis for future work in conflict prevention at the community level.

NGOs and Funding

Finally, funding organizations are crucial to the work of NGOs in the area of conflict prevention. Institutions such as Carnegie Corporation of New York, the Ford Foundation, the Hewlett Foundation, the McKnight Foundation, the MacArthur Foundation, the United States Institute of Peace, the Soros Foundation, the Pew Charitable Trust, the Rockefeller Foundation, and a number of others have played a vital role in this area. In some countries, governments provide the funding needed for NGOs to work in conflict prevention and resolution. Without their support, many efforts at developing both the theory and practice of conflict prevention and resolution would simply not materialize.

Other Opportunities for NGO-IGO Cooperation

The potential for complementary work between conflict prevention and resolution NGOs and IGOs has scarcely been touched. In this field, as in others, the quality of NGOs can vary dramatically, so careful case-by-case consideration is needed before entering into any kind of dialogue or cooperation. Nonetheless, a more thorough analysis of possible partnerships is warranted and could be very beneficial to the promotion of sustainable peace, as will be discussed in chapters 12 and 13.

The Carter Center

The Carter Center, founded in 1983 by President Jimmy Carter and his wife, Rosalynn, has, in a short time, become an impressive model of what an NGO can do in the areas of conflict resolution, good governance, and human rights. Although the center also offers a range of other programs in areas such as development and public health, only those directly related to sustainable peace will be discussed here.

The Conflict Resolution Program

The Carter Center's Conflict Resolution Program operates with six permanent staff members, who support the mediation efforts of the former president and Mrs. Carter. To provide overall direction and leadership for the program, the center has established the International Negotiation Network (INN), which is composed of world leaders and experts in conflict prevention and resolution from international organizations, universities, and foundations. Members of the network are brought together once a year, along with other experts, to identify and analyze situations that might require particular attention over the following year. Staff members in the conflict resolution program gather information and assess possibilities for effective intervention in these situations. Weekly bulletins, tracking events and highlighting wire and newspaper reports, are prepared and distributed to all center staff.

Most missions are undertaken by the former president and his wife on request from the parties. Before embarking on a mission, the staff considers the prospects for success and when involvement seems opportune, the center prepares briefing papers. Carter then consults with governments, as well as relevant intergovernmental and nongovernmental organizations, including the White House and the U.S. State Department, and the Secretary-General of the United Nations. The center sometimes flies in outside experts, such as special representatives of the UN Secretary-General, to brief Carter and his team.

Carter's missions have included talks with the late President Kim Il Sung in the Democratic People's Republic of Korea in 1994, where President Kim agreed to freeze his country's nuclear program in exchange for the resumption of dialogue with the United States. This breakthrough, in an otherwise stalled negotiation process, subsequently brought about an agreement that reduced the risk of horizontal nuclear proliferation. Another example was a mission undertaken by former President Carter (with Senator Sam Nunn and the former chairman of the Joint Chiefs of Staff, General Colin Powell) to negotiate the departure of Haiti's military leaders and the restoration to power of the rightfully elected president, Jean-Bertrand Aristide. This effort ended a three-year crisis and averted an invasion of the island. Carter and his team (along with many other NGOs and IGOs) have also been working in Rwanda and Burundi, in cooperation with African leaders.

Through these kinds of initiatives, the Carters have been able to fill a gap in the international system, especially where Track One efforts have broken down. Staff at the center sometimes call what Carter does "Track One and a Half Diplomacy," diplomacy at the highest level, provided in an unofficial capacity, but with official blessing. Of particular advantage to Jimmy Carter's initiatives is his status as a former president of the United States, but also important are his unique skill, enthusiasm, and experience as a mediator.

In establishing the International Negotiation Network, the hope was that council members would become involved in their own efforts at conflict prevention or resolution. This has occurred in a limited way, but the potential remains for the International Negotiation Network to be much more effective than it currently is.

In some cases center staff and the INN Core Group conduct projects without the direct involvement of Carter, such as their project on the Baltics, which is aimed at conflict prevention by bringing together different segments of Baltic society (including representatives from the highest level) to discuss issues related to the integration of the indigenous and Russian-speaking communities and to foster understanding of problems and the mutual sense of victimization. In addition, staff from the center take part in joint efforts with other institutions in carrying out problem-solving workshops. For example, the center, in conjunction with the Institute for Conflict Analysis and Resolution at George Mason University and the Institute for Multi-Track Diplomacy, conducted workshops for the various factions in Liberia.

The Human Rights Program

The Carter Center's human rights program operates at several levels. The first involves intervention by the Carters in cases of persecution, where a letter or a meeting with a government leader might make a difference to the fate of a human rights victim. Although the decision to act is made by the center staff, established human rights advocacy groups, such as Amnesty International or Human Rights Watch, regularly provide information. The center has had some success with these procedures.

A second aspect of the program involves technical assistance to governments in the establishment of human rights safeguards. For example, the center undertook a number of projects in Ethiopia, including a workshop for the country's new lay judges on the importance of maintaining the judiciary as an independent institution, police workshops on the incorporation of human rights protections into a police code of conduct, a workshop for education officials in charge of curriculum development, teacher training on human rights instruction in the schools, and a meeting to explore the feasibility of a human rights ombudsman for the country. Staff members have also worked with the government to include human rights protections in their new constitution.

The center also works to support United Nations efforts in human rights and put forward proposals to the World Conference on Human Rights, supporting the appointment of a UN High Commissioner for Human Rights. It was instrumental in setting up a support system for special rapporteurs at the UN Human Rights Center, providing interns from the Notre Dame Graduate Program. The Carter-Menil Human Rights Foundation regularly awards a prize of $100,000 to individuals or organizations for outstanding efforts in human rights. The Institute for Applied Social Science in Oslo was one of the recipients for its "Oslo Channel" to peace in the Middle East.

To assist its work, the center has recently established the high-level Human Rights Council, whose task will be to advance and protect human rights worldwide and to foster collaboration between world leaders and nongovernmental, international, and national organizations. The council has defined the following goals for itself:

- to bolster the influence of human rights in United Nations activities
- to find ways to assist understaffed UN offices in collecting and disseminating information on human rights violations
- to promote opportunities for domestic NGOs to have greater input to UN initiatives, including minimum standards of NGO participation in conferences and commissions
- to support and strengthen the efforts of the post of UN High Commissioner for Human Rights
- to stimulate greater dialogue between private sector businesses and human rights organizations
- to seek ways to bolster an early warning system for human rights abuse, preventing incipient situations from deteriorating into large-scale catastrophes

Electoral Assistance and Democratization

Electoral assistance and democratization are themes that run through several of the center's programs, including the Latin American and Caribbean Program, the African Governance Program, and the Commission on Radio and Television Policy.

The Latin American and Caribbean Program

This program specializes in inter-American relations and U.S. policy toward the region. One of its main activities has been electoral monitoring and mediation for countries in transition to democracy, such as Nicaragua,

Haiti, Panama, Guyana, Paraguay, and Mexico. Because of the center's independence, its judgment on the fairness of an electoral process is seen as free of governmental influence and, therefore, has been generally accepted. When irregularities are found, the Carter team can, as it did in Panama, declare fraud and propose action to rectify the situation.

To assist and carry out its work, the center has set up the Council of Freely Elected Heads of Government, composed primarily of former presidents and prime ministers. The presence of such high-level and eminent persons on an electoral team has had the benefit of ensuring that its actions are taken seriously by the government involved and has guaranteed immediate access to those at the top. In some cases, Carter has led the delegation. In Nicaragua, for example, Carter led a team, which included the prime minister of Belize, seven former presidents, and a bipartisan group of twelve members of the U.S. Congress. The high-level representation allowed the team a unique ability to resolve problems by dealing directly with the principal actors—President Ortega and Mrs. Chamorro (Pastor, 1990).

The center's activities go beyond pure electoral monitoring to a more active role in "electoral mediation," a service not typically offered by IGOs. This process involves helping the parties to overcome disagreements about the electoral process and to remain engaged in a constructive dialogue, so that they are willing to accept the outcome of the election, to cooperate in managing the transition (if the election results require it), and to negotiate with one another on issues needing coordination. In order to preserve its impartiality, the center makes certain that it is invited by all main parties to become involved—often orchestrating simultaneous invitations. In short, Carter Center staff and council members practice a kind of intervention that transcends electoral observation. The center is beginning to move into the area of electoral consolidation and is considering whether to establish a unit that would specialize in democratization.

The African Governance Program

The goal of this program is to promote democracy in Sub-Saharan Africa by monitoring multiparty elections and working with governments to build solid institutional and social foundations for emerging democracies. An international observer team was led by Carter to monitor registration and voting processes and to verify the first free and fair multiparty elections in Zambia. The center subsequently convened a workshop in conjunction with the Zambian Election Monitoring Coordinating Committee on the role of civil society in a plural democracy, from which a Zambian organization emerged to oversee the new democratic system, monitor future elections, and promote human rights and civil liberties. The program has also been involved in electoral monitoring and postelection projects to consolidate democracy in Ghana. It has also provided technical assistance to Liberian civic groups and the country's Electoral Commission, in the run-up to elections in that country.

Commission on Radio and Television Policy

In 1990, the Commission on Radio and Television Policy was established by the Carter Center. Composed of prominent policymakers and media specialists from the United States and the newly independent states of the former Soviet Union, its task is to examine the social, political, and economic impact of television and radio. Among other activities, the commission is engaged in "developing models of fair coverage of elections and of ethnic minorities for use by television stations and governmental policy-makers in countries where new press freedoms are being introduced." It has published material on elections and minorities and translated it into a number of languages. As well, the commission is drafting a Charter of Media Independence.

Summary and Possible Next Steps

The Carter Center is an interesting example of innovation in conflict prevention and the promotion of good governance. Its multilayered, multidimensional approach is somewhat unique for NGOs. Of particular interest, the center has developed a novel modus operandi to enhance its outcomes and expand its work. For each of its programs, it has established a group of high-level and knowledgeable individuals to become involved in both designing and carrying out the work of the center, with the support and guidance of the center staff. This methodology not only extends its reach, but also increases the chances that the center can sustain its influence with governments at the highest level after the Carters have retired.

Duplicating the Carter Center might, however, be another matter. Carter's charismatic and visionary leadership was essential to the center's establishment. While there are other world leaders with vision and skill, they would find it more difficult to secure the kind of financial resources that Carter has been able to attract, since no other country has the private funding resources of the United States. For example, the Arias Foundation of Costa Rica, while active in a number of very useful ways, is simply unable to achieve a funding base comparable to that of the Carter Center. The status of Carter, as a former president of the only remaining superpower, also lends a certain leverage and standing to his interventions, which is difficult to replicate. The head of the now-dormant African Leadership

Forum, the former Nigerian president, General Olusegun Obasanjo (now in prison), provides a sobering reminder that status as a former national leader does not, in itself, guarantee the success of an NGO.

Nonetheless, the potential for former leaders to create other models certainly exists. The South Center, which is an outcome of the South Commission, which former President Julius Nyerere of Tanzania championed and which is funded by a consortium of nonaligned countries, suggests that other types of initiatives by leaders or former leaders might present viable new options that can augment the other types of NGOs described above.

Part Three

Organizing for Sustainable Peace

12

Sharing Responsibility in Conflict Prevention

As DISCUSSED THROUGHOUT this book, the shadow cast by the cold war was so profound that when, suddenly, it was no longer there, every region of the world was faced with a dramatic shift in its view of its security problematique. Until that time, the major threat to states was perceived to be "external," and even when internal problems arose, they were frequently blamed on external agents (sometimes, of course, as a matter of political expediency). Security was defined in terms of "state security," and, in this context, intrastate problems tended to be seen as having less to do with real grievances or a state's own policies and shortcomings, than with "communist," "capitalist," or "extremist" influence and support. In fact, this view was not entirely without foundation, since the superpower rivalry did, indeed, permeate and contaminate conflict nearly everywhere.

Nonetheless, the prevailing view so neglected the "root causes" of problems that, when the ideological struggle was over, there was a real perplexity as to why so many conflicts continued, and why so many new ones were cropping up. Some could still be blamed on the fallout of the cold war, which had set in motion trends that polarized factions, entrenched the dynamics of escalation and created an excess of arms. Others, however, were less simple to explain. Regional organizations and the United Nations had to take a much closer look at the new situation, to redefine the underlying causes of conflict. Moreover, without the cold war as the overarching attribution for their inability to be effective, these organizations had to search for new ways to meet the objectives that they had set for themselves when they were founded. This task, however, entailed a number of problems. Not only did regional organizations and the UN have to reappraise the causes of conflict and the mechanisms they had created to deal with it, but also the legal mandate and normative agreement upon which they were established was based on the premise that the problems they would be facing would be *interstate*. Even more problematic, in the process of establishing rules for controlling interstate conflict, member states had created a number of provisions in their charters that legally prohibited "interference" in their internal affairs. Now, however, this became a major stumbling block to their efforts to respond to the new challenges.

Finding a New Definition for Conflict Prevention

In looking for a new, more holistic understanding of the problem of conflict, two concepts have been particularly useful—the first is the notion of "human security" as a means for addressing basic "human needs" and as a way for governments to increase "state security." This concept thus provides a bridge between the two Charter concepts of "we the peoples" and state sovereignty, reminding governments that their *raison d'être* is to work to achieve human security for all of their people.

Indeed, member states of the United Nations have worked hard to find a definition of human security that they could agree upon and regard as "universal." They have accomplished this through the Universal Declaration of Human Rights, the International Covenant on Civil and Political Rights, the International Covenant on Economic, Social and Cultural Rights, and the more than 70 other human rights declarations that have been the result of this cooperative labor. Together, these instruments provide a precise definition of human security and prescribe the agenda to which governments are obliged to aspire.

The second useful concept that has received more attention than ever before is the linkage between human rights, democracy, development, and peace that was articulated by Boutros Boutros-Ghali in *An Agenda for Democratization* (1996), *An Agenda for Development* (1994), and *Building Peace and Democracy* (1994). Simply stated, this linkage suggests that human needs can be best satisfied by good governance based on human rights. Good governance, in turn, fosters both peace and development.

Indeed, governance based on human rights necessarily implies a participatory democratic process, since both the Universal Declaration of Human Rights and the International Covenant on Civil and Political Rights describe the process from which the authority of governments should derive as follows: *"The will of the people shall be the basis of the authority of governments; this will shall be expressed by periodic and genuine elections, which shall be by universal and equal suffrage and shall be held by secret vote or by the equivalent free voting procedures"* (Article 21, Universal Declaration of Human Rights, 1948; emphasis added). Thus, participation in the democratic process is unequivocally declared as a universal and fundamental human right.

The relationship between participatory governance and peace is supported by the data discussed earlier. Within states, democracy is the most likely form of governance to facilitate peace since it provides a self-correcting system of dispute settlement that allows negotiations between constituents and leaders (e.g., via the ballot box), and forums for ongoing negotiations between different interest groups within the society (e.g., through representative parliaments). As Boutros-Ghali notes, "Democracy within States thus fosters the evolution of the social contract upon which lasting peace can be built. In this way, a culture of democracy is fundamentally a culture of peace."

The data also support a positive relationship between democracy, and peace between states. Recent studies have gone beyond the earlier work, which showed that democracies are less likely to wage war against one another, to demonstrate that democracies are also *less likely to be the targets of military intervention* by either other democracies *or* nondemocracies (Hermann and Kegley, 1996). Apparently this is due to the fact that democracies convey the expectation that they value negotiation, mediation, compromise, and consensus over the use of force. Hermann and Kegley conclude simply that "democracy served as a shield from military intervention by another state."

The relationship between development and democracy has been summarized in *An Agenda for Democratization* (1996) as follows:

> By providing legitimacy for government and encouraging peoples' participation in decision-making on the issues that affect their lives, democratic processes contribute to the effectiveness of State policies and development strategies. Democratic institutions and practices foster the governmental accountability and transparency necessary to deter national and transnational crime and corruption and encourage increased responsiveness to popular concerns. In development, they increase the likelihood that State goals reflect broad societal concerns and that government is sensitive to the societal and environmental costs of its development policies.

As discussed earlier, transitions to democracy can be difficult, especially when a culture of democracy is nonexistent or weak, and if not managed appropriately can even cause conflict. Moreover, democracy does not lead automatically to development, but simply provides conditions that are conducive to it. Thus, the twin goals of sustainable peace and sustainable development both need to be supported by the international community if they are to have any hope of being realized. Governance based on the goal of human security is needed at all levels—locally, nationally, regionally, and internationally. Mechanisms are needed to provide assistance in promoting long-term structural change, as well as short-term problem solving. Most important of all will be the bridge between these two goals. Efforts aimed at solving short-term problems will need to be linked to the establishment of long-term structures that will eventually make assistance less necessary, as actors develop the necessary processes and means to resolve their own problems.

Finding a New Mandate for Conflict Prevention

Because its objective has always been the promotion of democracy and human rights within its member states, the Council of Europe (as discussed in chapter 6) is the only intergovernmental organization reviewed in this book that has not had to face the problem of its mandate being out of step with current challenges. It is little wonder, therefore, that it is the most advanced in its development of the methodology of assistance in promoting good governance.

Over the past few years, however, most other intergovernmental organizations have been struggling with the sovereignty issue and the barrier that this has caused to effective prevention. As Boutros-Ghali (1992) states in his oft-quoted passage from *An Agenda for Peace*, "The time of absolute and exclusive sovereignty . . . has passed; its theory was never matched by reality. It is the task of leaders of states today to understand this and to find a balance between the needs of good internal governance and the requirements of an ever more interdependent world."

Interestingly, the first forays against the concept of absolute sovereignty were the development of human rights reporting, monitoring, and enforcement. In the Council of Europe, the OAS, the UN, and the OAU, Special Rapporteurs or Commissions on Human Rights (and Courts of Human Rights, in the case of the COE and OAS) were able to carry out on-site visits, report on their findings to the international community, and require governments to change their practices and/or make restitution for grievances.

As discussed in chapter 8, the OAS was the first regional organization to include democracy as part of the organization's mandate. Its charter was already unique in stating that one of its aims was "to promote and consolidate representative democracy." In 1985, it added to the charter the statement, "Representative democracy is an indispensable condition for the stability of peace and development in the region." In 1991, the Santiago Commitment declared that member states had an "inescapable commitment" to democracy. To help states fulfill this commitment, the Unit for the Promotion of Democracy was established to provide election monitoring and assistance. Later, its mandate was extended to include the provision of assistance in democratic institution building. Also in 1991, Resolution 1080 was passed, giving the OAS the authority to become involved in cases where a coup or other interruption of the legitimately elected government had occurred. The Protocol of Managua also calls on member states to "modernize domestic administrative and political structures and systems; improve public administration; protect minorities and political opposition groups; achieve national reconciliation and consolidate a democratic culture; meet basic needs; safeguard human rights and ensure the subordination of armed forces to legitimately constituted civilian authority." This is a rather dramatic change for a regional organization whose charter is replete with nonintervention clauses.

The OSCE has made similar moves. In 1991, its right to be involved in certain internal matters was explicitly declared in the preamble to the Moscow Document, where participating states agreed that "commitments undertaken in the human dimension of the CSCE are matters of direct and legitimate concern to all participating states and do not belong to the internal affairs of the states concerned." To help implement this policy, the organization established a High Commissioner on National Minorities to work with governments to find solutions to minority problems, as outlined in chapter 7. Long-term missions were also created to further this work and to assist governments in bringing their laws, regulations, and practices into line with their OSCE commitments. Its Office for Free Elections was set up to provide electoral assistance and developed quickly into the Office for Democratic Institutions and Human Rights, which offers a wide range of assistance in democratic consolidation. The OSCE Permanent Council meets weekly to discuss developments and to take action to assist its members with problems, and the Budapest Document authorized it to assume a greater role in dialogue on the human dimension and to take action "in case of non-implementation."

The 1990 OAU Declaration of the Assembly of Heads of State and Government of the Organization of African Unity on the Political and Socio-Economic Situation in Africa and the Fundamental Changes Taking Place in the World noted that:

> We are fully aware that in order to facilitate this process of socio-economic transformation and integration, it is necessary to promote popular participation of our peoples in the processes of government and development. A political environment which guarantees human rights and the observance of the rule of law would assure high standards of probity and accountability particularly on the part of those who hold public office. . . . We accordingly recommit ourselves to the further democratization of our societies and to the

consolidation of democratic institutions in our countries. We reaffirm the right of our countries to determine, in all sovereignty, their system of democracy on the basis of their socio-cultural values, taking into account the realities of each of our countries and the necessity to ensure development and satisfy the basic needs of our peoples. We therefore assert that democracy and development should go together and should be mutually reinforcing.

The OAU has since set up the Unit for Elections, and the Mechanism for Conflict Prevention, Management, and Resolution. Further, the secretary-general of the OAU has been given greater powers for carrying out preventive diplomacy and peacemaking, and although not explicitly stated, there seems to be an understanding that this could extend to intrastate problems.

As mentioned in chapter 10, a security agenda is relatively new to ASEAN, which, characteristically, is approaching the issue in a carefully considered, step-by-step manner. Nonetheless, ideas for implementing preventive diplomacy are being actively discussed, especially in its Track Two process.

The United Nations has made considerable progress in the setting of universal standards for human rights, as well as establishing a set of human rights machinery. Although far from perfect, instrumentalities such as the UN Commission on Human Rights, the Sub-Commission on the Prevention of Discrimination and the Protection of Minorities, the Human Rights Committee, the Committee on Economic, Social, and Cultural Rights, and the many other commissions, working groups, special rapporteurs, and the Center for Human Rights have kept human rights constantly at the top of the UN agenda for many years, thus requiring governments to respond to this agenda. The creation of the post of UN High Commissioner for Human Rights expanded authority in this area, since the High Commissioner can report directly to the Security Council. Thus, human rights are linked to security issues more directly than ever before.

But in spite of these promising signs, there has remained a reluctance on the part of some states to see the UN become involved in preventive diplomacy. In short, Article 2(7) continues to block agreement on the full development of preventive diplomacy.

The Security Council's involvement in intrastate problems has occurred largely through individual case decisions (usually in extreme crisis situations) rather than through formal resolutions or changes to its mandate or Charter. The Security Council has in recent years become involved in a number of decisions, including the authorization of large-scale peacekeeping operations related to intrastate conflict (although often only after long discussion and tortuous rationales).

It is noteworthy, however, that there has been less resistance to the idea of assistance in the development of good governance. The development of the UN Center for Human Rights Advisory Services, Technical Assistance, and Information Branch, and of the Division of Electoral Assistance mark a movement in the direction of involvement in internal affairs through advisory and technical assistance. This kind of assistance, with particular reference to human rights, was enthusiastically called for at the 1993 Vienna Conference on Human Rights. Of course, assistance is provided upon the request of a member state.

In summary, in Europe, the Americas, and Africa, states are becoming (albeit guardedly) more open to the idea that regional organizations have a role to play in helping to resolve internal problems, as well as in assisting with the development of processes that are designed for conflict prevention, with the proviso, of course, that government consent is fundamental. The fact that this remains a more sensitive issue in the United Nations is due not only to the greater diversity among member states, but also to the Security Council's wide range of coercive powers, and the perennial concern over Great Power domination. Therefore, in finding a new mandate, regional organizations may have an advantage over the UN. In short, their members may be more willing to allow their regional organization the authority to assist them in preventing intrastate conflict.

Finding a New Methodology for Conflict Prevention

Over the last few years, there has been a growing consensus that the international community should assume greater responsibility for assisting states that have serious problems that they cannot solve on their own. Most agree that simply following developments and admonishing governments that are having difficulties is insufficient. As noted by Zaagman (1995b), "a more positive commitment is needed." Moreover, Boutros-Ghali in *An Agenda for Democratization* (1996) points out the very real peril of not assisting states when "there is also a danger that strengthening civil society without also addressing state capacity may undermine governability or overwhelm the state."

Several organizations have taken steps to meet this challenge. The OAU, OAS, and OSCE have given their leadership additional authority and encouragement to become involved in preventive diplomacy by enhancing the role of their secretaries-general (or in the case of the OSCE, the chairman-in-office) and by establishing decision-making forums (the Central Organ of the OAU, the permanent councils of the OSCE and OAS), which meet on a frequent basis to discuss emerging problems and recommend action. The UN has improved its tracking of problems; the Secretary-General has made wider use of special representatives (especially for peacemaking); and a High Commissioner for Human Rights has been appointed. ASEAN has created a new, and more widely based, regional forum for dialogue, which plans to utilize confidence building and preventive diplomacy to achieve regional peace between states. The OSCE has also set up the Court of Conciliation and Arbitration to assist its members with dispute resolution.

Tables 12.1 to 12.3 provide an overview of both old and new mechanisms that exist in the international organizations examined here with regard to the peaceful settlement of disputes, the promotion of democracy, and the protection of human rights. As described in chapters 5 to 10 and as can be seen in these tables, there is considerable variability between them. As a consequence, IGOs could learn much from one another and a more strategic partnership between them could benefit all regions.

In addition to strengthening their traditional methodologies, regional organizations and the UN have been exploring a series of new approaches. As reviewed briefly in chapter 2, these include regional and international socialization, assistance, and problem solving, each of which will be discussed more fully below.

Socialization

One of the most powerful processes in terms of effecting change is that of socialization by peers. The democratization of Eastern and Central Europe, Latin America, and Africa can be attributed largely to regional and international socialization. Observation (by individuals and governments) of models of governance that appear to be more successful than their own, makes them want to reform their own structures, in the hope that reform will bring them the same advantages.

The seeds for this latest wave of democratization were laid not only by the relatively successful economic and political track record of many democracies around the world, but also by attempts to develop a common set of standards for human rights, and by subsequent efforts to monitor and implement them. Human rights standards not only set forth a prescription for democracy, but also highlighted the failings of authoritarian regimes. Thus, as discussed in chapter 7, the enjoyment of human rights in some countries has led to a desire for the same entitlements elsewhere. Moreover, when states are successful in making the transition to democracy and an improved economy with or without assistance from the international community, this also provides a powerful pull for peoples and governments elsewhere.

A second socialization process has evolved in several regional organizations, where states with a common agenda exert a pull on the other states

TABLE 12.1 Mechanisms for the Peaceful Settlement of Disputes within the Intergovernmental Organizations Reviewed in This Book

	Legal Instruments for Peaceful Settlement of Disputes	Decision-making Political Forum which Monitors Conflict and Can Act	Consensual Approach to Decision Making in Political Forums	Secretariat Systematically Monitors Potential Problems	Use of Good Offices by the Political Leadership of the Organization	Use of Good Offices by the Secretary-General	Use of Personal or Special Representatives	Use of Committees of "Wise Men"	Use of High Commissioner on National Minorities	Use of Short-term Missions (fact-finding and mediation)	Use of Long-term Missions (preventive diplomacy and peace-making)	Use of Conference Diplomacy	Emergency Provisions for Dispute Settlement	Availability of Judicial or Quasi-Judicial Mechanism for Dispute Settlement	Possibility of Imposing Coercive Sanctions
UN	X	X		X	X	X	X			X		X	X	X (ICJ)	X
COE															
OSCE	X	X	X		X	X	X	X (Ad Hoc Steering Committees)	X	X	X		X	X (Court of Conciliation and Arbitration)	
OAS	X	X		(plans to develop the capacity)	X	X	X			X					X
OAU	X	X			X	X	X	X (Ad Hoc Committees of the Assembly)		X			X	(Commission of Reconciliation, Conciliation and Arbitration were never used)	X
ASEAN	X		X					(High Council has never been used)				X			

TABLE 12.2 Mechanisms for the Promotion of Democracy within the Intergovernmental Organizations Reviewed in This Book

	Electoral Monitoring and Assistance	Technical or Advisory Assistance (Democratic institution building)	Active Liaison with NGOs	Emergency Defense of Democracy Mechanisms
UN	X		X	
COE	X	X	X	
OSCE	X	X	(beginning)	X
OAS	X	X	X	X
OAU	X		X	
ASEAN			X	

TABLE 12.3 Mechanisms for the Protection of Human Rights within the Intergovernmental Organizations Reviewed in This Book

	General Human Rights Instruments	Minority or Indigeneous Human Rights Instruments	Availability of Technical and Advisory Assistance in Human Rights	General Monitoring Mechanisms for Implementation of Human Rights	Use of Special Human Rights Rapporteurs	High Commissioner for Human Rights	Commission on Human Rights (quasi-judicial)	Court of Human Rights (judicial)	Emergency Human Rights Mechanism
UN	X	X (declaration)	X	X (treaty based)	X	X	X (political)		X (High Commissioner)
COE	X	X	X	X			X (expert)	X	
OSCE	X	X	X						X
OAS	X	X (draft convention)	X		X		X (expert)	X	
OAU	X						X (expert)		
ASEAN									

in the region. This has been particularly strong when accompanied by an expectation of related economic or political advantages. The pull toward democratization in Eastern Europe is an example of this phenomenon.

A third socialization process takes place through the political bodies of IGOs (such as the OSCE and OAS Permanent Councils or the OAU Central Organ), which meet frequently to discuss problems, offer guidance, and apply pressure on their members to comply with the obligations that they have jointly undertaken. This process provides ongoing feedback, which helps governments conform to the group's norms.

Assistance

A complementary approach has been the provision of expert advice and assistance to governments in the use of democratic processes to find structural solutions to their problems. As noted in *An Agenda for Democratization*, democratization offers a new area for technical assistance that was not possible during the political climate of the cold war. But since then, member states have been reorienting their requests for technical assistance to areas relevant to democratization. The United Nations and regional organizations (along with NGOs) were quick to respond and began to offer their services in observing elections and assisting in the electoral process. The UN established the small Division of Electoral Assistance; the OAS set up its Unit for the Promotion of Democracy; the OSCE established its Office for Free Elections; and the OAU created the Unit for Elections.

The idea of offering broader forms of advisory and technical assistance followed quickly on the heels of the success of electoral assistance. The UN Center for Human Rights set up its Advisory Services, Technical Assistance, and Information Branch. The Council of Europe and the OSCE established special programs for Eastern and Central Europe (and Central Asia in the case of the OSCE). These programs offered legal advice and many kinds of training to those sectors of the society that are important to the establishment and maintenance of a democratic process. The OAS Unit for the Promotion of Democracy now plans to carry out a similar (although more targeted) program to assist its members with the building of democratic institutions.

The attractiveness of this approach has been that it is elective (although the political bodies of some organizations encourage states to make use of such services—the UN Commission on Human Rights and the OSCE Permanent Council, for example, have both adopted this practice). Because advisory and technical assistance programs are low key and noncoercive, and because they tend to add to a country's "capacity," they have been welcomed by established democracies, emerging democracies, and nondemocratic states alike. At the same time, they assist in building a "culture of democracy" by encouraging tolerance and moderation, by strengthening beliefs about the rights and dignity of all citizens, and by helping to enshrine fair practices and laws. Some of these programs also attempt to facilitate the development and strengthening of NGOs, which helps to ensure that the process of change will be self-sustaining. Although this approach is still new, it offers considerable promise since it provides an *acceptable basis for an international organization to become involved in conflict prevention within a country.*

It is worthy of note that both the OSCE High Commissioner on National Minorities and long-term preventive diplomacy missions effectively offer advisory and technical assistance to help participating states find democratic solutions to their ethnic and minority problems. By making specific recommendations regarding legislation, regulation, and practice, and by offering support for their implementation, they provide governments with clear options, which they are free to reject, but which they usually accept. As discussed earlier, the High Commissioner and long-term missions also attempt to establish an ongoing forum for dialogue, thereby providing a democratic process by which future grievances can be managed and addressed. This has proven to be an acceptable way of approaching intrastate disputes, which appears to satisfy both governments and minority groups and leads to satisfactory solutions.

A Problem-Solving Methodology

Underpinning the strategies outlined above is a problem-solving approach, which seeks to reconcile parties' legitimate interests through innovative solutions. Building systems for addressing grievances before they can escalate into conflict is, indeed, quintessential to sustainable peace.

Of the three types of approaches to disputes that have been identified by scholars—power-based, rights-based, and interest-based (referred to here as problem solving)—sustainable peace depends on the latter two: the establishment of the rule of law, and the institutionalization of problem solving (to replace power-based methods). Since, in any dispute, the interaction between the disputing parties determines what processes will be used, both governments and disaffected groups will need to learn how to use a problem-solving approach. In chapter 3, it was noted that in democratic societies, most grievances are expressed initially through nonviolent protest, leaving ample time for problem solving. Disputes tend to escalate into violent protest when nonviolent protest is either ignored or suppressed. Thus, the methodology for problem solving will need to be institutionalized as a normative practice that can replace the power-based approach and act early in a dispute as a support to the rule of law.

A Noncoercive Approach

What is needed is a set of strategies that will be effective in reducing the level of conflict and which states will accept because they see it as in their own best interest to do so. It is well known that both positive influence strategies (so-called carrots) and negative influence strategies (so-called sticks) can influence behavior. Considerable work at the theoretical level, however, has shown that obligations that are accepted voluntarily are more likely to be adhered to and integrated into long-term practice. On the other hand, coercive attempts at influence have been shown to sometimes cause "reactance," in which attempts at influence are resisted (even when it is irrational to do so), in an effort to maintain freedom of action and control. In the peace and security field, the international community has, on the whole (through both its bilateral and multilateral efforts), tended to place a greater emphasis on coercive influence strategies (often because it has waited too long to address a problem). Indeed, this may be a contributing factor to many of its failures.

It is important to note, however, that positive influence strategies can also create "reactance" (although usually in a less-severe form), if they imply a loss of freedom of action (as, for example, when the imposition of another party's agenda is perceived to be compelled through "bribery"). Thus, the blunt use of "carrots" with explicit "conditionalities" is likely to be less effective than a more nuanced approach that relies on socialization or assistance. Ultimately, the greatest success will be achieved by demonstrating to governments the advantages of providing human security and good governance for their people. These goals can be achieved through technical, advisory, and economic assistance.

It is also essential that new methodologies for sustainable peace through the promotion of good governance not be a neocolonial imposition of "Western democracy" or the "Western system" on the rest of the world. Rather, it should be a means of empowerment for local peoples and local ideas. Good governance, therefore, must be tailored to local cultural norms and practices, as well as to local issues.

With this in mind, the UN Secretary-General's Special Representative to Mozambique, Aldo Ajello, consulted with local cultural anthropologists before considering how to make democratic elections compatible with the cultural traditions of the area. This is not to say that information on how systems work elsewhere is not an important tool for democracy building. Ajello (who is a former Italian parliamentarian) also spent many hours discussing democratic and parliamentary practices with the leading members of Renamo, who were unfamiliar with how democracies worked. In brief, what is needed is information about how to establish a fair process; but the agenda that process addresses and the way it will evolve in a given context must be decided by the local and regional community.

Boutros-Ghali (1996) provides a cogent argument for assisting democratic processes as they develop, but not imposing democratization:

> While democratization is a new force in world affairs, and while democracy can and should be assimilated by all cultures and traditions, it is not for the United Nations to offer a model of democratization or democracy or to promote democracy in a specific case. Indeed, to do so could be counterproductive to the process of democratization which, in order to take root and to flourish, must derive from the society itself. Each society must be able to choose the form, pace and character of its democratization process. Imposition of foreign models not only contravenes the Charter principle of nonintervention in internal affairs, it may also generate resentment among both the Government and the public, which may in turn feed internal forces inimical to democratization and to the idea of democracy.

The development of an assistance approach will not, of course, replace the need to monitor and enforce human rights or the collective security approaches needed to influence states that do not live up to international law and do not respond to a positive socialization process. Indeed, the two can work most effectively together when the modalities for implementing the two approaches are kept *separate* (although coordinated) as described by Chigas and her colleagues in the chapter on the OSCE. This provides a wider-ranging and ultimately more powerful set of options from which the international community and governments can choose. If governments wish to avoid the international community's more punitive censure, they can choose to avail themselves of its more positive assistance—to live up to the international commitments they have made for the peaceful settlement of disputes and for observance of human rights in becoming part of the United Nations.

But What about "Bad Guys"?

The bottom line in the thinking of many is the question of what to do about the "bad guys." The first stumbling block often occurs, however, in agreeing on *who* the "bad guys" are. Opinions within the international community can and do vary, sometimes making it difficult for member states to decide what should be done and to whom. Partisan perceptions often lead to a part of the international or regional community seeing one group as in the right and the other in the wrong, whereas another part may construe the situation differently. As has often been said, one person's "guerilla" is another's "freedom fighter."

Moreover, the violent confrontations that occur during the powerful dynamics of conflict escalation often result in all sides committing atrocities in their fight to achieve their interests, thereby blurring the distinction, since in the process, all become "bad guys." Nevertheless, there are objective criteria for determining universally condemned action, such as war crimes and crimes against humanity, and the development of the Permanent International Criminal Court proposed by the International Law Commission will be a welcome addition to the UN's repertoire in this regard, in terms of both deterrence and in helping to identify and prosecute those who are responsible (in a legal rather than political manner), when such crimes do occur. Beyond this, however, the international system must be equipped with a full repertoire of responses for dealing with "political entrepreneurs."

But as argued earlier, the first line of defense against those who would advocate or promulgate violence is a system for preventing the conditions that give rise to their ability to come to power in the first place. Since extremists tend to gain credibility in situations of unresolved conflict, it is precisely the kind of cooperative security approaches advocated here that should be most effective at discouraging the emergence of bad leadership. Moreover, even in cases where the "bad guys" do gain a foothold, such arrangements should help to dampen or head off extremist policies or actions.

When the "bad guys" do succeed in gaining power and in inciting their followers to violence, thus creating a threat to international peace and security, a breach of the peace, or an act of aggression, the power-based approaches of collective security are available to be used. Hence, in creating effective dispute settlement within the international system, the development of a full range of cooperative security approaches, backed up by a full complement of collective security approaches, is needed. A better understanding is also required of how these approaches interact, so that the international community can better orchestrate the pull of socialization, assistance, and problem solving and the push of power-based approaches—to encourage moderation and the nonviolent resolution of grievances.

The UN system already has in its current repertoire a range of power-based methods available for use, even if the political will has not always been there to use them, or to extend them to intrastate situations. What has been largely missing from the UN's dispute settlement system, however, is the availability of a full complement of cooperative security approaches.

Choosing the Right Actors for Conflict Prevention

Following Secretary-General Boutros-Ghali's call for a greater reliance on Chapter VIII of the UN Charter ("Regional Arrangements"), there has been a steady stream of articles debating the advantages and disadvantages of the UN versus regional organizations in various types of action. Typically, these discussions pose the question of which organization is best placed to carry out preventive diplomacy, peacemaking, or peacekeeping. There have also been a few articles arguing that NGOs are better suited than IGOs for some types of involvement. Rather than enter into this either-or debate, it would seem more useful to consider how all these organizations could work together to achieve a whole greater than the sum of their parts. An understanding of the advantages and disadvantages of each will allow a more thoughtful consideration of how this might be done.

Advantages and Disadvantages of the United Nations as an Actor in Conflict Prevention

As the only global intergovernmental organization whose primary function is the peaceful settlement of disputes, the UN has a number of distinct advantages. One is that all 185 member states have, by virtue of becoming members of the organization, agreed to resolve their disputes peacefully, to respect human rights, to work for social and economic justice, to practice tolerance, and to live together in peace. Because some regions do not yet have regional organizations, and because a number of states that are members of the UN do not belong to any regional arrangement, the coverage of the United Nations is greater than that of regional organizations, singly or collectively.

A second advantage is that the UN provides the most comprehensive dispute settlement system available, with a full range of organs (the Secretary-General, the International Court of Justice, and the Security Council) and a wide range of methods (ranging from good offices through peace enforcement). Its system essentially embodies the three different approaches to dispute settlement discussed above—an interest-based approach, a rights-based approach, and a power-based approach, with each corresponding roughly to the organs of the United Nations—good offices of the Secretary-General and his envoys representing the organization's interest-based approach, the judicial functions of the World Court and the UN's human rights machinery representing its rights-based approach, and the Security Council and its repertoire of potential responses under Chapter VII representing its power-based approach.

The availability of power-based instruments, however, acts as both an advantage and disadvantage in different circumstances. In some cases, it encourages member states to abide by their obligation to resolve their disputes peacefully in order to avoid the consequences of the Security Council becoming involved. In other situations, fear of Security Council involvement actually discourages member states from using the UN system and from availing themselves of, for example, the Secretary-General's good offices. Of course, it is not only the Security Council's power-based instruments that make member states concerned about its involvement, but also its composition. The Council's lack of adequate representation, as well as the privileges of the Great Powers (including permanent membership and the veto) cause some members to feel that the Security Council could or sometimes does act inconsistently and in the self-interest of its members.

Another factor that is both advantageous and disadvantageous is that the basic medium of discourse and action within the UN system is that of governments. The advantage is that the various activities of the United Nations constantly socialize governments to conform to developing international norms. As well, intergovernmental leverage, when properly applied, can be considerable. But because governments have bilateral and multilateral relationships outside the UN system, they also typically bring political baggage to their interactions within the UN, which leads to political trade-offs against principles of the Charter, and results in inconsistent decision making, motivated by national or coalitional political and economic interests rather than "the greater good."

Although in recent years the UN has become involved in many situations that might be construed as intrastate, as discussed above, this remains a highly sensitive issue that has presented a major obstacle to preventive diplomacy.

In spite of these problems, the UN has more institutional experience than any other organization in attempting to prevent and resolve conflict (even though this experience has not been preserved as well as it might have been). The UN's human and financial resources, although small in relation to its enormous mandate, are considerably greater than those of any other intergovernmental or nongovernmental organization operating in the field of conflict prevention and resolution (see table 12.4).

Advantages and Disadvantages of Regional Organizations as Actors in Conflict Prevention

Chapter VIII of the UN Charter not only includes regional organizations and arrangements as part of its system, but also explicitly encourages their development and use in furthering the aims of the Charter. Like the UN, however, regional organizations have their advantages and disadvantages. One advantage is that they are likely to be familiar with the actors in a dispute, as well as with the situation on the ground and how it is developing.

Proximity itself can make a situation more salient. Neighbors are likely to take a greater interest in conflict prevention in an adjacent state if they fear that fighting could spread or result in uncontrolled flows of arms or refugees through their territory. On the other hand, neighbors sometimes

TABLE 12.4
**1997 Budget Estimates of the Organizations Reviewed in This Book and
Their Programs That Promote Sustainable Peace**

	($ in millions)
UN Regular Budget (partly unpaid)	1,200.0
ASEAN	5.0
OAS	91.2
OAU (partly unpaid)	30.0
COE	161.1
OSCE	49.4
Regional Divisions in the UN Department of Political Affairs	8.7
UN Centre for Human Rights Advisory Services, Technical Assistance and Information Branch	3.1
UN High Commissioner for Human Rights	<1.0
OSCE High Commissioner on National Minorities	1.1
OSCE Office of Democratic Institutions and Human Rights (ODIHR)	3.9
COE Programs for Assistance to Central and Eastern Europe	10.7
OAS Unit for the Promotion of Democracy	2.0
OAU Peace Fund	6.0

Source: Personal communications from each organization.

have a vested interest in a dispute, such as when members of an aggrieved group in a neighboring state are ethnic "kin."

In terms of long-term conflict prevention and resolution, regional organizations can have an even more effective socializing role than the United Nations because of the importance of regional relationships. Regional politics, however, may also play a less-helpful role. Regional cleavages can cause some governments to side with one party and others with the other party or parties, which can widen a dispute. Regional hegemones can also use their weight to unduly influence the organization in a direction favorable to themselves.

Similarity of norms and values between states in a region and a low level of conflict within a regional organization may promote consensus and overcome such problems. However, regional norms and values can sometimes evolve in a manner that deviates from universal norms. In certain instances, for example, a majority of governments in a region might agree to condone or overlook certain abuses by a member state in the interest of regional harmony.

Finally, most regional organizations have even more meager human and financial resources than the United Nations. This necessarily limits their reach and effectiveness. The exception to the rule is the OSCE, which is evolving more quickly than any other IGO in conflict prevention, despite a relatively small budget (see table 12.4).

Advantages and Disadvantages of NGOs as Actors in Conflict Prevention

In general, NGOs tend to be less constrained than IGOs in being able to relate freely to the nongovernmental parties involved in a dispute (although governments sometimes discourage such dialogue). With their work in the field, many NGOs also have the ability to bring about dispute resolution (and even reconciliation) at the community level, as various organizations are currently attempting to do in South Africa. Further, they can serve as the eyes, ears, and conscience of the international community, highlighting, for example, abuses of human rights, minority discrimination, or impending or actual humanitarian crises, and prodding the rest of the world, including IGOs, to respond.

Other NGOs work at the level of Track Two diplomacy, bringing together, in an unofficial capacity, influential members of the policy-making community or those who have other forms of access to decision makers, as mentioned in chapter 11. A limited number of NGOs, such as the Carter Center and its International Negotiation Network, are also working in the realm of "Track One and a Half," finding a path between official and unofficial approaches. Research institutes also play an important role in terms of analysis of security issues and problems and the exploration of potential solutions that can have an influence on policymaking.

The advantage of NGOs is that they can take many forms and play many roles. Their multidimensional character and flexibility allows them to highlight specific problems and work on issues in ways that IGOs usually do not. Local NGOs and those that work extensively in the field are often more aware than IGOs of the root causes of problems. Normally, however, they do not have the same face validity with governments as IGOs, due to their lack of official status, their tendency to take a more uncompromising stand, and their lack of high-status interlocutors. There are exceptions to this rule, of course, as with the Carter Center, which sometimes finds itself more welcomed by governments than are IGOs. Finally, NGOs are often even more resource-poor than the UN or regional organizations and are usually dependent entirely on voluntary contributions, making their staying power more tenuous.

Complementarity of the Three Models

Given the advantages and disadvantages of each of the models described above, the potential exists for the formation of a coalition of actors whose work could complement and augment one another. As already discussed, Secretary-General Boutros-Ghali took initial steps toward this goal through his promotion of a larger role for regional organizations alongside that of the UN, thereby giving greater meaning to Chapter VIII. There has also been a growing recognition of the need for IGOs and NGOs to work together.

More often than not, however, these three types of actors either do not coordinate properly or appear to actively obstruct one another. A problem of *diffusion of responsibility* sometimes occurs, when the UN believes a situation should be handled by the regional organization and the regional organization abdicates responsibility to the UN. Other times, two or more actors become involved in an uncoordinated manner and work at cross-purposes. Equally problematic are bureaucratic jealousies and interinstitutional rivalries, which too often plague efforts at coordination, exacerbate problems, and waste time.

Potentially, all three kinds of organizations could be substantially developed, and a much more coordinated approach taken to conflict prevention. Ideally, the advantages and disadvantages that each actor could bring should be carefully considered in every situation and they should work cooperatively, delineating how tasks should be divided, and how work should be integrated. Such a multilayered approach will require careful coordination, which would no doubt be facilitated by proximity.

Sisk (1996) argues for both a broadening and deepening of conflict prevention and the peace process. He notes that the elite-mass dichotomy has been too simplified and suggests that the mobilized midlevel elites whose interests may be threatened by either conflict or peace should be considered:

> Increasingly, international participants in ethnic conflict management processes are focussing simultaneously on bottom-up efforts (usually through the activities of nongovernmental organizations) and top-down, or diplomatic efforts. Perhaps an important missing link is the middle range of local- and regional-level group leaders whose direct interests—power and control—are at stake. . . . Successful policies aimed at peaceful management of ethnic conflicts must be targeted at multiple levels of society, more or less simultaneously.

The next chapter will consider how these different actors might begin to work together more strategically to accomplish this goal.

13

Regional Centers for Sustainable Peace

I N THE SHORT TIME since the end of the cold war, the emergence of a greater multilateralism has resulted in the UN and regional organizations being given increased responsibility for the whole domain of peace and security. In grappling with this new role, these organizations (as discussed in the previous chapters) have begun to develop some rudimentary bases upon which conflict prevention might be built, although an effective and coherent set of international mechanisms is still far from becoming a reality. Nonetheless, the initial efforts by these organizations and their preliminary successes and failures can help point the way toward a more appropriate methodology. This chapter will draw upon the embyronic developments of the UN and regional organizations to propose a more coordinated and strategic approach.

As argued in the previous chapter, sustainable peace is dependent upon addressing human security needs through the development of a fair process that can foster and maintain that security. Assistance in the creation of sustainable peace must therefore be based first on a thorough understanding of human security needs at the local level, and second on knowledge about how these might be best addressed through appropriate institutional and structural mechanisms.

To achieve success at both of these fundamental tasks, the locus of action for conflict prevention might benefit by being moved to the regional level. This chapter will propose, therefore, that UN Regional Centers for Sustainable Peace be created. Such centers would allow the UN to develop a more intimate knowledge of regional problems and actors; create maximal cooperation with regional and subregional organizations, as well as other regional actors; and provide the opportunity to offer assistance in an ongoing manner. UN Regional Centers would also overcome past difficulties of trying to understand what is happening in the field from UN Headquarters in New York. Moreover, a regional assistance focus should allow governments to become more familiar with the services offered, thus reducing their fears and misunderstandings.

Regional centers could be established as an extension of the United Nations Department of Political Affairs. Their creation not only would extend the department geographically, but also would expand its current approach. UN Regional Centers for Sustainable Peace would have two foci. The first would be to maintain peace through the provision of assistance in dispute resolution. The second would be to assist governments at all levels in the development of institutions and structural processes that could promote good governance and address human security. Thus, a Program for Assistance in Dispute Settlement could be established with one or more dispute settlement teams headed by a full-time Special Adviser in Dispute Settlement, which could offer a range of services in conflict prevention and dispute resolution. Second, a Program for Assistance in Developing Good Governance could be composed of good governance teams, headed by a Special Adviser in Good Governance. In effect, Special Advisers would be like Permanent Special Representatives for each region. Centers for Sustainable Peace could report to the Secretary-General of the UN, through the Under-Secretary-General for Political Affairs, and thus be tied closely to the rest of the UN system.

To maximize their effectiveness, UN Regional Centers would need to maintain an exclusive focus on conflict prevention. This would overcome problems of the past, where full-blown conflicts absorbed all of the capacity of political staff, leaving little time for prevention. Also, centers would need to concentrate their efforts at the *early* stage of prevention when assistance is likely to be most effective.

When the assistance methodology of the center is not effective and a dispute has escalated to a crisis, the situation would be referred to UN Headquarters and managed by the Under-Secretary-General for Political Affairs and the Secretary-General (through, for example, the appointment of a Special Representative for that situation, consultation with the Security Council, etc.). Operations such as preventive deployment and peacekeeping would *not* be part of the center's mandate and would be handled elsewhere in the system. Thus, centers would focus on disputes before they developed into serious crises and/or turned violent; other parts of the UN system would handle their management if they escalated beyond that stage.

Centers would also need to adopt a *quiet, proactive assistance* approach, offering help and support, and relying on regional and international socialization to provide positive incentives for cooperation. Even if governments or disputing parties were at first uninterested, they could be urged (through repeated contacts) to take advantage of such assistance. This would differ from the traditional approach in which the UN has tended to wait to be asked for assistance. The reason to adopt a more proactive approach is that while parties are often reluctant to *request* help (fearing that it might be viewed as a sign of weakness), they may be willing to *accept* assistance that is quietly offered.

Staff from both programs could make regular visits throughout their region to discuss problems with relevant actors. Since such visits would be routine, they would not call attention to themselves or "internationalize" situations (fears that have presented obstacles in the past). Visits would allow staff to become acquainted with local and regional problems, and would help to develop relationships of trust and a reputation for fairness.

Expert knowledge and skill would be *fundamental* to the work of these programs. Senior staff with specialist knowledge and experience in dispute settlement would be required, along with regional or area experts who are well versed in the cultural, historical, and political perspectives of states and actors in the region. Those with expertise in governance will also be necessary. Staff would need excellent political skills and judgment, and those heading teams would require considerable stature, so that they could gain access to governments at the highest levels. This would mean recruiting staff (to supplement existing personnel) from the upper echelons of the diplomatic corps, from the senior levels of academia, and from experienced professionals who have been working in similar settings.

In implementing its work, each center could draw upon the full UN system, helping to mobilize resources and expertise from the various specialized agencies. Regional centers would ideally involve close cooperation between the United Nations and the relevant regional organization. Working together would allow both organizations to pool their expertise, use their comparative advantages, and be better informed about individual situations as well as the overall causes of conflict within a region. A joint approach would also provide an opportunity to share responsibility and truly coordinate activities, thus fulfilling the spirit of Chapter VIII of the UN Charter.

Further, the centers could work closely with NGOs, research institutions, and think tanks in the region, to extend their knowledge base and "reach" into all levels of civil society. This would ensure that learning proceeds in both directions (i.e., bottom up as well as top down), so that the constructive ideas of those at all levels are heard and incorporated into solutions that are acceptable and well tailored to local concerns, culture, and circumstances. Equally important would be the *horizontal transfer of knowledge and experience within each region*. Thus, those within the region who have found solutions to their local problems or have developed relatively successful models for good governance could be tapped to assist others in this endeavor. Figures 13.1, 13.2, and 13.3 provide an overview of how a strategic coalition of actors could be formed and interact to form Regional Centers for Sustainable Peace, as well as offer a sample of the potential functions of each. These are discussed more fully below.

Regional Programs for Assistance in Dispute Settlement

Regional Programs for Assistance in Dispute Settlement could offer expert assistance to help in reducing tension between groups, whether within or between states. Since the methodology for each is slightly different, they are described separately below.

Providing Assistance in Intrastate Disputes

Listening to and Understanding Concerns

A vital issue will be how each center's mandate is defined. One model to consider might be that of the OSCE High Commissioner on National Minorities, as developed by the incumbent, Max Van der Stoel. When he believes that a case needs attention, he typically informs a government that he would like to visit in order to obtain a better understanding of the situation of minorities in the country. Although the High Commissioner does not "ask" to visit, a state can, in theory, always refuse him entry, government officials can refuse to meet with him or refuse to comply with his recommendations. Thus, the procedure is proactive, but ultimately *remains subject to a state's consent.*

If Regional Centers for Sustainable Peace were to adopt a similar approach, the first step would be an on-site visit to assess the problem. The special adviser would need to travel not only to the capital, but also to areas where problems exist. Discussions would be required with a wide range of interlocutors, including those in government, those in the opposition, representatives of minority groups, NGOs, members of the local public, and trade union representatives. Relevant statistics would also need to be gathered.

The special adviser would also need to listen carefully to the problem that governments face in meeting these challenges, since it is only by taking such factors into account and finding ways to help governments deal with them, that the solutions that are proposed will be considered to be realistic. Thus, the special adviser and team will need (at all times) to maintain an aura of impartiality, while also developing relationships with all parties in

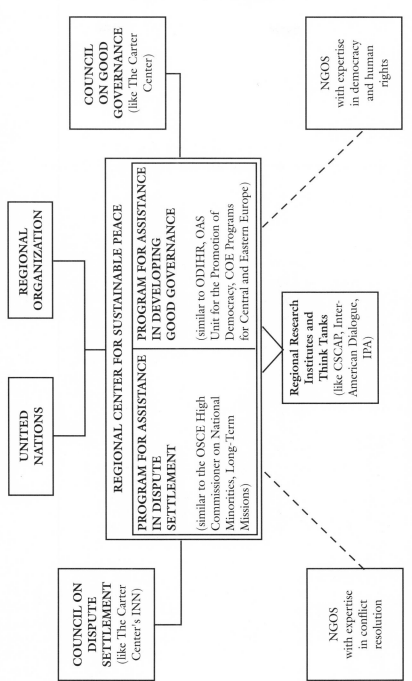

Fig. 13.1 Proposed Organizational Structure for Regional Centers for Sustainable Peace

PROGRAM FOR ASSISTANCE IN DISPUTE SETTLEMENT

Special Adviser on Dispute Settlement and Team in Intrastate Disputes:
- carry out on-site visits and discuss issues with a wide range of interlocutors to understand grievances and concerns
- encourage constructive approach on all sides
- advise all parties of their obligations, consequences of actions and recommend structural solutions to governments—i.e., changes in laws, practice, etc.
- follow-up/assist with implementation of recommendations
- establish ongoing forums for dialogue and problem solving
- act as "trip wire" to UN and regional organization if situation deteriorates

Special Adviser on Dispute Settlement and Team in Interstate Disputes:
- carry out on-site visits to gain an in-depth understanding of the problems
- offer assistance with dispute settlement, e.g.,
  – facilitate Track Two workshops
  – encourage and support negotiations
  – provide good offices/mediation
  – help parties seek conciliation, arbitration, or adjudication
- assist in implementing and monitoring agreements
- act as "trip wire" if dispute escalates and recommend options to UN and regional organization
- provide ongoing monitoring of events

Long-Term Preventive Diplomacy Missions:
- develop in-depth understanding of the situation through assessment "on the ground"
- recommend structural solutions to government
- help government implement recommendations
- establish ongoing forums for dialogue and problem solving

PROGRAM FOR ASSISTANCE IN DEVELOPING GOOD GOVERNANCE

Special Adviser on Good Governance and Team:
- advise government and parliament on reform of constitutions, laws, regulations, practices
- work with government ministries to help implement reform
- provide consultants when specialized expertise is required
- offer training, study visits to observe procedures elsewhere and support to key institutional actors, e.g.,
  – executive branch
  – judiciary
  – parliament
  – police
  – local officials
  – media
- assist military in defining a new role within civilian society through contact with model military structures elsewhere
- assist in establishing new institutions, e.g., national human rights commissions, ombudsmen, electoral commissions
- assist at all levels in the development of pluralism
- provide training at all levels in problem-solving approaches to dispute settlement

Fig. 13.2 Sample of Functions to Be Carried Out by Regional Centers for Sustainable Peace

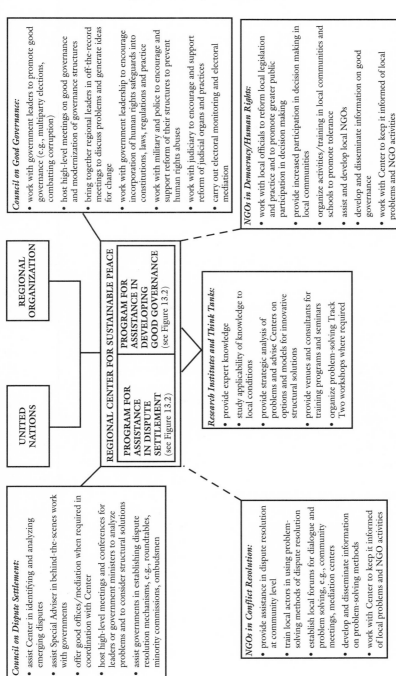

Fig. 13.3 Sample of Functions to Be Carried Out by Actors Associated with Regional Centers for Sustainable Peace

Council on Good Governance:

- work with government leaders to promote good governance (e.g., multiparty elections, combatting corruption)
- host high-level meetings on good governance and modernization of governance structures
- bring together regional leaders in off-the-record meetings to discuss problems and generate ideas for change
- work with government leadership to encourage incorporation of human rights safeguards into constitutions, laws, regulations and practice
- work with military and police to encourage and support reform of their structures to prevent human rights abuses
- work with judiciary to encourage and support reform of judicial organs and practices
- carry out electoral monitoring and electoral mediation

NGOs in Democracy/Human Rights:

- work with local officials to reform local legislation and practice and to promote greater public participation in decision making
- provide increased participation in decision making in local communities
- organize activities/training in local communities and schools to promote tolerance
- assist and develop local NGOs
- develop and disseminate information on good governance
- work with Center to keep it informed of local problems and NGO activities

REGIONAL ORGANIZATION

UNITED NATIONS

REGIONAL CENTER FOR SUSTAINABLE PEACE

PROGRAM FOR ASSISTANCE IN DISPUTE SETTLEMENT (see Figure 13.2)

PROGRAM FOR ASSISTANCE IN DEVELOPING GOOD GOVERNANCE (see Figure 13.2)

Research Institutes and Think Tanks:

- provide expert knowledge
- study applicability of knowledge to local conditions
- provide strategic analysis of problems and advise Centers on options and models for innovative structural solutions
- provide venues and consultants for training programs and seminars
- organize problem-solving Track Two workshops where required

Council on Dispute Settlement:

- assist Center in identifying and analyzing emerging disputes
- assist Special Adviser in behind-the-scenes work with governments
- offer good offices/mediation when required in coordination with Center
- host high-level meetings and conferences for leaders or government ministers to analyze problems and to consider structural solutions
- assist governments in establishing dispute resolution mechanisms, e.g., roundtables, minority commissions, ombudsmen

NGOs in Conflict Resolution:

- provide assistance in dispute resolution at community level
- train local actors in using problem-solving methods of dispute resolution
- establish local forums for dialogue and problem solving, e.g., community meetings, mediation centers
- develop and disseminate information on problem-solving methods
- work with Center to keep it informed of local problems and NGO activities

order to maximize influence. In short, adequate time spent listening to the concerns of all sides before making recommendations is likely to be time well spent.

The OSCE High Commissioner has found that, while grievances vary from situation to situation, most relate to the issues covered in chapters 3 and 4: that is, access to political decision making, as well as greater economic, social, and cultural rights. Of course, each individual situation and region can be expected to display its own particular manifestations of these basic issues, depending on the unique situational and environmental factors involved.

Providing New Ideas and Recommendations

The special adviser and team could then take the next step, much as the OSCE High Commissioner on National Minorities has done. After obtaining a thorough understanding of the causes of the problem, the High Commissioner offers nonbinding recommendations to the government in a purposefully low-key manner, by writing a letter to the foreign minister, thanking him or her for the government's helpfulness, defining the problems, and offering suggestions for change. Such letters often legitimize a minority group's most important concerns, but also may express an understanding of the difficulties from the government's perspective. When merited, the High Commissioner may commend previous efforts by the government to solve specific problems. Most important, however, these letters typically offer sets of specific, nonbinding recommendations, citing international or regional obligations and standards and expressing the High Commissioner's belief that the government will, naturally, wish to live up to these. This approach, developed with a high level of diplomatic and problem-solving skill by the OSCE High Commissioner, has been called "one-way mediation," since the government in question is the only interlocutor with whom the international organization has any formal status. Within the OSCE, this approach has been widely accepted by participating states, with *no* state refusing the High Commissioner's visit to date, and most adopting his recommendations.

At the same time, on an informal basis, the High Commissioner and his advisers usually have considerable influence with minority groups, and often remind them of their obligation to use constructive means in pursuing their interests. Indeed, the mere presence of a high-level representative of the international community, who is offering his or her services in problem solving, can calm a situation. Minority groups feel less desperate and more willing and empowered to pursue legal or politically constructive means of redress.

Encouraging the Establishment of Forums for Ongoing Dialogue

In addition to suggesting ways that governments might address an existing set of tensions, such a program should also recommend the establishment of forums for ongoing dialogue and problem solving. This may involve creating new institutional mechanisms or strengthening existing ones. Although forums for dialogue between groups exist in interstate situations (through international, regional, and subregional organizations), they are often lacking in intrastate situations. Especially in newly emerging democracies or nondemocratic states, it may be necessary to propose the creation of special conferences, or commissions, to allow parties to enter into a constructive dialogue and to begin a search for ways of resolving problems on their own. Such forums may begin to establish much-needed "habits of dialogue." This may be needed not only at the national level, but also at the community level. In Estonia, for example, the OSCE High Commissioner suggested the creation of an Ombudsman's Office, as well as a National Commissioner on Ethnic and Language Questions. In the Former Yugoslav Republic of Macedonia, he called for the strengthening of the Council for Inter-Ethnic Relations.

In a few cases, the OSCE High Commissioner himself has been involved in organizing the first step in this process. In Kyrgyzstan (with financial support from two governments and an NGO), he brought together government officials, NGO representatives of ethnic communities, representatives from Kazakhstan, Russia, and Tajikistan, and international experts on minority issues to examine international legal principles and practices that could be applied to their problems.

As necessary, the Regional Program for Assistance in Dispute Settlement would need to follow up its recommendations—through communication with key actors or further on-site visits—to check on progress toward their implementation and to offer new suggestions as new problems arise.

Providing Good Offices

In cases where tensions were escalating, the special adviser and team might need to engage in good offices to avert violence. This could entail formal or informal meetings with both sides, or shuttle diplomacy. Through intensive shuttle diplomacy, the OSCE High Commissioner was able to resolve a problem in Estonia between the Estonian government and the Russian ethnic group that was threatening to secede. In the case of the dispute between Ukraine and the Autonomous Republic of Crimea, government officials and parliamentarians from both sides were brought together (with financial assistance from the Swiss government) for discussion under the chairmanship of the OSCE High Commissioner and the

OSCE Head of Mission. The meetings' recommendations were subsequently forwarded to both parliaments.

Providing Access to Expert Assistance

Sometimes problems may be so complex that outside experts are needed to study a situation. In this case, the eventual recommendations may have greater face validity and carry more weight, since they will be backed by the authority of a "team of experts." Outside experts may be especially useful when a problem is highly technical.

The OSCE High Commissioner has used this approach in tackling the dual problem of the Hungarian minority in Slovakia and the Slovak minority in Hungary, where he utilized a team of three experts to study the situation in both countries over several visits and to provide him with recommendations, which he passed on to both governments. In Ukraine, the High Commissioner sent a team of constitutional experts to help in the drafting of the new constitution. The Regional Program for Assistance in Developing Good Governance might need to work with the Program for Assistance in Dispute Settlement in such situations.

Special advisers should be able to call upon the full range of regional or UN agencies (including the Bretton Woods institutions), as well as member states, to provide economic or technical assistance. Within the UN, the practice of using "Friends of the Secretary-General," typically a group of interested member states, to offer political, economic, or technical assistance, has filled this niche in peacemaking and might in some cases be considered as a potentially useful adjunct to preventive diplomacy: for example, in providing needed economic assistance for a given reform.

The OSCE High Commissioner has also, on a number of occasions, appealed to OSCE states for financial aid. In Estonia, small donations were sought to provide language training in the dominant language to help individuals from the minority group qualify for citizenship. In Albania, funds were raised for Greek language instruction for the Greek minority in the schools. The OSCE High Commissioner has stressed the usefulness of even small amounts of strategically placed economic assistance in preventing conflict. It might, therefore, be useful to establish a central fund that could be tapped by regional programs for such projects.

Providing Assistance in Interstate Disputes

Detecting and Analyzing Disputes

Regular and routine visits throughout each region would also allow special advisers and their teams to become familiar with emerging or simmering interstate disputes as well as the larger regional causes of conflict, and to offer timely assistance. A careful analysis of emerging situations would allow teams to offer the most appropriate kind of innovative assistance, a sample of which is outlined below.

Encouraging Parties to De-escalate Tensions

In some cases, it may be necessary to de-escalate tension before the parties will agree to talk. Special advisers could work with parties individually to suggest a range of de-escalation tactics. Parties could also be encouraged to identify and implement a series of confidence-building initiatives, which do not jeopardize their own interests but which might reduce hostility. Where necessary, program staff could offer specific ideas for consideration.

Facilitating Multitrack Diplomacy

In cases where parties are not ready to accept negotiation or mediation, the special adviser could encourage, or even initiate, Track Two diplomacy, in order to establish a better relationship between the parties, break down incorrect perceptions of the other side, and begin the process of inventing new solutions. The special adviser could ask one of the appropriate research institutes or universities associated with the program to host problem-solving workshops, with experts skilled in this methodology being invited to lead the workshop. The team could help identify participants (including influential persons or officials who might attend in an unofficial capacity) and provide briefing or background material to the facilitators.

Encouraging and Supporting Negotiation

Even with the introduction of assistance, it is likely that negotiation will remain the most popular method of dispute settlement, since it allows disputing parties to maintain maximum decision-making control over both the process and outcome of dispute resolution. Although negotiation does not involve an intermediary, program staff could still be helpful in initiating and speeding up the process.

While parties are sometimes reluctant to suggest negotiation for fear that they will be seen as "weak" by the other side, acceptance of the negotiation process as a result of urging by a special adviser could reframe the situation and serve as a face-saving entry into negotiation. Staff could assist by advising the parties on how to structure negotiations to maximize a constructive process. They could provide model procedural rules and help the parties locate an acceptable neutral site. In addition, program staff could act as observers during negotiations, to introduce a moderating effect on the process. In some cases, a special adviser and team might be able to provide technical information or expertise that could expand the range of ideas (for example, by offering a catalogue of solutions that parties in other situations have agreed upon).

Offering "Good Offices" or Mediation Directly

In some situations, a special adviser and team might offer their own services to facilitate the initial contacts between disputing parties, assist in beginning a dialogue, or establish "talks about talks." Using a problem-solving approach to mediation, the special adviser and team could help parties identify, prioritize, and communicate interests and work with them to develop and refine a range of innovative proposals that might meet parties' concerns. They could also assist in searching for objective criteria and principles of fairness or precedent that could be used as a basis for settlement. If a solution were still not forthcoming, they could encourage parties to invent further options, change the scope of the negotiation, or negotiate a procedural solution. Alternatively, teams could suggest provisional, contingent, partial, or nonbinding measures. Throughout mediation, the special adviser could maintain procedural control by carefully managing the mediation process, providing a neutral site, discouraging discussion of hard-line positions, keeping emotions under control, encouraging acts of good will, and excluding audiences.

Meetings of experts could also be used as a source of new ideas and input. Such meetings could be organized to target problematic aspects of the process and provide a fresh perspective.

Acting as a Referral Source for Third-Party Mediation

In other cases, the parties or the special advisor may feel that another third party should provide mediation. Program staff could assist the parties in approaching other intermediaries, such as eminent persons from the region (for example those on the Council for Dispute Settlement to be discussed below), a leader of a neighboring state, or an NGO. Program staff could offer to host or facilitate initial exploratory meetings with a prospective mediator. They might also act as observers and once mediation was underway, as an ongoing resource.

Helping Parties Seek Conciliation, Arbitration, or Adjudication

In appropriate instances, the special adviser might propose a process of conciliation, arbitration, or adjudication. In such cases, the parties could be helped to understand the steps involved in setting up a conciliation or arbitration procedure. Staff might also assist by providing a standard set of procedures or by finding conciliators or arbiters acceptable to both sides. The special adviser could advise parties as to whether their case was suitable for referral to the International Court of Justice and help them find the necessary financial or legal assistance to approach the Court. Where warranted, parties might be encouraged to use the Court's chambers option to simplify and speed up the proceedings.

Monitoring Compliance with Agreements

Once agreement of any kind has been reached, the special adviser could assist in monitoring compliance with agreements, intervene to prevent slippage, or mediate disputes arising from breaches of an agreement. Such a function would keep problems from recycling by providing timely assistance before the reemergence of a dispute could deteriorate into a larger problem.

Acting as a "Trip Wire"

When disputes are escalating rapidly, the special adviser would be able to provide timely, well-researched assessments of the situation and recommendations to the Secretary-General, the Security Council, and the relevant regional organization. Regional programs could provide a much more effective approach than "fact-finding missions" sent in the past from New York, since they would have been tracking the dispute for some time and would bring to the assessment a more in-depth knowledge of the situation and the actors. In certain cases, disputing parties might be invited to send delegations to either the UN's or the regional organization's headquarters, or the Secretary-General of one of these organizations might visit the area. Where necessary, the special adviser could inform the Security Council through the Secretary-General that the situation had reached the late prevention stage and that the imminent outbreak of violence was likely.

Providing Continuous Monitoring of Events

When a crisis did occur, program staff would be able to provide a communication link between the parties and the international community, and act as a source of continuous, up-to-date information and advice to the parties, as well as to the Secretary-General and Security Council, and to the relevant regional organization.

Regional Programs for Assistance in Developing Good Governance

The creation of Regional Programs for Assistance in Developing Good Governance would require a multidisciplinary staff with a high level of expertise in a range of topics (e.g., constitutional lawyers, experts in governance, economists, jurists, experienced trainers). A wide range of consultants would also be needed, so that specialized regional and extraregional expertise could be extensively tapped, both for advisory and educational purposes. A special adviser on good governance could coordinate the activities in each region.

The program could respond to requests from governments, although it would also be able to offer its services in a proactive manner. In either case, when governments expressed interest, a team could undertake an on-site "needs assessment." Such an assessment would involve wide-ranging discussion, not only with those in government, but with key institutional actors at all levels (for example, judges, military, police, the media, local authorities), as well as with the people—representatives of minorities, NGOs, trade unions, and private citizens. In some cases, a team might be asked to assess a country's constitution, laws, and governance structures. A subsequent report on the kinds of activities that the program could offer to the requesting government could be discussed and letters of understanding with the government exchanged before programs began. In an attempt to sketch how assistance in good governance might contribute to conflict prevention, some of the kinds of assistance will be outlined briefly below. Both the COE programs and the OSCE's ODIHR provide models for the kinds of work that might be provided.

Providing Assistance for Transition to Democracy

Over the past decade, there has been a marked increase in the number of countries making the transition to democracy. While ultimately this may lead to a reduced incidence of violent conflict, the transition process itself can be fraught with danger unless carefully managed. As discussed in chapter 3, on the whole, the evidence suggests that transitions are more likely to succeed if democracy is approached gradually, if the authoritarian regime is liberalized rather than overthrown, and if pluralist groups and associations are allowed and encouraged to develop. When a regime is overthrown suddenly, power struggles between opposition parties are likely to develop. Negotiated solutions are often thrashed out hurriedly and risk being unstable. One of the dangers is the absence of conflict-regulating institutions to contain the rise of nationalism, which often occurs at these times.

In multiethnic states, one of the most important factors in avoiding ethnic conflict in periods of transition has been the willingness to address ethnic issues *early* in the process, through the writing of an appropriate constitution and the inclusion of ethnic groups in a power-sharing arrangement. Thus, when transitions do occur, assistance from expert staff in the Regional Program for Assistance in Developing Good Governance could be invaluable. Staff could offer information about the need to ensure participation through representatives from all significant groups in central and local governments. They could help governments consider autonomy arrangements, proportional systems of voting, the advantages of a parliamentary system with grand coalition cabinets representing different parties, the dangers of the "winner takes all" presidential system, and the utility of mechanisms such as a minority veto (over issues of particular importance to a minority group). Advice on establishing different kinds of territorial and nonterritorial forms of autonomy and on which might be best suited to a given ethnic distribution may also be helpful. In particular, approaches arrived at by other governments could be reviewed, along with their outcomes, downside risks, and so on. Visits to countries to observe a given model might also be useful for key actors. In such cases, assistance, offered on a timely basis, could mean the difference between a functioning society and civil war.

In new democracies, those who are supposed to be representing the will of the people may also need special assistance in understanding their role and in learning how to carry it out. An assistance program could do much to help accelerate this process through, for example, opportunities to observe parliaments or local governments in action elsewhere.

Providing Assistance in the Development of Fair Rules, Law, and Practice

Assistance could also be provided in studying a state's constitution, laws, regulations, and practices, and specific changes could be recommended to bring them into line with regional or international standards. Relevant models or reference to similar laws in other countries could be provided. Advice could be offered in the drafting of constitutions or legislation. The separation of government powers; freedom of expression, association, or assembly; independence of the judiciary; the role of the judiciary in overseeing the police and prison systems; protection of national minorities; electoral laws; and citizenship and asylum laws represent a few of the kinds of issues about which recommendations and suggestions might be offered.

Also, assistance could be provided in helping relevant ministries or departments draw up plans for the implementation of reforms, and in considering how obstacles to these reforms might be overcome. Once plans were developed, their implementation could be monitored and further advice and assistance provided upon request. Workshops or seminars could be held to familiarize government officials with proposed reforms or to anticipate potential problems and discuss how they should be handled.

Providing Assistance in the Development of a Full Range of Institutions to Administer Laws and Regulate Conflict

Since certain institutions within a society have a fundamental role to play in good governance through the administration of law and the regulation of conflict, it is crucial that these institutions be encouraged to function in a manner that upholds individual freedoms and due process of law, and safeguards human rights. Technical and financial assistance could be provided for special training programs for judges, magistrates, lawyers, prosecutors, police officers, prison personnel, ombudsmen, or mediators. Seminars and workshops with experienced professionals could be arranged to discuss issues related to fair and independent systems for administering justice; professional ethics; independence of the judges and lawyers; fair trial procedures; human rights during investigations; use of force; torture; crowd control; police command, management and control; treatment of prisoners; prison administration and discipline; or community policing. Other key institutions, such as the media, could also benefit from workshops on topics such as freedom of information and expression, access to information, professional codes of ethics, censorship, and the importance of the press in developing multicultural understanding.

Exposure to systems where these institutions function smoothly and fairly is another means of introducing such concepts, and study visits to observe how things are done elsewhere might be useful. The Council of Europe, for example, sponsors study programs in which judges visit a host country and observe court proceedings, attend the questioning of suspects, and meet with other judges, lawyers, police, prison personnel, social and probation workers, and clerks of court for extensive discussion about how the system works. Such programs are likely to provide a powerful modeling effect. Civil servants and local authorities might also benefit from training in civil administration, financing local government, combating corruption, or involving local communities in decision making.

Separating Military Institutions from Civilian Administration

When states are in transition to civilian rule from a military regime, or where the military has been actively involved in governing a state in the recent past, providing assistance to the military in finding a new role for itself in relation to the civil authority may be vital. This is, of course, a most delicate task that must be handled with extreme sensitivity. Exchanges with other military establishments that enjoy a good relationship with civilian government might be one low-key approach that could offer a new vision of how such relationships might operate in different configurations. While some military-to-military discussions are already taking place bilaterally, carefully structured multilateral workshops could provide an opportunity to explore this topic. Such concepts could be routinely introduced into training programs for military personnel and new recruits through the development of regional training institutions or curricula.

Encouraging More Honest Governance

Corruption and organized crime are presenting new and serious challenges to states in transition as well to weak states. Both financial and technical assistance could be provided to governments in fighting these destructive forces. Assistance could be provided in the establishment of anticorruption legislation, monitoring, and enforcement. Successful experience from other societies could be shared with local and national officials, and special training in anticorruption investigation and prosecution offered. As well, assistance with campaigns to change public attitudes and behavior could be offered, based on campaigns carried out elsewhere to change community norms. The programs could also arrange grants to assist such initiatives (with built-in appropriate human rights protection).

Promoting Greater Economic Opportunity and Access

Minority and ethnic grievances within states are often related to economic discrimination and injustice, as previously discussed. In the same way that democracy is sometimes inappropriately considered to be a panacea for these problems, development has often been considered the key to minority groups' economic concerns. But just as a more nuanced approach is needed in the structuring of democracy in multiethnic societies, so a more sophisticated answer is needed for development policy—since, if not properly controlled, development can actually exacerbate rather than ameliorate ethnic problems. Unmanaged, rapid growth–oriented development strategies, for example, can lead to the deepening of a dual economy when the modern sector becomes prosperous, while the urban and rural poor are further marginalized, sowing the seeds for discontent. This can also occur regionally within a country.

Thus, assistance in how to minimize such problems may be helpful. More specifically, advice could be offered to governments in how to achieve sectoral, regional, or communal balance in development. Assistance might also be provided in initiating and implementing programs of land reform, where expert assistance can point to successful land reform programs elsewhere and help governments develop appropriate programs of compensation and distribution. Also, advice and assistance might be offered in devising more individualistic policies of economic opportunity, such as special rights for members of minority groups through quotas for government hiring or military recruitment, special loans, or special arrangements for entry to university.

Assistance might also be made available by means of redistributing expenditures within government budgets. In the belief that ethnic conflicts can be controlled through a strong military, many governments commit inordinately large proportions of their budgets to military forces and arms purchases. Good governance teams may be able to gradually help governments realize that reallocating even part of these funds toward social policy initiatives that address the root causes of the same conflicts could be more effective.

Promoting Pluralism, Cultural Understanding, and Tolerance

Encouragement could be given in the adoption of policies more conducive to tolerance and cross-cultural understanding. Models for multiculturalism in use elsewhere could be introduced through seminars for officials from government ministries, the media, local authorities, representatives of minority groups, and others, who could be offered the opportunity to consider which parts of these models might most effectively be adopted locally.

In societies where the mass media are pervasive, encouragement (including financial incentives) could be provided for multicultural programming, which might have far-reaching effects, particularly when targeted at developing understanding between groups. Pluralism could also be encouraged at the community level. Even with small amounts of financial assistance, such programs might be useful where ethnic tension is high.

Where historical situations have created deep fissures, more intensive work may be required. Special programs for promoting community reconciliation may need to be introduced by those with experience in this area.

In particular, schools offer an excellent venue for programs that foster tolerance and an appreciation of other cultures. In mixed communities, education and awareness training for ethnic groups in one another's language and culture could be promoted. Teachers and curriculum planners could be urged to introduce specially designed programs to inoculate against racial or ethnic discrimination and hatred. Where appropriate, assistance could be provided for the introduction of laws and judicial practices that prohibit incitement to ethnic or racial hatred, discrimination, or violence.

Augmenting the Work of Regional Centers

Using Small Assistance Missions

In some situations, it might be advantageous to deploy small, expert assistance missions, as the OSCE has done, as a further extension of both the good governance and dispute resolution programs. Typically, OSCE missions have ranged from eight to twenty persons, and regional center missions could be similar in size. In the area of assistance in the development of good governance, such missions could provide a greater degree of ongoing support during the establishment of some new good governance reform. For example, to assist a government that wished to strengthen its own capacity in fighting corruption, a small anticorruption mission might be deployed to work alongside local staff until local capacity was sufficient to carry on the task alone. A police training mission might be sent to a country that wanted training for local police supervisors or desired assistance in developing training curriculum for police instruction. A multicultural team might be deployed to work with government ministries and/or local governments in devising a multicultural program that would promote pluralism and ameliorate local ethnic tensions. An economic opportunity team might be sent to help governments devise ways to provide minorities with greater economic opportunity and access within the society. It should be stressed, however, that such teams would need to be composed of individuals with a high level of expertise.

Small assistance missions might also be helpful in dispute settlement by providing an "on-the-ground" presence, which could serve as a calming influence by showing that the international community was aware of the problems and interested in helping to resolve them. Such missions could work with both minorities and the government to help resolve short-term problems, as well as to put in place long-term institutional mechanisms that would allow the parties to discuss and eventually resolve their own problems. Small assistance missions would provide an inexpensive and flexible response, which would be less formal and cumbersome, and more targeted to specific needs than the preventive deployment of large military forces. Rather than being passive observers, members of such missions would be given an active mandate to help governments find ways to resolve their problems. Of course, this would not rule out the use of large-scale preventive deployment missions when they were needed, but this would be a quite different approach and *not* part of the assistance program's mandate.

Using the Expertise of Regional and International Scholars

To tailor skills to local conditions and to draw upon a wide range of potential solutions, regional research institutes, universities, and think tanks could support both programs in a variety of ways. A network of regional and international specialists and scholars with relevant expertise could be established to assist each program. They could be called upon to act as consultants in specific cases, to help program staff members sharpen their analysis of problems, and to broaden their consideration of possible solutions.

A small team of experts could also be chosen to work with each of the programs to help it continuously refine its methodology through the review of specific case experience and to help design regular evaluation of its training programs. By adopting a self-analytical approach to both successes and failures, valuable lessons could be learned that would improve the center's practice. To further this effort, meetings between all regional center programs could take place on a regular basis, so that insights could be shared. These meetings could be attended not only by program staff, but also by those scholars involved in helping to refine each program's effectiveness.

As experience accumulated, a deeper understanding of the "root causes" of conflict in each region would emerge, and as a consequence, program staff could work with scholars to develop a more effective long-term agenda for addressing them. This agenda might form the basis for the more effective marshaling of resources (both human and economic), including recommendations to the General Assembly, other relevant bodies of the UN and regional organizations, as well as to the international and regional financial institutions.

Using the Expertise of NGOs and Civil Society

NGOs working in the area of conflict resolution, democracy, human rights, and development also could be utilized to extend the work of both programs. NGOs with appropriate expertise in conflict resolution could, for example, help to provide assistance in dispute resolution at the community level—training local actors in problem solving and establishing local forums for dialogue. Also, they could develop and disseminate information on problem-solving methods throughout all levels of the community and help program staff keep in touch with local problems. Finally, NGOs and other civil society groups could keep the program staff informed of local issues that might need other kinds of attention. Where local NGOs do not exist and could help to promote sustainable peace, national or international NGOs could assist in their creation and development, thus contributing to the development of an active civil society.

NGOs with expertise in human rights and democracy could work with local governments and local peoples to make them aware of the need to incorporate human rights safeguards into local laws and practice, and to help them understand the advantages of greater local participation in decision making. Additionally, NGOs could encourage those at the local level to work toward a communal consensus of what is required for good governance. Development NGOs could help define local priorities for development and support local initiatives.

Nongovernmental organizations can also foster efforts in intercultural understanding and pluralism, initiating and supporting local community activities, helping schools incorporate the topic into their curriculum, and encouraging the development of forums for community dialogue and problem solving.

Using the Experience of Regional Leaders

Borrowing from the Carter Center's innovation in this area, high-level councils could be formed to work alongside program staff. These could be composed of former prime ministers, presidents, supreme court judges, Nobel laureates, prominent intellectuals, and other high-profile persons, who could provide the necessary status and political expertise to extend the program's work upward into the highest levels of government.

A Regional Council on Dispute Settlement could work with the Program for Assistance in Dispute Settlement and be convened on a regular basis (with the network of regional and international scholars) for off-the-record meetings to identify and analyze emerging or existing disputes. This council could also host high-level meetings of leaders or government ministers, to analyze regional or subregional problems and to consider a range of possible structural solutions. Individual council members could select particular situations where they might work quietly (behind-the-scenes) with reluctant governments to encourage the acceptance of recommendations made by program staff. In dispute settlement, council members might be asked to provide good offices or mediation (with backup, where needed, from program staff).

Drawing together these different actors into a strategic alliance would help to overcome the obstacle that IGOs always face—that of having to gain a government's consent before its staff can do anything. Although the activities of the program itself would be subject to the direct consent of governments, the other three sets of actors (scholars, NGOs, and council members) would be able to promote the program's agenda even in cases where a country has not been formally involved with the program. Thus, this alliance not only extends the reach in terms of finding ways to tackle a problem at all levels of society, but it also finds a way around the common barriers to IGO influence.

A Regional Council on Good Governance could meet regularly with program staff from the Program for Assistance in Developing Good Governance, scholars, and selected NGO and civil society representatives, to ascertain which areas might be most in need of the program's assistance, and to analyze issues upon which the program should focus as a priority. Council members could then work quietly behind-the-scenes with government leaders, to urge them to move in the direction of good governance. They could help to make good governance issues salient in the region by hosting high-level conferences within and between states. Council members could also host off-the-record meetings on regionwide problems, bringing together leaders to consider what could be done to overcome problems. Such meetings could gradually create regional norms of good governance and help governments consider practical steps to move in this direction.

Finally, much like the Carter Center's Council of Freely-Elected Heads of Government, the Council on Good Governance could assist with electoral monitoring and mediation, where needed. The presence of high-level council members who could obtain access to the leadership of political parties could help smooth the transition of power from one political party to another.

Because of their status, council members could also play a role in working with the military, police, or judiciary, encouraging and supporting them in the reform of their structures and practice. This could be carried out through behind-the-scenes urging or through hosting high-level meetings to discuss topics such as the role of these institutions in modern governance structures.

In addition, the strategic interaction of these actors should provide a synergetic effect. For example, scholars, through association with program staff, should become more adept at packaging their knowledge in a form that is more practical and useful to practitioners. In turn, program staff, NGO staff, and regional leaders should be able to refine and expand their own expertise through contact with scholars and other experts.

Location of Centers

Although all regions require the kind of assistance that regional centers could provide, Europe (including Eastern and Central Europe), with its better endowed regional organizations, is already receiving this kind of help from both the OSCE and the COE. Therefore, the regions most in need would be Africa, Asia, and the Americas. With their legacy of colonialism, however, all three of these regions remain understandably sensitive to any outside interference. Thus, it would be essential for those UN member states from each region, as well as for the regional organizations, to be intimately involved in the development of each center. Centers could either grow out of or work closely with the embryonic structures already developing in Africa and the Americas (e.g., the Conflict Management Division and the Central Organ in the OAU and the Unit for the Promotion of Democracy in the OAS).

In some regions, more than one center may be useful. Indeed, it can be argued that Europe already has two such programs in the area of good governance (the OSCE and the COE programs). Since both Africa and Asia have the greatest number of conflicts and since both cover huge territories, Africa might profit from two centers (for example, one in East Africa and one in West Africa). In Asia, it might be useful to have one center that focuses on Northeast Asia and another that encompasses Southeast Asia. The Americas, on the other hand, with its larger number of governments in transition to democracy but relatively fewer number of conflicts might require one center. (Although not covered in this book, the Middle East might also profit from a regional center of this type. Indeed, the Middle East Arms Control and Regional Security process discussed the establishment of a conflict-prevention center). Although most disputes are likely to be within states or regions, where a problem develops between regions, centers could liaise with one another.

Financing Regional Centers for Sustainable Peace

A summary of the budgets for the UN and the five regional organizations reviewed here is presented in table 12.4, as well as a budget for the various programs related to prevention. It is noteworthy that every one of the latter programs was created in the last six years and that the amount spent on them is still exceedingly small.

Since it is proposed that Regional Centers for Sustainable Peace be developed according to regional needs, it is difficult to set a precise figure on their cost. A rough estimate could be obtained, however, by drawing budget figures from the best two models available. The office of the OSCE High Commissioner on National Minorities (taking into account the value of positions seconded by governments) costs around $2 million; and the COE's Programs for Assistance to Central and Eastern Europe have a budget of about $10 million. The total of $12 million could, therefore, be an approximate cost for each regional center, comprising the two programs working on dispute settlement and good governance. Thus, regional centers for Africa, Asia, and the Americas would cost around $36 million.

If Regional Centers for Sustainable Peace were to be set up as a joint venture between the UN and regional organizations, funding could come from both. Such broad-based funding would avoid the implication that one part of the world was attempting to impose its agenda on another part.

The larger issue, however, and, indeed, the one that *must* be tackled, if sustainable peace and sustainable development are to be considered as the new agenda, is a more viable financial basis for international good governance. This will be considered further in chapter 14, where it will be pointed out that, although adequate funding *could* be made available, whether it *is* made available will depend on the "political will" of the international community. Usually absent from discussions of "political will," however, is the notion that it is something that must be *generated*. By contrast, it is normally treated as if it were an unchangeable trait of governments and IGOs, which is either present or absent. In fact, "lack of political will" simply refers to a government's current estimate of the advantages and disadvantages of following a certain course of action. It is essential to remember that such estimates are open to influence—from other governments and from civil society. A better understanding of "political will" and its determinants is needed if those interested in promoting an agenda for sustainable peace and sustainable development are to have the resources needed to pursue such goals.

14

The First Half of the Twenty-first Century: Promoting Good Governance Regionally and Internationally

A S PROPOSED EARLIER, sustainable peace will depend on the development of good governance at all levels—local, national, regional, and global. Chapter 13 addressed how national and local good governance might be assisted by regional and global structures (the United Nations and regional organizations). This chapter will consider how regional and global governance structures themselves could be improved. It will be argued that the development of more democratic and equitable regional and international governance would support and reinforce more effective local and national governance.

The last part of the twentieth century has seen the abatement of the East-West conflict, which had eroded the international system's ability to tackle other serious problems on its agenda. The beginning of the twenty-first century could provide a corresponding opportunity to overcome the structural problems that are the root causes of the North-South conflict.

It is noteworthy that the North-South conflict (based as it is on an asymmetrical power balance) mirrors the dynamics between dominant and nondominant groups discussed in chapters 3 and 4. The less-powerful groups of the South desire greater access to political decision making, want their economic needs more equitably met, and wish to protect their culture against incursion from the dominant culture. For its part, the dominant groups of the North fear loss of control and privilege. In beginning to address these grievances and discrepancies, solutions similar to those presented earlier could be applied regionally and globally. A sample is set out below.

Establishing Consensus and a More Integrative Agenda

Since the twin concepts of sustainable peace and sustainable development integrate the concerns and preoccupations of both developed and developing countries, such an agenda should help to bridge the North-South divide. It highlights the fact that peace and environmentally responsible development are intimately intertwined and ultimately must go hand in hand, since the absence of one undermines the presence of the other. As Willy Brandt put it, "He who wants to ban war must also ban poverty" (Brandt, 1990). A fuller rationale for the inherent linkages between peace, development, and democracy is explored in *An Agenda for Development* (1994) and *An Agenda for Democratization* (1996).

Indeed, it can be argued that much of the agenda for tackling the structural causes of conflict at an international level has already been widely canvassed and even agreed upon at various large UN conferences, including those held in recent years on sustainable development, human rights, social development, population control, human habitats, and the status of women. These meetings were themselves a model of global participation, involving wide dialogue, consultation, and participation from both governments and civil society. The resulting action plans from these conferences offer an excellent place to begin a more comprehensive program for sustainable peace and sustainable development.

Providing More Satisfactory Power-Sharing Arrangements

With the rise of problems beyond the control of any one state or group of states, there is a growing imperative for international democratization and involvement by all states in global decision making. *An Agenda for Democratization* (1996) comments that:

> For all States, democratization at the international level has become an indispensable mechanism for global problem-solving in a way that is accountable and acceptable to all and with the participation of all concerned. Dominance by one country or group of countries must over time evolve into a democratic international system in which all countries can participate, along with new non-State actors.

It notes that only a few states currently play their full role on the world stage and calls upon all member states to increase their level of engagement in international affairs.

Founded on the principle of "sovereign equality" among members, the United Nations is also in need of a better power-sharing arrangement. Although the UN General Assembly is a democratic structure, the Security Council no longer adequately meets the standards for representation and legitimacy in today's world. Many proposals have been put forward and debated for reform of its composition and practice, but the hard bargaining approach by those advocating one position over another has done little to resolve the problem. Yet finding a set of satisfactory solutions to this ongoing irritant would do much to build confidence and create a better relationship between member states. Hence, application of a problem-solving approach to the diverse interests may offer the only real chance of obtaining Security Council reform and the benefits that would ensue.

International economic forums such as the IMF, the World Bank, and others could be made more democratic with more adequate representation from the poorer, less-powerful segments of the international community. As Boutros-Ghali (1996) notes, democratizing economic participation at the international level would "help guarantee that, through the United Nations, the poorest countries will have an ever growing voice in the international system. It can help ensure that the international system does not leave a vast portion of the world to fend for itself but truly promotes the integration and participation of all peoples."

There is also a need to expand participation to a greater range of actors beyond member states. *An Agenda for Democratization* suggests that regional organizations, nongovernmental organizations, academia, business and industry, the media, parliamentarians, and local authorities all represent groups that should be included in global decision making and that new ways should be found to integrate them into existing and newly developing international structures and mechanisms.

Providing More Equitable Economic Opportunity through Macroeconomic Reform

It is a tragic but well-documented fact that the debt burden imposed by the IMF has undone much of the progress achieved by both UN and bilateral development assistance in the developing world. The debt burden of developing countries has increased fifteenfold over the past 20 years, while the GNP for the whole continent of Africa is about 50 percent less today than it was at the beginning of the 1970s—when Africa was already considered to be in the grip of severe poverty (UNDP Development Report, 1994; Sahnoun, 1996). Moreover, it is clear that many of the conflict-prone areas are also some of the poorest, since competition over resources is greatest in these regions.

A more equitable macroeconomic policy is required, with special attention to assisting the poorer segments of international society in obtaining
greater economic opportunity and access, in order to be able to better
satisfy basic human needs. This would require a major overhaul and restructuring of macroeconomic policy and a reorientation of the international system toward conflict prevention through more effective sectoral
development among states.

A number of proposals have also been made for restructuring ECOSOC
into two separate councils that could more effectively guide macroeconomic and social policy (UNDP Human Development Report, 1994;
Commission on Global Governance, 1995; Report of the Independent
Working Group on the Future of the United Nations, 1995). The task of
an economic council would be to focus on sustainable human development
and to act as a watchdog over the policy direction of international and
regional financial institutions. A social council could work closely with the
new economic council but focus on integrating and promoting issues related to social development.

The Bretton Woods institutions would need to adopt policies more
closely tied to the goals of the United Nations Charter and to a sustainable
peace and sustainable development agenda. A first confidence-building
step might be for developed countries to cancel the debt of the poorest
countries, if agreement could be reached that funds released would be
spent on social development and good governance (UNDP Development
Report, 1994). Sahnoun (1996) has also proposed a Marshall Plan for
the South, and such an idea should be developed further with adequate
representation of all concerned in high-level or expert working groups (indeed, this could be taken up by a new or reformed economic council).

In addition, existing UN structures could work more closely with the
Bretton Woods institutions, such as the World Bank and the IMF, as well
as with regional development banks and other bilateral and multilateral
donor organizations, to create a more unified approach to conflict prevention through the provision of financial support for national and local good
governance initiatives, as well as through more appropriate sectoral development policies.

Reorienting the UN and Regional Organizations to a More Preventive Approach

An overall reorientation of the UN and regional organizations to a more
preventive approach could also be undertaken. All relevant departments,
agencies, and organizations within these systems could be asked to review
their programs in the light of the twin objectives of sustainable peace and
sustainable development and to report on how their efforts could be

strengthened, both at current levels and with increased levels of funding. A task force within each organization could be asked to study these proposals and to consider ways that linkages might be built between programs on a regional basis to build synergy. The process might also generate new ideas that could be pursued.

Building Regional Capacity

As outlined in chapters 6 through 10 and summarized in tables 12.1–12.3, regional organizations have begun to develop a number of interesting and innovative cooperative security approaches to conflict prevention, with each organization adopting a unique array of instruments. A closer alliance between regional organizations and the United Nations, as proposed in chapter 13, would help to develop regional capacity, as well as a better understanding of regional problems.

Greater horizontal sharing of solutions between regions could also offer an opportunity for building regional capacity. A first step might be to bring together senior diplomats and Secretariat staff from the UN and different regional organizations to share information about their unique and developing methodologies. (Such a meeting would have a different purpose than the two meetings with regional organizations that were organized by the UN Secretary-General and dealt with issues of coordination.) A series of small seminars could focus on sharing information and experience about respective approaches to different topics, such as electoral monitoring and assistance, assistance in the promotion of good governance, dispute settlement or human rights machinery. Indeed, it is surprising how little senior staff members in regional organizations know about related programs in other regional organizations. A horizontal exchange of information could lead to a more comprehensive plan for regional capacity building within and between regions.

Strengthening the Capacity and Effectiveness of IGO Secretariats

Good leadership is as vital to good global and regional governance as it is to good national and local governance. Leaders are needed who are intelligent, knowledgeable, and experienced; who possess the capacity for clear, strategic thinking and vision; who are motivated by a profound sense of collective responsibility; and who possess good managerial and diplomatic skills, including sensitivity to diverse needs and creativity in finding ways to address and reconcile them.

Of course, much has been said about the need for a more professional approach in choosing the UN Secretary-General. Reforms such as those urged by Urquhart and Childers (1996) and the Commission on Global Governance (1995) are urgently required to ensure a more-professional selection process for this most important of all posts. Similar care should also be given to the selection of leadership in regional organizations.

The Secretariats of the UN and regional organizations also need access to the best professional candidates for the difficult and demanding tasks that they are asked to perform. Some of these organizations could benefit from a major overhaul of their system of recruitment, promotion, and assignment to posts (see Urquhart and Childers [1996] for a detailed account of what is required within the UN). Most would also profit from greater specialized professional expertise and from an increase in experienced senior staff. Appropriate training and continuing educational opportunities will also be vital if staff are to be up-to-date with the latest rapidly-advancing knowledge needed to maximize their performance.

Some intergovernmental organizations also require a complete modernization of their administrative practice. Irrational and redundant bureaucratic practices have evolved over time—ironically, in some cases, additional layers of bureaucracy have been added in an effort to respond to criticism about alleged bureaucratic waste. A new and streamlined system of administration and management and access to more modern communication and research technologies and equipment would also assist in increasing staff productivity and effectiveness. Also, most of these organizations could profit from more strategic planning and better intra- and interdepartmental or agency communication and coordination.

Strengthening the Capacity and Effectiveness of Foreign Ministries

Equal attention, however, should be given to the administration of foreign ministries and the choice of senior diplomats involved in regional and global decision making. Although some countries have established foreign services based on merit, it is still common practice in too many countries to appoint ambassadors or other diplomats to senior posts because they come from a well-connected family, have the right political connections, or have contributed heavily to a given political party or campaign. Indeed, many committed and effective diplomats and officials in the international community express serious frustration about the poor quality of too many of their colleagues, a condition that impedes effective mutilateral negotiation and decision making. More rigorous selection criteria are clearly needed for those who hold the fate of the world and its peoples in their hands.

Diplomats should also be encouraged to have more direct contact with the problems on which they are working and the people whose lives are affected by their decision making. Diplomats chosen for their financial connections may have little appreciation of the problems of the disadvantaged, even in their own country, and the diplomatic lifestyle often does little to expose them to such circumstances. Thus, where possible, diplomatic staff should be encouraged to carry out on-site visits to see situations first-hand. When this is not possible, they should at least be more effectively and realistically briefed, so that the decisions made at the center are the right ones for the problems being experienced in the field.

It can be argued that changes are also needed to diplomatic protocol and practice. More effective and streamlined meeting rules with clearly defined objectives for outcome, as well as new norms for shorter, more-to-the-point interventions in the endless round of multilateral meetings might be an advantage to all concerned.

Moreover, if the new objectives for the international community are to be sustainable peace and sustainable development through good governance, and if state prestige is to be measured by a government's efforts toward such goals, foreign ministries, along with other government ministries, may wish to consider reorienting their budgets to devote more of their resources to these goals at home or abroad rather than to the expenses associated with the trappings of prestige in New York, Geneva, or other foreign capitals. These new, more socially responsible norms, tailored to today's problems rather than to the exigencies of past centuries of diplomatic practice in the courts of Europe, would need to be developed through self-regulation and a renewed commitment to securing a greater degree of human security for all.

Finally, a corresponding argument to that leveled at IGOs can be made for the administration of the foreign services or ministries of many member states. Government policy is too often insufficiently coordinated between sections of a ministry and between ministries, resulting in contradictory directives. Policy decisions are frequently made with deficient information or by those without adequate knowledge, and bureaucratic practices at all levels often slow down the decision-making process. Efforts to streamline and improve the quality of national decision making would be likely to have a corresponding salutary effect on international decision making.

Revitalizing the UN by Expanding Its Resource Base

It is well known that resource shortages exacerbate conflict, and within the United Nations a large part of the North-South conflict has been waged over this issue. Not only have member states argued about how much of the UN's budget should be paid by whom and when, but they have also long battled over how to spend the limited funds which are available.

Throughout its existence, the UN has been plagued by financial crises, largely because various member states have, over the years, refused to pay major sums that they legally owe to the organization. In recent years, the crisis has deepened as arrearages have accumulated and demands on the UN have increased sharply.

Two reasons exist for the nonpayment of dues. The first is that some developing countries have found it increasingly difficult to pay as their indebtedness has grown. The second, more serious problem, however, is the deliberate withholding of dues as "a destructive way of exercising influence" (Commission on Global Governance, 1995). Childers and Urquhart (1994) argue that the current system of disproportionate assessment has contributed to the problem: "A similar mentality of 'contributing the most' or 'most of' the assessed budgets of the UN system has long distorted attitudes in some countries toward UN financing. It has provoked public antagonisms against the UN, has given apparent legitimacy to the withholding of dues, and has reinforced continuing demands for special influence both in governing bodies and in secretariats. It creates tensions within the overall membership that could yet tear the United Nations apart."

Furthermore, the constant pressure on its financial base has forced the UN to operate on a minimalist approach, which has steadily frustrated its ability to meet its Charter objectives. The Ogata-Volcker Report, a 1993 study by eminent financiers commissioned by the Ford Foundation to study the UN's financial crisis, points out the disparity between the organization's mandate and its resources:

> We have been impressed in particular by the contrast between the demands placed on the United Nations and the smallness and precariousness of its financial base. Any great political institution has to develop with the times, and that development often causes growing pains. In the post-cold war era, the United Nations is being asked to develop very fast and to take on vital responsibility of a kind, and on a scale, undreamed of in its earlier years. Many of the tasks the UN is now undertaking are pioneering efforts in new fields. They will set precedents for vital activities in the future. It is essential that the world organization have the financial backing, as well as the administrative and operational capacity, to make these efforts successful and workable models for the difficult years to come. The UN remains the only existing framework for building the institutions of a global society. While practicing all the requisite managerial rigor and financial economy, it must have the resources—a pittance by comparison with our society's expenditure on

arms—to serve the great objectives set forth in its Charter. Surely the world is ready for, and urgently in need of, a more effective United Nations.

Clearly, if the international community is to more effectively tackle the enormous problems that it faces, an innovative solution is needed to overcome this impasse. One approach might be for member states to devise an entirely new means of financing that would obviate the debate over the size of member states' share of assessment and provide the system with the sustainable resource base that it needs. The Ogata-Volcker Report suggested that additional means of financing the UN may be needed in the future, and they and many others have offered a range of ideas, including various forms of global taxation of airline tickets, oil, pollution, or the arms trade. The Tobin Tax, a plan offered by James Tobin, winner of the 1981 Nobel Prize for economics, proposes that a very small fractional levy be imposed on the trillions of dollars of daily foreign exchange transactions. This would raise multiples of the current UN budget, with minimal cost to any one sector, and with the added benefit of helping to protect the world economy from excessive currency speculation (UNDP Development Report, 1994).

The major concern expressed against taxation proposals has been the fear that member states might lose control over decision making. But as Childers and Urquhart (1994) point out, each member state would be responsible for the collection and transfer of taxation raised in this way, thus leaving members in control of the funds at their source. Moreover, the General Assembly would retain its control over budget allocations.

Although it is beyond the scope of this book to review the merits of these proposals, further study is clearly needed, so that a more effective financial base can be secured and a more constructive relationship between member states established. It is worthy of note, however, that Evans (1996) has mentioned that his informal "soundings" suggest that a great many countries now favor some form of global taxation.

Developing a Vision of the Possible

The sense of crisis that currently pervades the United Nations system has arisen, in part, from the total mismatch between expectations for the organization and its current capacity. With the existing funding base, it has been impossible for the UN to fulfill its mandate. As the organization has struggled against the odds, a loss of confidence has led to a vicious downward spiral of institutional decline. Problems have appeared increasingly insurmountable and a vision of the possible has been lost.

If, however, resources could be brought into line with expectations, the

United Nations could be transformed almost overnight into a more vibrant institution. It could regain the confidence and respect needed to meet the challenges of the next century. The benefits to the international community of a greatly increased budget for the UN would be enormous.

The very process of deciding to make the UN function fully and effectively would create a new climate of hope. A new relationship could develop between member states from the North and South as they began working together to restructure the system and to use the augmented resources wisely to meet the goals of the Charter. A large-scale restructuring could provide an opportunity for a systemwide reshaping and streamlining to make the UN and regional organizations more interactive and efficient. It could bring about a complete rethinking, overhaul, and modernization of the system.

Where required, human resources could be augmented and the ideal of the international civil service revitalized. During the mid-1980s, half the world's scientists worked in the military–industrial complex. There is no reason why, in the interests of sustainable peace and sustainable development, the United Nations and regional organizations should not have similar access to the most highly experienced, knowledgeable, skilled, and dedicated men and women around the world.

With more adequate resources, the United Nations and regional organizations would be better able to assist governments in meeting the basic human needs of their populations and in eliminating the root causes of conflict. With the UN working in partnership with NGOs and research institutions, results would begin to appear that would reinforce the idea that problems, even enormous ones, can be tackled.

In the area of good governance, assistance could be provided to help governments better address the basic human needs of all their people. Services could be offered to strengthen fair laws and institutions. Resources could be used to support governments in providing economic access and opportunities to minorities (including indigenous groups), as well as in addressing their need for cultural expression and identity. As local and national governments became more responsive to the needs of all their citizens, ethnic tension would be reduced. The development of an active civil society and fairer, more democratic processes would provide the built-in corrective mechanisms needed to enhance and maintain good governance and accountability. Habits of dialogue, accommodation, and problem solving would gradually replace violent protest, civil war, insurgency, states of emergency, and gross violations of human rights, such as genocide, "ethnic cleansing," forced expulsion, torture, disappearances, arbitrary detentions, and executions.

The goal of sustainable development could also come closer to reality. A new era of development cooperation could be opened between North and South, as they work together to genuinely tackle the world's problems. Appropriate institutions, guided by suitable macroeconomic policy, could be established to achieve the goals that had been jointly agreed upon. Through the strategic use of resources, economies could be strengthened, employment opportunities created, and poverty greatly reduced. Education could be expanded and developed, enhancing people's prospects of being able to support themselves and their families and to build strong communities.

All of these developments would mean that human needs for security and safety, physical well-being, identity, recognition, and distributive justice could be better addressed, which would reduce the likelihood that groups would turn to violent confrontation. As tensions were reduced, greater demilitarization and disarmament could proceed, freeing up funds that could be spent on developing more just societies. Reduction in the surfeit of weapons would make resort to violence less likely.

When serious disputes between and within countries did arise, expert assistance in preventive diplomacy would be available to help the parties resolve problems before they became violent. Teams of well-trained personnel could be used to calm or stabilize a situation or to actively promote problem solving. Additional resources could also be used to contribute in various ways to a solution. Tracking and studying disputes within each region could lead to a deeper understanding of their causes, and eventually to long-term programs for their reduction. Dispute resolution knowledge would be sharpened and problem-solving skills could be more widely adopted as a more constructive means of approaching problems.

When disputes were not responsive to such methods, a more representative Security Council would be able to take effective preventive or corrective action, including the rapid deployment of military and civilian missions to help prevent or ameliorate the escalation of conflict. Those engaged in peacemaking would be given appropriate support financially and politically to assist the parties in a search for solutions. Adequate humanitarian assistance could also be readily available early in a crisis for both man-made and natural disasters.

International law could be further developed and strengthened. The International Court of Justice could be equipped to handle an increased caseload and complementary tribunals established for specific purposes to deepen the dispute resolution structure.

By placing emphasis "upstream" on prevention rather than "downstream" on management, the international community would find that less of its resources were expended on rehabilitating war-torn societies. Groups would learn that war and violence are not the most effective ways to pursue their interests and that alternative, more effective, and less costly means are available.

Increasing resources and shifting the focus to a more preventive, assistance approach could go a long way toward helping member states of the United Nations and regional organizations work more effectively with each other and with civil society to tackle the many problems besetting the planet. Childers and Urquhart (1994) note that the problems facing the international community "cannot be resolved by individuals, or even, in most instances, regional groups of states; they have worldwide causes and effects. They are not 'sectoral', or single-phenomenon problems; they have multiple socioeconomic and political causes and effects. These problems will not find their own solutions." The authors suggest that the UN provides "the only set of institutions in the world that have the capability to reflect the aspirations, fears, and material needs of the whole of humankind. These are also the only institutions mandated by virtually all governments to respond, in equity and sensitivity, to universal problems and needs."

If the challenge of designing a more effective approach to good international and regional governance is met, sustainable peace and sustainable development could be realized in the twenty-first century. Good global and regional governance would have prepared the way for good national and local governance, whose goal would be the satisfaction of the basic human needs of all the world's peoples.

Acronyms

AMM	ASEAN Ministerial Meeting
ARF	ASEAN Regional Forum
ARF-SOM	ASEAN Regional Forum, Senior Officials Meeting
ASEAN	Association of Southeast Asian Nations
CIO	Chairman-in-Office (of the Organization for Security and Cooperation in Europe)
CIS	Commonwealth of Independent States
COE	Council of Europe
CSCAP	Council for Security Cooperation in the Asia-Pacific Region
CSCE	Conference on Security and Cooperation in Europe (now called the Organization for Security and Cooperation in Europe)
DPA	Department of Political Affairs (of the United Nations)
DPRK	Democratic People's Republic of Korea
ECOSOC	Economic and Social Council (of the United Nations)
EU	European Union
GNP	Gross National Product
HCNM	High Commissioner on National Minorities (of the Organization for Security and Cooperation in Europe)
IGO	Inter-governmental organization
IMF	International Monetary Fund
INN	International Negotiation Network (of the Carter Center)
IPA	International Peace Academy
ISIS	Institute of Strategic and International Studies
LODE	Local Democracy Program (of the Council of Europe)
NGO	Nongovernmental organization
OAS	Organization of American States
OAU	Organization of African Unity

ODIHR	Office for Democratic Institutions and Human Rights
ORCI	Office for Research and the Collection of Information
OSCE	Organization for Security and Cooperation in Europe
PMC	Post-Ministerial Conferences (of the Association of Southeast Asian Nations)
UNDP	United Nations Development Programme
USIP	United States Institute of Peace
ZOPFAN	Zone of Peace, Freedom and Neutrality (of the Association of Southeast Asian Nations)

References

Acharya, A. 1991. The Association of Southeast Asian Nations: "Security community" or "defense community"? *Pacific Affairs* 64, no. 2:159–77.

———. 1992. Regional military-security cooperation in the Third World: A conceptual analysis of the relevance and limitations of ASEAN. *Journal of Peace Research* 29, no. 1:7–22.

———. 1993. *A new regional order in South-East Asia: ASEAN in the post-cold war era*. London: International Institute for Strategic Studies.

———. 1994a. ASEAN-UN cooperation in peace and preventive diplomacy: Its contribution to regional security. *The Indonesian Quarterly* 22, no. 3:215–26.

———. 1994b. Human rights and regional order: ASEAN and human rights management in post-cold war Southeast Asia. In *ASEAN and Human Rights Management in Southeast Asia,* ed. J. T. H. Tang. London: Cassell Publishers.

Adeniji, O. 1993. Regionalism in Africa. *Security Dialogue* 24:211–20.

af Ugglas, M. 1993. *The challenge of preventive diplomacy: The experience of the CSCE*. Stockholm, Sweden: Ministry for Foreign Affairs.

Alagappa, M. 1993. Regionalism and the quest for security: ASEAN and the Cambodian conflict. *Journal of International Affairs* 46, no. 2:439–67.

Almond, H. H. 1993. Human rights, international humanitarian law, and the peaceable adjustment of differences in Africa. *East Africa Journal of Peace and Human Rights* 1, no. 2:137–63.

Alston, P. 1992a. Critical appraisal of the UN human rights regime. In *The United Nations and human rights,* ed. P. Alston. Oxford: Clarendon Press.

———. 1992b. The Commission on Human Rights. In *The United Nations and human rights,* ed. P. Alston. Oxford: Clarendon Press.

———. 1992c. The Committee on Economic, Social and Cultural Rights. In *The United Nations and human rights,* ed. P. Alston. Oxford: Clarendon Press.

Amoah, P. 1992. The African Charter on Human and Peoples' Rights—An effective weapon for human rights? *The African Journal of International and Comparative Law* 4:226–40.

Amoo, S. G. 1993. Role of the OAU: Past, present, and future. In *Making war and waging peace,* ed. D. Smock. Washington, D.C.: United States Institute of Peace Press.

Arat, Z. F. 1991. *Democracy and human rights in developing countries.* Boulder, Colo.: Lynne Rienner Publishers.

Archibugi, D. 1993. The reform of the UN and cosmopolitan democracy: A critical review. *Journal of Peace Research* 30:301–16.

Askandar, K. 1994. ASEAN and conflict management: The formative years of 1967–1976. *Pacifica Review: Peace, Security and Global Change* 6:43–56.

Association of Southeast Asian Nations. 1967. The ASEAN Declaration. Declaration establishing the organization, Bangkok.

———. 1971. Zone of Peace, Freedom and Neutrality Declaration. Declaration of the 1971 meeting of ASEAN, Kuala Lumpur.

———. 1976. Treaty of Amity and Cooperation in Southeast Asia. Agreement reached at the 1976 meeting, Bali.

———. 1992. The ASEAN Declaration on the South China Sea. Declaration of the 1992 meeting of ASEAN, Manila.

———. 1994. Twenty-seventh ASEAN ministerial meeting; ASEAN Regional Forum; and post-ministerial conferences with dialogue partners.

———. 1995a. The ASEAN Regional Forum: A concept paper. Paper prepared by the Secretariat of ASEAN.

———3—. 1995b. *Report of the secretary-general of ASEAN.* Jakarta, Indonesia: ASEAN Secretariat.

Austin, D. 1992. Kennst du das Land? In *Resolving third world conflict: Challenges for a new era,* eds. S. J. Brown and K. M. Schraub. Washington, D.C.: The United States Institute of Peace Press.

Azar, E. E. 1990. *The management of protracted social conflict: Theory and cases.* Hampshire, England: Dartmouth Publishing Company, Ltd.

Bakwesegha, C. J. 1993. The need to strengthen regional organizations: A rejoinder. *Security Dialogue* 24, no. 4:377–81.

———. 1995. The role of the Organization of African Unity in conflict prevention, management and resolution. *International Journal of Refugee Law Special Issue,* 207–19.

———. 1996. The role of the Organization of African Unity in conflict prevention, management and resolution in the context of the political evolution of Africa. *African Journal on Conflict Prevention, Management and Resolution* 1:4–22.

Benedek, W. 1993. The African Charter and Commission on Human and Peoples' Rights: How to make it more effective. *Netherlands Quarterly of Human Rights* 1, 25–40.

Bercovitch, J. 1992. The structure and diversity of mediation in international relations. In *Mediation in international relations,* eds. J. Bercovitch and J. Z. Rubin. New York: St. Martin's Press.

Bercovitch, J., and J. Langley. 1993. The nature of the dispute and the effectiveness of international mediation. *The Journal of Conflict Resolution,* 37, 670–91.

Bercovitch, J., and J. Z. Rubin. 1992. *Mediation in international relations.* New York: St. Martin's Press.

Berhe-Tesfu, C. 1995. Humanitarian action, preventive diplomacy and advocacy: The emerging role of CBOs and NGOs. *International Journal of Refugee Law Special Edition*, 220–34.

Boutros-Ghali, B. 1992a. *An agenda for peace*. New York: United Nations.

———. 1992b. Empowering the United Nations. *Foreign Affairs* 71:89–102.

———. 1994a. *An agenda for development*. New York: United Nations.

———. 1994b. Report of the secretary-general on the work of the organization (A/49/1).

———. 1995a. Report of the secretary-general on the work of the organization (A/50/1).

———. 1995b. Supplement to an agenda for peace: Position paper of the secretary-general on the occasion of the fiftieth anniversary of the United Nations (A/50/60).

———. 1996. *An agenda for democratization*. New York: United Nations.

Brecher, M., and J. Wilkenfeld. 1989. *Crisis, conflict and instability*. Oxford: Pergamon Press.

Brinkley, D. 1995. Jimmy Carter's modest quest for global peace. *Foreign Affairs* 74:90–100.

Brockner, J., and J. Z. Rubin. 1985. *The social psychology of conflict escalation and entrapment*. New York: Springer-Verlag.

Brölmann, C., R. Lefeber, and M. Zieck, eds. 1992. *Peoples and minorities in international law*. Dordrecht: Kluwer Academic Publishers.

Brown, M. E. 1993. Causes and implications of ethnic conflict. In *Ethnic conflict and international security*, ed. M. E. Brown. Princeton, N.J.: Princeton University Press.

———. 1996. *The international dimensions of internal conflict*. Cambridge, Mass.: The MIT Press.

Brown, S. J., and K. M. Schraub. 1992. *Resolving third world conflict: Challenges for a new era*. Washington, D.C.: United States Institute of Peace Press.

Buergenthal, T., R. Norris, and D. Shelton. 1990. *Protecting human rights in the Americas: Selected problems*. Arlington, Va.: N. P. Engel, Publisher.

Burton, J. 1984. *Global conflict*. London: Wheatsheaf Books.

———. 1990. *Conflict: Human needs theory*. New York: St. Martin's Press.

Buszynski, L. 1992. Southeast Asia in the post-cold war era. *Asian Survey* 32, no. 9:830–47.

———. 1993. ASEAN security dilemmas. *Survival* 34, no. 4:90–107.

Camilleri, J. A. 1994. Human rights, cultural diversity, and conflict resolution: The Asia-Pacific Context. *Pacifica Review: Peace, Security and Global Change* 6:17–42.

Carment, D. 1993. The International dimensions of ethnic conflict: Concepts, indicators, and theory. *Journal of Peace Research* 30:137–50.

Carter Center. 1992–93. *Waging peace around the world*. Atlanta, Ga.: Carter Center of Emory University.

———. 1994–95. *State of the world conflict report*. Atlanta, Ga.: Carter Center of Emory University.

Center for Human Rights. 1994. *United Nations action in the field of human rights*. Geneva: United Nations.

Cerna, C. M. 1992. The structure and functioning of the Inter-American Court of Human Rights. In *The British year book of international law*. Oxford: The Clarendon Press.

Chigas, D., E. McClintock, and C. Kamp. 1995. Preventive diplomacy and the Organization for Security and Cooperation in Europe: Creating incentives for dialogue and cooperation. In *Preventing conflict in the post-communist world*, eds. A. H. Chayes and A. Chayes. Washington, D.C.: The Brookings Institution.

Childers, E., and B. Urquhart. 1994. *Renewing the United Nations system*. Uppsala, Sweden: Dag Hammarskjold Foundation.

Claude, I. L. 1993. Reflections on the role of the UN secretary-general. In *The Challenging role of the UN secretary-general*, eds. B. Rivlin and L. Gordenker. Westport, Conn.: Praeger.

Clements, K. 1994. Conflict and conflict resolution in the Asia Pacific region: Culture, problem solving, and peacemaking. *Pacifica Review: Peace Security and Global Change* 6:1–15.

Clements, L. J. 1994. *European human rights: Taking a case under the convention*. London: Sweet & Maxwell.

Coakley, J. 1993. Introduction: The territorial management of ethnic conflict. In *The territorial management of ethnic conflict*, ed. J. Coakley. London: Frank Cass & Co., Ltd.

Commission on Global Governance. 1995. *Our global neighbourhood*. Oxford: Oxford University Press.

Commission on Inter-American Dialogue. 1994. The Organization of American States: Advancing democracy, human rights and the rule of law in the Americas. A report of the Commission on Inter-American Dialogue on the OAS. Washington, D.C.

Conference on Security and Cooperation in Europe. 1975. Final Act: Document of the CSCE, adopted by high officials of participating states, Helsinki.

———. 1990. Charter of Paris for a New Europe. Document of the Paris Meeting of Heads of State or Government, Paris.

———. 1991a. Report of the CSCE Meeting of Experts on Peaceful Settlement of Disputes. Report adopted by the representatives of the CSCE, Valetta.

———. 1991b. Summary of conclusions. CSCE council meeting, Berlin.

———. 1992a. Convention on conciliation and arbitration within the CSCE. Agreement reached at the third meeting of the council, Stockholm.

———. 1992b. Helsinki summit declaration: The challenges of change. Declaration of the Meeting of Heads of State or Government, Helsinki.

———. 1992c. Prague Document on Further Development of the CSCE Institutions and Structures. Summary of the conclusions of the CSCE Council Meeting, Prague.

———. 1992d. Shaping a new Europe—The role of the CSCE. Summary of the conclusions of the CSCE council meeting, Stockholm.

———. 1993. CSCE mechanisms: Overview of implementation. Document prepared by the CSCE secretariat, Vienna.

———. 1994a. Annual report of the secretary general, Vienna.

———. 1994b. Budapest summit declaration: Toward a genuine partnership in a new era. Declaration of the Meeting of Heads of State or Government, Budapest.

Consultation of the International Negotiation Network. 1993. *Revolving intranational conflicts: A strengthening role for intergovernmental organizations.* Conference Report Series of the Carter Center of Emory University, 5 (1).

Cooper, R., and M. Berdal. 1993. Outside intervention in ethnic conflicts. In *Ethnic conflict and international security,* ed. M. E. Brown. Princeton, N.J.: Princeton University Press.

Cooperation Agreement between the Secretariat of the United Nations and the General Secretariat of the Organization of American States. 1995. Unpublished Document.

Coulter, R. T. 1995. The Draft UN Document on the Rights of Indigenous Peoples: What is it? What does it mean? *Netherlands Quarterly of Human Rights* 2:123–37.

Council of Europe. 1985. *European Charter of Local Self-Government.* European Treaty Series, No. 122.

———. 1992a. *Convention on the Participation of Foreigners in Public Life at Local Level.* European Treaty Series, No. 144.

———. 1992b. *European Charter for Regional and Minority Languages.* European Treaty Series, No. 148.

———. 1995a. *Assistance to the development and consolidation of Democratic security.* 1994 Annual Report of the Cooperation and Assistance Programmes with Countries of Central and Eastern Europe. Strasbourg, France: Division of Pan-European Cooperation Programme.

———. 1995b. *The Council of Europe: Achievements and activities:* Strasbourg, France: Publishing and Documentation Service of the Council of Europe.

———. 1995c. *Human rights: A continuing challenge for the Council of Europe.* Strasbourg, France: Council of Europe Press.

Council of Freely Elected Heads of Government. 1990. *Observing Nicaragua's elections, 1989–1990.* Atlanta, Ga.: Carter Center of Emory University.

Cullen, R. 1992. Human rights quandary. *Foreign Affairs* 71:79–88.

da Costa, P. 1995. Keeping the peace. *Africa Report,* May–June, 27–29.

Davidson, S. 1992. *The Inter-American Court of Human Rights.* Aldershot, England: Dartmouth Publishing Company, Ltd.

———. 1995. Remedies for violations of the American Convention on Human Rights. *International and Comparative Law Quarterly* 44:405–14.

de Nevers, R. 1993. Democratization and ethnic conflict. In *Ethnic conflict and international security,* ed. M. E. Brown. Princeton, N.J.: Princeton University Press.

de Silva, K. M., and S. W. R. de A. Samarasinghe. 1993. Introduction. In *Peace accords and ethnic conflict,* eds. K. M. Silva and S. W. R. de A. Samarasinghe. London: Pinter Publishers.

de Soto, A., and G. Castillo. 1994. Obstacles to peacebuilding. *Foreign Policy* 94:69–83.

Deng, F. M., and I. W. Zartman. 1991. *Conflict resolution in Africa.* Washington, D.C.: The Brookings Institution.

Deutch, K. W. 1984. Space and freedom: Conditions for the temporary separation of incompatible groups. *International Political Science Review* 5:125–38.

Diamond, L. 1995. *Promoting democracy in the 1990s: Actors and instruments, issues and imperatives.* A report to the Carnegie Commission on Preventing Deadly Conflict. New York: Carnegie Corporation of New York.

Djiwandono, J. S. 1994. Cooperative security in the Asia-Pacific region: An ASEAN perspective. *The Indonesian Quarterly* 22, no. 3:205–9.

Donnelly, J. 1993. *International human rights.* Boulder, Colo.: Westview Press.

Drzemczewksi, A. 1993. The Council of Europe's cooperation and assistance programmes with Central and Eastern European countries in the human rights field. *Human Rights Law Journal* 14, no. 7–8:229–47.

Drzemczewksi, A., and J. Meyer-Ladewig. 1994. Principal characteristics of the new ECHR control mechanism, as established by Protocol No. 11, signed on 11 May 1994. *Human Rights Law Journal* 15, no. 3:81–115.

Dwyer, A. S. 1990. The Inter-American Court of Human Rights: Toward establishing an effective regional contentious jurisdiction. *Boston College International and Comparative Law Review* 13, no. 1:127–66.

Egeland, J. 1994. Norway's Middle East peace channel. *Security Dialogue* 25, no. 3:349–51.

Eide, A., and B. Hagtvet. 1992. *Human rights in perspective: A global assessment.* Oxford: Basil Blackwell, Ltd.

El-Ayouty, Y. 1994. *The Organization of African Unity after thirty years.* Westport, Conn.: Praeger.

Elias, T. O. 1989. The role of the International Court of Justice in Africa. *The African Journal of International and Comparative Law* 1:1–12.

Emmerson, D. K., and S. W. Simon. 1993. *Regional issues in Southeast Asian security: Scenarios and regimes.* Seattle, Wash.: National Bureau of Asian Research.

Esman, M. J. 1990a. Economic performance and ethnic conflict. In *Conflict and peacemaking in multiethnic societies,* ed. J. Montville. Lexington, Mass.: Lexington Books.

———. 1990b. Political and psychological factors in ethnic conflict. In *Conflict and peacemaking in multiethnic societies,* ed. J. Montville. Lexington, Mass.: Lexington Books.

———. 1994. *Ethnic politics.* Ithaca, N.Y.: Cornell University Press.

Etzioni, Z. 1993. The evils of self-determination. *Foreign Policy* 89:21–35.

Evans, G. 1993. *Cooperating for peace: The global agenda for the 1990s and beyond.* Sydney, Australia: Allen and Unwin.

———. 1994. Cooperative security and intrastate conflict. *Foreign Policy* 96:3–20.

Falk, R. 1994. Democratizing, internationalizing, and globalizing. In *Global transformation: Challenges to the state system,* ed. Y. Sakamoto. Tokyo: United Nations University Press.

———. 1995. Regionalism and world order after the cold war. *Australian Journal of International Affairs* 49, no. 1:1–15.

Farer, T. 1991. Finding the facts: The procedures of the Inter-American Commission on Human Rights of the Organization of American States. In *Fact-finding before international tribunals,* 11th Sokol Colloquium, Ardsley-on-Hudson: Transnational Publishers.

Faure, G. O., and J. Z. Rubin. 1993. *Culture and negotiation.* Newbury Park, Calif.: Sage Publications.

Findlay, T. 1994a. Multilateral conflict prevention, management and resolution. *SIPRI yearbook 1994.* Oxford: Oxford University Press.

————. 1994b. South-East Asia and the new Asia-Pacific security dialogue. *SIPRI yearbook 1994.* Oxford: Oxford University Press.

Forsythe, D. P. 1993. The UN secretary-general and human rights: The question of leadership in a changing context. In *The challenging role of the UN secretary-general,* eds. B. Rivlin and L. Gordenker. Westport, Conn.: Praeger.

Franck, T. M. 1990. *The power of legitimacy among nations.* Oxford: Oxford University Press.

————. 1994. *Fairness in the international legal and institutional system.* Dordrecht: Kluwer Academic Publishers.

Fromuth, P. 1993. The making of a security community: The United Nations after the cold war. *Journal of International Affairs,* 341–66.

Gaer, F. D. 1992. First fruits: Reporting by states under the African Charter on Human and Peoples' Rights. *Netherlands Quarterly of Human Rights* 1, no. 10:29–42.

————. 1993. The United Nations and the CSCE: Cooperation, competition, or confusion? In *The CSCE in the 1990s: Constructing European security and cooperation,* ed. M. R. Lucas. Baden-Baden: Nomos Verlag.

Galtung, J. 1980. The Basic needs approach. In *Human needs: A contribution to the current debate,* eds. K. Lederer, J. Galtung, and D. Antal. Cambridge, Mass.: Oelgeschlager, Gunn, and Hain.

————. 1990. International development in human perspective. In *Conflict: Human needs theory,* ed. J. Burton. New York: St. Martin's Press.

Ganesan, N. 1994. Taking stock of post–cold war developments in ASEAN. *Security Dialogue* 25, no. 4:457–68.

Gaviria, C. 1995a. Annual report of the secretary-general, 1994–1995. General Secretariat Organization of American States. Washington, D.C.

————. 1995b. A new vision of the OAS: Working paper of the general secretariat for the permanent council. Washington, D.C.: OAS.

George, A. L. 1993. *Bridging the gap: Theory and practice in foreign policy.* Washington, D.C.: The United States Institute of Peace Press.

Ghebali, V. Y. 1993. The CSCE Forum for Security Cooperation: The opening gambits. *NATO Review* 41:23–27.

————. 1995. After the Budapest conference: The Organization for Security and Cooperation in Europe. *NATO Review,* March, 24–27.

Glover, A. 1995a. The human dimension of the OSCE: From standard-setting to implementation. *Helsinki Monitor* 3:31–39.

————. 1995b. Natonal minorities in Europe. *Studia Diplomatica* 48, no. 3:52–61.

Gordenker, L. 1993. The UN secretary-generalship: Limits, potentials and leadership. In *The challenging role of the UN Secretary-General,* eds. B. Rivlin and L. Gordenker. Westport, Conn.: Praeger.

Groom, A. J. R., and P. Taylor. 1993. Beyond the agenda for peace. *Peace and the Sciences* 24:11–19.

Grossman, C. 1989. Proposals to strengthen the inter-American system of protection of human rights. *German Yearbook of International Law* 32:264–79.

Guest, I. 1990. *Behind the disappearances: Argentina's dirty war against human rights and the United Nations*. Philadelphia: University of Pennsylvania Press.

Gupta, D. K., A. J. Jongman, and A. Schmid. 1994. Creating a composite index for assessing country performance in the field of human rights. *Human Rights Quarterly* 16:131–62.

Gurr, T. R. 1992. Third world minorities at risk since 1945. In *Resolving third world conflict: Challenges for a new era*, eds. S. J. Brown and K. M. Schraub. Washington, D.C.: The United States Institute of Peace Press.

———. 1993. *Minorities at risk: A global view of ethnopolitical conflicts*. Washington, D.C.: The United States Institute of Peace Press.

———. 1994. Peoples against states: Ethnopolitical conflict and the changing world system. *International Studies Quarterly* 38:347–77.

Gurr, T. R., and B. Harff. 1994. *Ethnic conflict in world politics*. Boulder, Colo.: Westview Press.

Gutlove, P., and G. Thompson. 1995. The potential for cooperation by the OSCE and nongovernmental actors on conflict management. *Helsinki Monitor* 3:52–64.

Gye-Wado, O. 1990. A comparative analysis of the institutional framework for the enforcement of human rights in Africa and Western Europe. *African Journal of International and Comparative Law* 2:187–201.

———. 1991. The rule of admissibility under the African Charter of Human and Peoples' Rights. *African Journal of International and Comparative Law* 3:742–54.

Habeeb, W. M. 1988. *Power and tactics in international negotiation: How weak nations bargain with strong nations*. Baltimore, Md.: The Johns Hopkins University Press.

Haggag, A. 1993. The role of regional organizations in conflict resolution, prevention and management: The example of the OAU. Paper presented to the International Roundtable Conference on Preventive Conflict Management, Vienna.

———. 1995. OAU mechanism for conflict prevention, management and resolution in Africa: An example of regional preventive diplomacy? Paper presented at the Fellowship Programme in Peacemaking and Preventive Diplomacy, Burg Schlaining, Austria, July 1995.

Hamburg, D. A. 1993. Preventing contemporary intergroup violence. *1993 annual report of the Carnegie Corporation of New York*. New York: Carnegie Corporation of New York.

Hannum, H. 1990. *Autonomy, sovereignty, and self-determination: The accommodation of conflicting rights*. Philadelphia: University of Pennsylvania Press.

Hassner, P. 1993. Beyond nationalism and internationalism: Ethnicity and world order. In *Ethnic conflict and international security*, ed. M. E. Brown. Princeton, N.J.: Princeton University Press.

Hemming, A. M. 1992. ASEAN security cooperation after the cold war: Problems and prospects. *The Indonesian Quarterly* 20, no. 3:286–97.

Hermann, M. G., and C. W. Kegley. 1996. Ballots, a barrier against the use of bullets and bombs. *Journal of Conflict Resolution* 40:436–60.

Horowitz, D. L. 1981. Patterns of ethnic separatism. *Comparative studies in society and history* 23:165–95.

———. 1985. *Ethnic groups in conflict.* Berkeley: University of California Press.

———. 1990a. Ethnic conflict management for policymakers. In *Conflict and peacemaking in multiethnic societies,* ed. J. Montville. Lexington, Mass.: Lexington Books.

———. 1990b. Making moderation pay: The comparative politics of ethnic conflict management. In *Conflict and peacemaking in multiethnic soceities,* ed. J. Montville. Lexington, Mass.: Lexington Books.

Höynck, W. 1994. CSCE works to develop its conflict prevention potential. *NATO Review* 42, no. 2:16–22.

———. 1995a. CSCE contribution to early warning, conflict prevention and crisis management. *Janes International Defense Review,* 1995, 30–35.

———. 1995b. From the CSCE to the OSCE: The challenges of building new stability. *Helsinki Monitor* 3:11–22.

———. 1995c. New challenges on the OSCE conflict resolution agenda. Speech by the secretary general of the OSCE at the 1995 NATO Crisis Management Seminar, Brussels.

———. 1995d. The OSCE's contribution to new stability. Speech by the secretary general of the OSCE at the 1995 Seminar, Post–Cold War Europe—Organizations in Search of New Roles, Helsinki.

———. 1995e. What can the OSCE do to manage crises in Europe? Speech by the secretary general of the OSCE, Pielavesi, Finland.

Huber, K. 1994. The CSCE's new role in the East: Conflict prevention. *RFE/RL Research Report* 3, no. 31:23–30.

Hume, C. 1994. *Ending Mozambique's war: The role of mediation and good offices.* Washington, D.C.: United States Institute of Peace Press.

Huxley, T. 1993. *Insecurity in the ASEAN regime.* London: Royal United Services Institute for Defense Studies.

Ibok, S. B. 1996. The dynamics of conflicts in Africa: Evaluating the OAU's past and present approaches for conflict prevention, management and resolution and future prospects. *African Journal on Conflict Prevention, Management and Resolution* 1:64–83.

Independent Working Group on the Future of the United Nations. 1995. *The United Nations in its second half-century: A report of the Independent Working Group on the Future of the United Nations.* New York: The Ford Foundation.

Inter-American Commission on Human Rights. 1992. *Basic documents pertaining to human rights in the Inter-American system.* Washington, D.C.: Organization of American States.

———. 1994. *Annual report of the Inter-American Commission on Human Rights.* Washington, D.C.: Organization of American States.

———. 1995. Draft of the Inter-American Declaration on the Rights of Indigenous Peoples, 21 September 1995. Washington, D.C.: Organization of American States.

Inter-American Commission on Human Rights and the Inter-American Institute of Human Rights. 1995. *Human Rights: How to present a petition in the Inter-American system.* Washington, D.C.: Organization of American States.

Inter-American Juridical Committee. 1995. *Annual report to the General Assembly of the Organization of American States.* OEA/Ser G/CP/doc. 2556/95.

Jalali, R., and S. M. Lipset, 1992. Racial and ethnic conflicts: A global perspective. *Political Science Quarterly* 107:585–606.

James, A. 1993. The secretary-general as an independent political actor. In *The challenging role of the UN Secretary-General,* eds. B. Rivlin and L. Gordenker. Westport, Conn.: Praeger.

Jennings, I. 1956. *The approach to self-government.* Cambridge, Mass.: Cambridge University Press.

Johnston, I., and T. Nkiwane. 1993. The Organization of African Unity and conflict management in Africa. An International Peace Academy report.

Kelman, H. C. 1990. Applying a human needs perspective to the practice of conflict resolution: The Israeli-Palestinian case. In *Conflict: Human needs theory,* ed. J. Burton. New York: St. Martin's Press.

Kemp, W. 1995. The OSCE and the UN: A closer relationship. *Helsinki Monitor* 1:23–31.

Kennedy, P., and B. Russett. 1995. Reforming the United Nations. *Foreign Affairs* 74:56–71.

Kihl, Y. W. 1989. Intra-regional conflict and the ASEAN peace process. *International Journal* 44, no. 3:598–615.

Kim, S. Y., and B. Russett. 1996. The new politics of voting alignments in the United Nations General Assembly. *International Organization* 50:629–52.

Kodjo, E. 1990. The African Charter on Human and Peoples' Rights. *Human Rights Law Journal* 11:271–83.

Kooijman, P. H. 1991. Inter-state dispute settlement in the field of human rights. In *The United Nations decade of international law: Reflections on international dispute settlement,* eds. M. Brus, S. Muller, and S. Wiemers. Dordrecht: Martinus Nijhoff Publishers.

Kovacs, L. 1995. The OSCE: Present and future challenges. *Helsinki Monitor* 3:7–10.

Krüger, H. C., and W. Strasser. 1994. Combatting racial discrimination with the European Convention on the Protection of Human Rights and Fundamental Freedoms. Council of Europe. *The use of international conventions to protect the rights of migrants and ethnic minorities.* Strasbourg: Council of Europe.

Kuper, L. 1985. *The prevention of genocide.* New Haven, Conn.: Yale University Press.

———. 1989. The prevention of genocide: Cultural and structural indicators of genocidal threat. *Ethnic and Racial Studies* 12:157–73.

Kux, S. 1992. International approaches to the national minorities problem. *The Polish Quarterly of International Affairs* 1:7–26.

Lake, D. A., and D. Rothchild. 1996. Containing fear: The origins and management of ethnic conflict. *International Security* 21:41–75.

Lawson, S. 1994. Culture, democracy, and political conflict management in Asia and the Pacific: An agenda for research. *Pacifica Review: Peace, Security and Global Change* 6:84–89.

Leatherman, J. 1993. Conflict transformation in the CSCE: Learning and institutionalization. *Cooperation and Conflict* 28 no. 4:403–31.

Leng, R. J. 1993a. Influence techniques among nations. In *Behavior, society, and international conflict: Volume III*, eds. P. E. Tetlock, J. L. Husbands, R. Jervis, P. Stern, and C. Tilly. New York: Oxford University Press.

———. 1993b. Reciprocating influence strategies in interstate crisis bargaining. *The Journal of Conflict Resolution* 37:3–41.

Levine, A. 1996. Political accommodation and the prevention of secessionist violence. In *The international dimensions of internal conflict*, ed. M. E. Brown. Cambridge, Mass.: The MIT Press.

Lewis, P. M. 1996. Economic reform and political transitions in Africa: The quest for a politics of development. *World Politics* 49:92–129.

Licklider, R. 1995. The consequences of negotiated settlements in civil wars, 1945–1993. *American Political Science Review* 89:681–90.

Lijphart, A. 1984. *Democracies: Patterns of majoritarian and consensus government in twenty-one countries.* New Haven, Conn.: Yale University Press.

———. 1990. The power-sharing approach. In *Conflict and peacemaking in multiethnic societies*, ed. J. Montville. Lexington, Mass.: Lexington Books.

Livermore, J. D., and B. G. Ramcharan. 1993. Purposes and principles: The secretary-general's role in human rights. In *The challenging role of the UN secretary-general*, eds. B. Rivlin and L. Gordenker. Westport, Conn.: Praeger.

Luck, E. C. 1995. Layers of security: Regional arrangements, the United Nations, and the Japanese-American security treaty. *Asian Survey* 35, no. 3:237–52.

Lukashuk, I. I. 1991. The United Nations and illegitimate regimes: When to intervene to protect human rights. In *Law and force in the new international order*, eds. L. F. Damrosch and D. Scheffer. Boulder, Colo.: Westview Press.

MacFarlane, S. N., and T. B. Weiss. 1994. The United Nations, regional organizations and human security: Building theory in Central America. *Third World Quarterly* 15, no. 2:277–93.

Magnarella, P. J. 1993. Preventing interethnic conflict and promoting human rights through more effective legal, political and aid structures: Focus on Africa. *Georgia Journal of International and Comparative Law* 23:327–43.

Mahoney, K. E., and P. Mahoney. 1993. *Human rights in the twenty-first century: A global challenge.* Dordrecht: Martinus Nijhoff Publishers.

Martenson, J. 1993. The United Nations and human rights today and tomorrow. In *Human rights in the twenty-first century: A global challenge*, eds. K. E. Mahoney and P. Mahoney. Dordrecht: Martinus Nijhoff Publishers.

Maslow, A. H. 1962. *Toward a psychology of being.* Princeton, N.J.: Van Nostrand.

Mason, T. D., and P. J. Fett. 1996. How civil wars end. *Journal of Conflict Resolution* 40:546–68.

Maynes, C. W. 1993. Containing ethnic conflict. *Foreign Policy* 90:3–21.

Mazrui, A. A., O. Otunnu, and S. A. Salim. 1993. The OAU and conflict management in Africa. Chairmen's report of joint OAU/IPA consultation, Addis Ababa, May 1993.

McCoy, J., L. Garbert, and R. Pastor. 1991. Pollwatching and peacemaking. *Journal of Democracy* 2, no. 4:102–14.

McGarry, J., and B. O'Leary. 1993. Introduction: The macro-political regulation of ethnic conflict. In *The politics of ethnic conflict regulation*, eds. J. McGarry and B. O'Leary. London: Routledge.

McGoldrick, D., ed. 1995. Human dimension of the OSCE. Collection of documents prepared for the Office for Democratic Institutions and Human Rights, Warsaw, Poland.

McRae, K. D. 1990. Theories of power-sharing and conflict management. In *Conflict and peacemaking in multiethnic societies,* ed. J. Montville. Lexington, Mass.: Lexington Books.

Medina, C. 1990. The Inter-American Commission on Human Rights and the Inter-American Court of Human Rights: Reflections on a joint venture. *Human Rights Quarterly* 12:439–64.

Merrills, J. G. 1991. *International dispute settlement.* 2d ed., Cambridge, England: Grotius Publications Ltd.

Mitchell, C. 1990. Necessitous man and conflict resolution: More basic questions about basic human needs theory. In *Conflict: Human needs theory,* ed. J. Burton. New York: St. Martin's Press.

Montville, J. V. 1993. The healing function in political conflict resolution. In *Conflict resolution theory and practice: Integration and application,* eds. D. J. D. Sandole and H. van der Merwe. Manchester, England: Manchester University Press.

Mowbray, A. 1993. Reform of the control system of the European Convention on Human Rights. *Public Law,* Autumn, 419–27.

———. 1994. A new European Court of Human Rights. *Public Law,* Winter, 540–53.

Mralzek, J. 1994. European security on peaceful settlement of disputes. *Co-existence* 31:221–40.

Munoz, H. 1993. The OAS and democratic governance. *Journal of Democracy* 4:29.

Mustapha, B. M. 1989. *The OAU and the management of African crises.* Lagos, Nigeria: African Peace Research Institute Series.

Mutua, M. 1995. The Banjul Charter and the African cultural fingerprint: An evaluation of the language of duties. *Virginia Journal of International Law* 35:340–80.

National Institute for Dispute Resolution. 1992. A conversation on peacemaking with Jimmy Carter. Publication from the National Conference on Peacemaking and Conflict Resolution, Charlotte, N.C., 7 June 1991.

Nguema, I. 1990. Human rights perspectives in Africa. *Human Rights Law Journal* 11:261–71.

Nordic UN Project. 1991. *The United Nations: Issues and options.* Stockholm: Almquist & Wiksell International.

Nordlinger, E. A. 1972. *Conflict regulation in divided societies.* Occasional paper no. 29. Cambridge, Mass.: Harvard University Center for International Affairs.

Northedge, F. S., and M. D. Donelan. 1971. *International disputes: The political aspects.* London: Europa.

Ocaya-Lakidi, D. 1992. Africa's internal conflicts: The search for response. Report of the OAU/IPA high-level consultation, Arusha, Tanzania, March 1992.

Odinkalu, A. C. 1993. Proposals for review of the rules of procedure of the African Commission of Human and Peoples' Rights. *Human Rights Quarterly* 15:533–48.

Ogata, S., and P. Volcker. 1993. *Financing an effective United Nations.* New York: Ford Foundation.

Ojo, O., and A. Sasy. 1986. The OAU and human rights: Prospects for the 1980s and beyond. *Human Rights Quarterly* 8, no. 1:89–103.

O'Neill, R. J. 1992. *Security challenges for Southeast Asia after the cold war.* Singapore: Institute of Southeast Asian Studies.

Oraa, J. 1992. *Human rights in states of emergency in international law.* Oxford: Clarendon Press.

Organization for Security and Cooperation in Europe. 1995. Survey of OSCE long-term missions, local OSCE representatives and sanctions assistance missions. Report to the CPC, Vienna.

Organization of African Unity. 1981. Banjul Charter on Human and Peoples' Rights. Agreement of the Meeting of Heads of State and Government, Nairobi.

———. 1989. Rules of procedure of the African Commission on Human and Peoples' Rights. OAU Document 1 Proceed. Afric., 233.

———. 1990. Declaration of the Assembly of Heads of State and Government of the Organization of African Unity on the political and socio-economic situation in Africa and the fundamental changes taking place in the world. Declaration of Twenty-sixth Ordinary Session of the OAU, Addis Ababa.

———. 1992. Report of the secretary-general on conflicts in Africa: Proposals for a mechanism for conflict prevention and resolution. Report submitted to the Fifty-sixth Extraordinary Session of the Council of Ministers, Dakar.

———. 1993a. Declaration of the Assembly of Heads of State and Government on the establishment within the OAU of a mechanism for conflict prevention, management and resolution. Declaration of Twenty-ninth Ordinary Session of the OAU, Cairo.

———. 1993b. Draft declaration of the Assembly of Heads of State and Government on the establishment within the OAU of a mechanism for conflict prevention, management and resolution. Draft presented to the Thirtieth Assembly of Heads of State and Government, Cairo.

———. 1993c. Report of the secretary-general on the establishment within the OAU of a mechanism for conflict prevention, management and resolution. Report to the Thirtieth Assembly of Heads of State and Government, Cairo.

———. 1994. Report of the secretary-general on the activities of the general secretariat. Report to the Council of Ministers Meeting, Tunis.

———. 1995. Report of the secretary-general on the activities of the general secretariat. Report to the Council of Ministers Meeting, Addis Ababa.

Organization of African Unity/International Peace Academy. 1993. The OAU and conflict management in Africa. Chairmen's report of joint OAU/IPA consultation, Addis, Ababa.

Organization of American States. 1991. Representative democracy. Resolution adopted at the fifth plenary session of the OAS. OAS Official Records AG/RES. 1080 (XXI-)/91.

———. 1992. *Basic documents pertaining to human rights in the Inter-American system.* OAS Official Records OEA/Ser.L.V/II.82, doc. 6 rev. 1.

———. 1994a. Annual report of the secretary general, 1993–1994. OAS official records OEA/Ser.D/III-44.

————. 1994b. Charter of the Organization of American States: As amended by the Protocol of Buenos Aires in 1967 and by the Protocol of Cartagena de Indias in 1985. OAS Treaty Series No. 1-F, OEA/Ser.A/2 (English) Rev. 4.

————. 1994c. Cooperation between the United Nations and the Organization of American States. Report of the secretary-general. OAS Official Records A/49/450.

————. 1994d. Special report on the human rights situation in the so-called "Communities of Peoples in Resistance" in Guatemala. Report to the Eighty-sixth Special Session of the Inter-American Commission on Human Rights. OAS Official Records OEA/Ser.L/V/II.86, doc. 5 rev. 1.

————. 1995. A new vision of the OAS. Working paper of the general secretariat for the permanent council, Washington, D.C.

Organization for Security and Cooperation in Europe. 1996. Lisbon summit declaration.

————. 1996. Lisbon declaration on a common and comprehensive security model for Europe for the twenty-first century.

Otunnu, O. A. 1992. Preface. In D. Ocaya-Lakidi, *Africa's internal conflicts: The search for response*. Report of a High-Level Consultation, Arusha, Tanzania, March 1992.

Panel of High-Level Personalities on African Development. 1995. Priority Africa: Summary of the work of the Panel of High-Level Personalities on African development. Office of the Special Coordinator for Africa and the Least Developed Countries, United Nations, New York.

Pasqualucci, J. M. 1993. Provisional measures in the Inter-American human rights system: An innovative development in international law. *Vanderbilt Journal of Transnational Law* 26, no. 4:803–63.

Pastor, R. 1990. The making of a free election. *Journal of Democracy* 1:13–25.

————. 1995. With Carter in Haiti. *World View* 8:5–8.

Peck, C. 1991a. The case for a United Nations dispute settlement commission. *Interdisciplinary Peace Research* 3:73–87.

————. 1991b. Designing more cost-effective methods for resolving international disputes. In *Whose new world order? What role for the United Nations?* eds. M. R. Bustelo and P. Alston. Canberra, Australia: Federation Press.

————. 1993. Improving the UN system of preventive diplomacy and conflict resolution: Past experiences, current problems and future perspectives. In *Blauhelme in einer turbulenten Welt*, ed. W. Kühne. Baden-Baden: Nomos Verlagsgesellschaft.

————. 1996. *The United Nations as a dispute settlement system: Improving mechanisms for the prevention and resolution of conflict*. The Hague: Kluwer Law International.

Perkin, L. 1995. ASEAN-UN cooperation for peace and preventive diplomacy: A United Nations perspective. In *ASEAN-UN cooperation in preventive diplomacy*, eds. S. Viraphol and W. Pfenning. Ministry of Foreign Affairs: Bangkok, Thailand.

Permanent Council. 1995. Annual report of the OAS Permanent Council to the General Assembly, 1 June 1995, OAS, Washington, D.C.

Permanent Council of the OAS Working Group on Representative Democracy. 1994. Workplan for the Unit for the Promotion of Democracy, 1994–1995, 9 March 1994, OEA/Ser.G CP/CG-1326/93 rev. 3.

Peter, C. M. 1993. The proposed African Court of Justice-Jurisprudential, Procedural, Enforcement Problems and Beyond. *East African Journal of Peace and Human Rights* 1, no. 2:117–36.

Pinto, D. 1995. *From assistance to democracy to democratic security: Cooperation and assistance programmes for Central and Eastern Europe.* Strasbourg, France: COE Division of Pan-European Cooperation Programme.

Posen, B. R. 1993. The security dilemma and ethnic conflict. In *Ethnic conflict and international security,* ed. M. E. Brown. Princeton, N.J.: Princeton University Press.

Princen, T. 1987. International mediation—the view from the Vatican. *Negotiation Journal* 3:347–66.

Pruitt, D. G., and J. Z. Rubin. 1986. *Social conflict: Escalation, stalemate, and settlement.* New York: Random House.

Puchala, D. J. 1993. The secretary-general and his special representatives. In *The challenging role of the UN secretary-general,* eds. B. Rivlin and L. Gordenker. Westport, Conn.: Praeger.

Quashigah, E. K. 1995. Legitimacy of governments and the resolution of intranational conflicts in Africa. *African Journal of International and Comparative Law* 7, no. 2:284–304.

Ra-anan, U. 1990. The nation-state fallacy. In *Conflict and peacemaking in multiethnic societies,* ed. J. Montville. Lexington, Mass.: Lexington Books.

Ramcharan, B. G. 1989. *The concept and present status of international protection of human rights.* Dordrecht: Martinus Nijhoff Publishers.

Remacle, E. 1993. The Yugoslav crisis as a test case for CSCE's role in conflict prevention and crisis management. In *The CSCE in the 1990s: Constructing European security and cooperation,* ed. M. R. Lucas. Baden-Baden: Nomos Verlag.

Report of the third general meeting between representatives of the United Nations System and the Organization of American States, New York, 17 and 18 April 1995. Unpublished document.

Reychler, L. 1992. The price is surprise on preventive diplomacy. *Studia Diplomatica* 45:71–82.

Richardson, J. M., and J. Wang. 1993. Peace accords: Seeking conflict resolution in deeply divided societies. In *Peace accords and ethnic conflict,* eds. K. M. de Silva and S. W. R. de A. Samarasinghe. London: Pinter Publishers.

Roberts, A. 1993. The United Nations and international security. In *Ethnic conflict and international security,* ed. M. E. Brown. Princeton, N.J.: Princeton University Press.

Rönquist, A. 1995. The Council of Europe Framework Convention for the Protection of National Minorities. *Helsinki Monitor* 1:38–44.

Ropers, N., and P. Schlotter. 1993. Multilateral conflict management in a transforming world order. *Law and State* 47:65–92.

Rosecrance, R. 1991. Regionalism and the post-cold war era. *International Journal* 46, no. 3:373–93.

Rosenne, S. 1995. *The World Court: What it is and how it works.* Dordrecht: Martinus Nijhoff Publishers.

Rotfeld, A. D. 1992. European security structures in transition. *World Armaments and Disarmament,* 563–92.

———. 1994a. Europe: The multilateral security process. *SIPRI yearbook 1995.* Oxford: Oxford University Press.

———. 1994b. The search for a cooperative security system. *International Affairs* 12:45–51.

Rothchild, D. 1986. Interethnic conflict and policy analysis in Africa. *Ethnic and Racial Studies* 9:66–86.

Rothchild, D., and N. Chazan. 1988. *The precarious balance: State and society in Africa.* Boulder, Colo.: Westview Press.

Rothstein, R. L. 1992. Weak democracy and the prospect for peace and prosperity in the third world. In *Resolving third world conflict: Challenges for a new era,* eds. S. J. Brown and K. M. Schraub. Washington, D.C.: United States Institute of Peace Press.

Ryan, S. 1990. *Ethnic conflict and international relations.* Aldershot, England: Dartmouth Publishing Company.

Sahnoun, M. 1994. *Somalia: The missed opportunities.* Washington, D.C.: United States Institute of Peace Press.

———. 1996. Managing conflict after the cold war: The Catholic Institute for International Relations. Report of the annual general meeting.

Salim, S. A. 1992. A new agenda for the OAU. *Africa Report* 37, no. 3:36–40.

Samarasinghe, S. W. R. de A., and R. Coughlan. 1991. *Economic dimensions of ethnic conflict.* London: Pinter Publishers.

Sandole, D. 1990. The biological basis of needs in world society: The ultimate micro-macro nexus. In *Conflict: Human needs theory,* ed. J. Burton. New York: St. Martin's Press.

Sapiro, M. 1995. Changing the CSCE into the OSCE: Legal aspects of a political transformation. *American Journal of International Law* 89, no. 3:631–37.

Saravanamuttu, J. 1994. ASEAN: A rejoinder. *Security Dialogue* 25, no. 4:469–72.

Saunders, H. H. 1993. A political approach to ethnic and national conflict. *Mediterranean Quarterly* 4:11–23.

Scarritt, J. R. 1993. Communal conflict and contention for power in Africa South of the Sahara. In *Minorities at risk: A global view of ethnopolitical conflicts,* ed. T. R. Gurr. Washington, D.C.: United States Institute of Peace Press.

Schachter, O. 1991. *International law in theory and practice.* Dordrecht: Martinus Nijhoff Publishers.

Scheman, L. R. 1989. Rebuilding the OAS: A program for its second century. *Inter-American Review of Bibliography* 39, no. 4:527–34.

Schermers, H. 1990. The European Commission of Human Rights from the inside: Some thoughts on human rights in Western Europe. The Josephine Onoh Memorial Lecture. England: Hull University Press.

Schlager, E. B. 1991. The procedural framework of the CSCE: From the Helsinki Consultations to the Paris Charter, 1972–1990. *Human Rights Law Journal* 12:221–37.

Schumann, K. 1994. The role of the Council of Europe. In *Minority rights in Europe: The scope for a transnational regime,* ed. H. Miall. London: Pinter Publishers.

Senghaas, D. 1993. Global governance: How could it be conceived? *Security Dialogue* 24:247–56.

Shehadi, K. S. 1993. Ethnic self-determination and the break-up of states. *Adelphi Papers* 283:3–90.

Shivji, I. G. 1989. *The concept of human rights in Africa.* London: Codesria Books.

Singh, D. 1992. ASEAN and regional security. *New Zealand International Review* 17, no. 5:13–15.

———. 1994. The politics of peace: Preventive diplomacy in ASEAN. *Harvard International Review,* Spring, 32–35.

Sisk, T. D. 1996. *Power sharing and international mediation in ethnic conflicts.* Washington, D.C.: United States Institute of Peace Press.

Smith, A. D. 1993. The ethnic sources of nationalism. In *Ethnic conflict and international security,* ed. M. E. Brown. Princeton, N.J.: Princeton University Press.

Smock, D., ed. 1993. *Making war and waging peace: Foreign intervention in Africa.* Washington, D.C.: United States Institute of Peace Press.

Smock, D., and H. Gregorian. 1993. Introduction. In *Making war and waging peace: Foreign intervention in Africa,* ed. D. Smock. Washington, D.C.: United States Institute of Peace Press.

Snyder, J. 1993. Nationalism and the crisis of the post-Soviet state. In *Ethnic conflict and international security,* ed. M. E. Brown. Princeton, N.J.: Princeton University Press.

Soares, J. C. B. 1994. Annual report of the secretary-general, 1993–1994. Washington, D.C.: OAS.

South Commission. 1990. *The challenge to the South.* The report of the South Commission. Oxford: Oxford University Press.

Spencer, D. E., and W. J. Spencer. 1991. *The international negotiation network: A new method of approaching some very old problems.* Occasional Paper Series. Atlanta, Ga.: Carter Center of Emory University.

Stack, F. 1992. Judicial policy-making and the evolving protection of human rights: The European Court of Human Rights in comparative perspective. *West European Politics* 15, no. 3:137–55.

Stedman, S. J. 1996. Conflict and conciliation in Sub-Saharan Africa. In *The international dimensions of internal conflict,* ed. M. E. Brown. Cambridge, Mass.: The MIT Press.

Steele, R. 1995. Approaches to peace building and preventive diplomacy in the Asia Pacific region. Paper presented to the ARF Seminar on Preventive Diplomacy, Seoul.

Steiner, J. 1990. Power-sharing: Another Swiss "export product"? In *Conflict and peacemaking in multiethnic societies,* ed. J. Montville. Lexington, Mass.: Lexington Books.

Stremlau, J. 1995. Antidote to anarchy. *The Washington Quarterly* 18:29–44.

Strohal, C. 1993. The United Nations response to human rights violations. In *Human rights in the twenty-first century: A global challenge,* eds. K. E. Mahoney and P. Mahoney. Dordrecht: Martinus Nijhoff Publishers.

Summit of the Americas. 1994. Summit of the Americas: Declaration of principles. OAS summit documents, Washington, D.C.

Sutma, R. 1992. Security arrangements in Southeast Asia: A challenge for ASEAN in the post-cold war era. *The Indonesian Quarterly* 20, no. 3:273–85.

Switalski, P. 1993. The role of the CSCE in conflict settlement. *The Polish Quarterly of International Affairs* 2:27–50.

Syquia, E. P. 1989. Regional peace through peaceful coexistence—the ASEAN experience. *Korean Journal of International Studies* 20, no. 4:585.

Talbott S. 1994. ASEAN post-ministerial conference. *US Department of State Dispatch* 5, no.32:545–52.

Tarschys, D. 1995. The Council of Europe: The challenge of engagement. *World Today* 51, no. 4:62–64.

Taylor, P. 1990a. Regionalism and functionalism reconsidered: A critical theory. In *Frameworks for international cooperation,* eds. A. J. R. Groom and P. Taylor. London: Pinter Publishers.

———. 1990b. Regionalism: The thought and the deed. In *Frameworks for International Cooperation,* eds. A. J. R. Groom and P. Taylor. London: Pinter Publishers.

Tetzlaff, R. 1992. Politicized Ethnicity—An underestimated reality in post-colonial Africa. *Law and State* 46:24–53.

Thérien, J. P., M. Fortmann, and G. Gosselin. 1996. The Organization of American States: Restructuring Inter-American multilateralism. *Global Governance* 2:215–39.

Thompson, M. R. 1993. The limits of democratisation in ASEAN. *Third World Quarterly* 14, no. 3:469–84.

Thornberry, P. 1991. *International law and the rights of minorities.* Oxford: Clarendon Press.

———. 1994. International and European standards on human rights. In *Minority rights in Europe: The scope for a transnational regime,* ed. H. Miall. London: Pinter Publishers.

Thornberry, P., and M. Martin Estebanez. 1994. *The Council of Europe and minorities.* Strasbourg, France: COEMIN.

Tillema, H. K. 1989. Foreign overt military intervention in the nuclear age. *Journal of Peace Research* 26:179–95.

Udofia, O. E. 1989. The Organization of African Unity and conflicts in Africa: The Chadian crisis. *Journal of Asian and African Affairs* 1:19–33.

United Nations. 1992. *Handbook on the peaceful settlement of disputes.* New York: The United Nations.

———. 1995a. Cooperation between the United Nations and the Organization for Security and Cooperation in Europe. Report of the secretary-general to the fiftieth session of the General Assembly. UN Document, A/50/564.

———. 1995b. Report of the third general meeting between representatives of the United Nations system and the Organization of American States. New York, 3 May 1995.

———. 1995c. Report of the United Nations high commissioner for human rights. Official records of the General Assembly, fiftieth session, supplement no. 36.

————. 1995d. Cooperation between the United Nations and the Organization of African Unity. Report of the secretary-general to the fiftieth session of the General Assembly. UN Document, A/50/575/add.1.

————. 1996a. Report of the United Nations high commissioner for human rights. UN Document, A/51/36.

————. 1996b. Committee on Economic, Social, and Cultural Rights, UN Document E/1996/22; E/C.12/1995/18.

————. 1996c. Report on the Human Rights Committee. UN Document, A/51/ 40, September.

United Nations Development Programme. 1994. *Human development report, 1994*. Dehli: Oxford University Press.

United Nations Economic and Social Council. 1995. Report of the United Nations high commissioner for human rights. Report to the Commission on Human Rights, fifty-first session, agenda items 3 and 25.

United States Commission on Improving the Effectiveness of the United Nations. 1994. *Defining purpose: The UN and the health of nations*. Washington, D.C.: U.S. Printing Office.

United States Institute of Peace. 1994a. The future of the Conference on Security and Cooperation in Europe: A United States Institute of Peace roundtable. Special report of the United States Institute of Peace, Washington, D.C.

————. 1994b. The U.S. contribution to conflict prevention, management and resolution in Africa. Special report of a United States Institute of Peace symposium, September.

Urquhart, B. 1993. The United Nations and future peace. *South African Journal of International Affairs* 1:9–16.

Urquhart, B., and E. Childers. 1996. *A world in need of leadership: Tomorrow's United Nations: A fresh appraisal*. Uppsala, Sweden: The Dag Hammarskjöld Foundation.

Ury, W. L., J. M. Brett, and S. B. Goldberg. 1988. *Getting disputes resolved: Designing systems to cut the costs of conflict*. San Francisco: Jossey-Bass Publishers.

Vaky, V. P., and H. Munoz. 1993. *The future of the Organization of American States: Essays*. New York: Twentieth Century Fund Press.

van Boven, T. C. 1992. "Political" and "legal" control mechanisms: Their competition and coexistence. In *Human rights in perspective: A global assessment*, eds. A. Eide and B. Hagtvet. Oxford: Basil Blackwell, Ltd.

————. 1993. Prevention of human rights violations. In *Human rights in the twenty-first century: A global challenge*, eds. K. E. Mahoney and P. Mahoney. Dordrecht: Martinus Nijhoff Publishers.

van der Donckt, C. 1995. Looking forward by looking back: A pragmatic look at conflict and the regional option. Policy staff paper, Department of Foreign Affairs and International Trade, Canada.

van der Stoel, M. 1994a. Preventive diplomacy. *Forum*, December, 35–37.

————. 1994b. The role of the CSCE high commissioner on national minorities in CSCE preventive diplomacy. *The challenge of preventive diplomacy: The experience of the CSCE*. Stockholm: Ministry of Foreign Affairs.

————. 1995. The heart of the matter: The human dimension of the OSCE. *Helsinki Monitor* 3:23–30.

Vatikiotis, M. 1993. The first step: ASEAN takes the initiative on security coopera-tion. *Far Eastern Economic Review,* June, 18.

Vetschera, H. 1995. Cooperative security in the OSCE framework: Confidence-building measures, emergency mechanisms and conflict prevention. OSCE un-published paper.

Villagran de Leon, R. 1992. *The Organization of American States and democratic development.* Washington, D.C.: United States Institute of Peace Press.

———. 1993. The OAS and regional security. Washington, D.C.: United States Institute of Peace Press.

Viraphol, S., and W. Pfenning. eds. 1995. *ASEAN-UN cooperation in preventive diplomacy.* Bangkok, Thailand: Ministry of Foreign Affairs.

Walker, J. 1993. International mediation of ethnic conflicts. In *Ethnic Conflict and International Security,* ed. M. E. Brown. Princeton, N.J.: Princeton University Press.

Wallensteen, P., and K. Axell. 1994. Conflict resolution and the end of the cold war, 1989–93. *Journal of Peace Research* 31, no. 3:333–50.

Wallensteen, P., and M. Sollenberg. 1995. After the cold war: Emerging patterns of armed conflict, 1989–94. *Journal of Peace Research* 32, no. 3:345–60.

———. 1996. The end of international war? Armed conflict, 1989–95. *Journal of Peace Research* 33:353–70.

Walzer, M. 1983. *Spheres of justice: A defense of pluralism and equality.* New York: Basic Books.

Wanandi, J. 1991a. *ASEAN security cooperation in Southeast Asia.* Tokyo: Interna-tional Institute for Global Peace.

———. 1991b. Peace and security in Southeast Asia. *The Indonesian Quarterly* 19, no. 4:313–25.

———. 1993. *The ASEAN political and security cooperation.* Jakarta: Centre for Strategic and International Studies.

———. 1994. Security cooperation in the Asia-Pacific. *The Indonesian Quarterly* 22, no. 3:198–204.

Warren, R. L. 1987. American Friends' Service Committee mediation efforts in Germany and Korea. In *Conflict resolution: Track two diplomacy,* eds. J. W. Mc-Donald and D. B. Bendahmane. Washington, D.C.: U.S. State Department.

Weiss, T. G., and L. Gordenker. 1996. *NGOs, the UN, and global governance.* Boul-der, Colo.: Lynne Rienner Publishers.

Welch, C. E. 1991. The Organization of African Unity and the promotion of human rights. *The Journal of Modern African Studies* 29, no. 4:535–55.

———. 1992. The African Commission on Human and Peoples' Rights: A five-year report and assessment. *Human Rights Quarterly* 14, no. 1:43–61.

Welsh, D. 1993. Domestic politics and ethnic conflict. In *Ethnic conflict and inter-national security,* ed. M. E. Brown. Princeton, N.J.: Princeton University Press.

Wendt, D. 1994. The peacemakers: Lessons of conflict resolution for the post-cold war world. *The Washington Quarterly* 17:163–78.

Wilson, L. C. 1989. The OAS and promoting democracy and resolving disputes: Reactivation in the 1990s? *Inter-American Review of Bibliography* 39, no. 4:477–97.

Wiseman, G. 1992. Common security in the Asia-Pacific region. *The Pacific Review* 5, no. 1:42–59.

Wood, P., and J. Wheeler. 1990. *ASEAN in the 1990s: New challenges, new directions.* Indianapolis, Ind.: Hudson Institute.

Zaagman, R. 1995a. Focus on the future. *Helsinki Monitor* 3:40–50.

———. 1995b. The role of the high commissioner on national minorities in OSCE conflict prevention. Report of the OSCE commission on national minorities, The Hague.

Zartman, I. W. 1990. Negotiations and prenegotiations in ethnic conflict: The beginning, the middle, and the end. In *Conflict and peacemaking in multiethnic societies,* ed. J. Montville. Lexington, Mass.: Lexington Books.

Zartman, I. W., and S. Touval. 1992. Mediation: The role of third-party diplomacy and informal peacemaking. In *Resolving third world conflict: Challenges for a new era,* eds. S. J. Brown and K. M. Schraub. Washington, D.C.: The United States Institute of Peace Press.

Zwart, T. 1994. *The admissibility of human rights petitions: The case law of the European Commission of Human Rights and the Human Rights Committee.* Dordrecht: Martinus Nijhoff Publishers.

Index

About the Author

The author of six books and numerous articles, Dr. Connie Peck is currently the coordinator of the Fellowship Programme in Peacemaking and Preventive Diplomacy at the United Nations Institute for Training and Research (UNITAR) in Geneva, Switzerland. The Fellowship Programme, which she founded, is cosponsored by UNITAR and the International Peace Academy, and provides advanced training to UN staff and diplomats in conflict analysis, negotiation, and mediation. The Fellowship Programme evolved from her work during 1992 as a special consultant to the Australian Foreign Minister, Senator Gareth Evans, during which she studied ways of strengthening the UN's capacity for peacemaking and preventive diplomacy. Some of her proposals were incorporated into the developing practice of the new Department of Political Affairs and the ongoing work of the Australian Department of Foreign Affairs and Trade. Since coming to UNITAR, Dr. Peck has continued to carry out research on these topics. She is the author of *The UN as a Dispute Settlement System: Improving Mechanisms for the Prevention and Resolution of Conflict* (Kluwer Law International, 1996), and she edited, with Roy S. Lee, *Increasing the Effectiveness of the International Court of Justice* (Kluwer Law International, 1997).

Dr. Peck was previously a reader in the Psychology Department at La Trobe University in Australia. In 1985, she was instrumental in establishing the La Trobe University Institute for Peace Research and served as its first chairperson. In 1984, she founded Psychologists for the Prevention of War, which she built into an active organization within the Australian Psychological Society. In 1994 Queen Elizabeth II appointed her an Officer in the Order of Australia for her service to "psychology and conflict resolution, theory and practice." Dr. Peck received her Ph.D. from the University of Wisconsin.